Territorial Separatism in Global Politics

This volume examines the various aspects of territorial separatism, focusing on how and why separatist movements arise.

Featuring chapters by leading scholars from different disciplinary perspectives, the book aims to situate the question of separatism within the broader socio-political context of the international system, arguing that a set of historical events as well as local, regional and global dynamics have converged to provide the catalysts that often trigger separatist conflicts. In addition, the book marks progress towards a new conceptual framework for the study of territorial separatism, by linking the survival of communities in international politics with the effective control of territory and the consequent creation of new polities. Separatist conflicts challenge conventional wisdom concerning conflict resolution within the context of international relations by unpacking a number of questions with regard to conflict transformation. Through the use of case studies, including Cyprus, the Rakhine State in Myanmar, the Shia separatism in Iraq, the Uyghurs in China and the case of East Timor, the volume addresses key issues including the role of democracy, international law, intervention, post-conflict peacebuilding and the creation of new political entities.

The book will be of much interest to students of Intra-State Conflict, Conflict Resolution, International Law, Security Studies and International Relations.

Damien Kingsbury is the Director of the Centre for Citizenship, Development and Human Rights, Deakin University, Australia. He has authored/edited a number of books, including: *Sri Lanka and the Responsibility to Protect: Politics, Ethnicity, Genocide* (Routledge 2011), *East Timor: The Price of Liberty* (Macmillan 2009), *International Development: Issues and Challenges* (Macmillan 2008, 2012) and *Political Development* (Routledge 2007).

Costas Laoutides is a lecturer in International Relations, School of Humanities and Social Sciences, Deakin University, Australia. He is the author of *Self-Determination and Collective Responsibility in the Secessionist Struggle* (Ashgate 2015).

Territorial Separatism in Global Politics

Causes, outcomes and resolution

Edited by Damien Kingsbury and
Costas Laoutides

LONDON AND NEW YORK

First published 2015
by Routledge
2 Park Square, Milton Park, Abingdon, Oxon OX14 4RN

and by Routledge
711 Third Avenue, New York, NY 10017

Routledge is an imprint of the Taylor & Francis Group, an informa business

© 2015 selection and editorial material, Damien Kingsbury and Costas Laoutides; individual chapters, the contributors

The right of Damien Kingsbury and Costas Laoutides; to be identified as the authors of the editorial material, and of the authors for their individual chapters, has been asserted in accordance with sections 77 and 78 of the Copyright, Designs and Patents Act 1988.

All rights reserved. No part of this book may be reprinted or reproduced or utilized in any form or by any electronic, mechanical, or other means, now known or hereafter invented, including photocopying and recording, or in any information storage or retrieval system, without permission in writing from the publishers.

Trademark notice: Product or corporate names may be trademarks or registered trademarks, and are used only for identification and explanation without intent to infringe.

British Library Cataloguing-in-Publication Data
A catalogue record for this book is available from the British Library

Library of Congress Cataloging-in-Publication Data
Territorial separatism in global politics : causes, outcomes and resolution / edited by Damien Kingsbury, Costas Laoutides.
  pages cm. – (Routledge studies in civil wars and intra-state conflict)
  Includes bibliographical references and index.
  1. Secession–Case studies. 2. Sovereignty–Case studies. 3. Separatist movements–Case studies. I. Kingsbury, Damien. II. Laoutides, Costas.
  JC327.T48 2015
  327.1–dc23   2014037586

ISBN: 978-1-138-79783-3 (hbk)
ISBN: 978-1-315-75684-4 (ebk)

Typeset in Times New Roman
by Wearset Ltd, Boldon, Tyne and Wear

Contents

Notes on contributors   vii
List of abbreviations   x

Introduction: territorial separatism in context   1
DAMIEN KINGSBURY AND COSTAS LAOUTIDES

PART I
Territorial separatism in an interdisciplinary perspective   13

1 **Secession: a much contested concept**   15
ALEKSANDAR PAVKOVIĆ

2 **Secession: a question of law or fact?**   29
PETER RADAN

3 **Vertical distinction as civic failure: state–nation disjuncture**   44
DAMIEN KINGSBURY

4 **Negotiating sustainable peace in separatist context**   59
COSTAS LAOUTIDES

5 **Discursive peacebuilding and conflict transformation after separatist wars: a radical proposition**   75
RICHARD JACKSON

PART II
Case studies 91

6 Recognition as a political act: political considerations in recognizing Indonesia's annexation of East Timor 93
CLINTON FERNANDES

7 Containing separatism? Control and resistance in China's Xinjiang Uyghur autonomous region 108
TERRY NARRAMORE

8 The anathema of partition: the quandary of division, secession and reunification in Cyprus 123
MICHÁLIS S MICHAEL

9 Succeeding and seceding in Iraq: the case for a Shiite state 139
BENJAMIN ISAKHAN

10 Secessionist aspects to the Buddhist–Muslim conflict in Rakhine State, Myanmar 153
ANTHONY WARE

Conclusion 169
COSTAS LAOUTIDES AND DAMIEN KINGSBURY

Index 177

Contributors

Clinton Fernandes is an associate professor at the International and Political Studies Program, School of Humanities and Social Sciences, University of New South Wales. His principal research area is 'International Relations and Strategy' with emphasis on the 'National Interest' in Australia's external relations. His most recent publications include (ed.) (2012) *Peace with Justice: Noam Chomsky in Australia*, Monash University Publishing; (2011) *The Independence of East Timor: Multidimensional Perspectives – Occupation, Resistance and International Political Activism*, Sussex Academic Press.

Benjamin Isakhan is Australian Research Council Discovery Early Career Research Award (DECRA) Research Fellow at the Centre for Citizenship and Globalization at Deakin University, Australia. He is the author of (2012) *Democracy in Iraq: History, Politics and Discourse*, Ashgate. He is also the editor and co-editor of (2011) *The Secret History of Democracy*, Palgrave Macmillan; (2012) *The Arab Revolutions in Context: Civil Society and Democracy in a Changing Middle East*, Melbourne University Press; (2012) *The Edinburgh Companion to the History of Democracy*, Edinburgh University Press.

Richard Jackson is Deputy Director at the National Centre for Peace and Conflict Studies, University of Otago. He is the founding editor and current editor-in-chief of the journal, *Critical Studies on Terrorism*, and the former convener of the BISA Critical Studies on Terrorism Working Group. He is the author and editor of numerous publications including: with SJ Sinclair (eds) (2012) *Contemporary Debates on Terrorism*, Routledge; with MB Smyth, J Gunning and L Jarvis (2011) *Terrorism: A Critical Introduction*, Palgrave Macmillan; with E Murphy and S Poynting (eds) (2010) *Contemporary State Terrorism: Theory and Cases*, Routledge; with J Bercovitch (2009) *Conflict Resolution in the Twenty-first Century: Principles, Methods and Approaches*, Michigan University Press; with MB Smyth and J Gunning (eds) (2009) *Critical Terrorism Studies: A New Research Agenda*, Routledge; (2005) *Writing the War on Terrorism: Language, Politics and Counterterrorism*, Manchester University Press.

viii *Contributors*

Damien Kingsbury is the Director of the Centre for Citizenship, Development and Human Rights and he is also with the School of Humanities and Social Sciences, Deakin University, Australia. Professor's Kingsbury research has focused on South-East Asian/Indonesia/East Timor/Sri Lanka politics, political development, the role of the military in politics, security and terrorism, post-colonial political structures and nation formation, assertions of self-determination, and civil and political rights. Prof. Kingsbury has written and edited or co-edited a number of books, including: (2011) *Sri Lanka and the Responsibility to Protect: Politics, Ethnicity, Genocide*, Routledge; (2009) *East Timor: The Price of Liberty*, Palgrave; (2012) *International Development: Issues and Challenges*, 2nd edn, Palgrave; (2007) *Political Development*, Routledge; (2003) *Key Issues in Development*, Palgrave; (2003) *Power Politics and the Indonesian Military*, Routledge/Curzon; (2002) *Autonomy and Disintegration in Indonesia*, Routledge/Curzon; (2005) *The Politics of Indonesia*, 3rd edn, Oxford University Press; (2005) *South-East Asia: A Political Profile*, 2nd edn, Oxford University Press.

Costas Laoutides is a lecturer in International Relations, School of Humanities and Social Sciences, Deakin University, Australia. Dr Laoutides' research focuses on the relation between peace and justice in secessionist conflicts. His publications include: (2015) *Self-Determination and Collective Responsibility in the Secessionist Struggle*, Ashgate; (2014) 'Surviving in a Difficult Context: The Quest for Development in Unrecognized States,' in A Ware (ed.) *Development in Difficult Sociopolitical Contexts*, Palgrave Macmillan; (2010) 'Preliminary Remarks on the Institutional Structures of Secessionist Movements: The Cases of PKK, Iraqi Kurdistan, and Transnistria,' *Citizenship and Globalization Research Papers*, vol. 1, no. 1; (2008) 'The Collective Moral Agency of Secessionist Groups,' in A Pavković and P Radan (eds), *On the Way to Statehood: Secession and Globalisation*, Ashgate; 'The Orphans of the Universe: Secession and World Politics,' in S Totman and S Burchill (eds), *Global Crises and Risks*, Oxford University Press; (2008) 'Hegemony and Secession: The Case of Transnistria,' *Science and Society: Journal of Political and Moral Theory*, no. 20.

Michális S Michael is the Deputy Director of the Centre for Dialogue, La Trobe University. Dr Michael's current research involves the careful study of intergroup and international conflict and how to transform its adversarial nature away from narrow notions of state-bound security. His recent publications include (2011) *Resolving the Cyprus Conflict: Negotiating History*, Palgrave Macmillan; with F Petito (eds) (2009) *Civilizational Dialogue and World Order: The Other Politics of Cultures, Religions and Civilizations in International Relations*, Palgrave Macmillan.

Terry Narramore is lecturer in International Relations, University of Tasmania. His research interests are in security and conflict in China and South-east Asia.

Aleksandar Pavković is an associate professor, Department of Modern History, Politics and International Relations, Macquarie University. His research interests are the theory and practice of secession, nationalism and nationalist movements. He has published widely on topics of secession, nationalism and the use of violence.

Peter Radan is with the Macquarie Law School, his research interests are self-determination and secession and he has published widely on these topics. His most recent publication is (2012) 'Secessionist Referenda in International and Domestic Law,' *Nationalism & International Politics*, vol. 18, pp. 8–21.

Anthony Ware is lecturer in International and Community Development, School of Humanities and Social Sciences, Deakin University. His research interests include the socio-political context and reform in Myanmar, aid effectiveness (particularly in relation to capacity building of civil society), and religious communities, faith-based organizations and inter-religious partnerships in development. Recent publications include (2012) *Context-Sensitive Development: How International NGOs Operate in Myanmar*, Kumarian Press, Sterling; (2012) 'Context Sensitivity by Development INGOs in Myanmar,' in M Skidmore, N Cheesman and T Wilson (eds), *Myanmar's Transition: Openings, Obstacles and Opportunities*, Institute of Southeast Asian Studies, Singapore.

Abbreviations

AA	Arakan Army
AFC	African National Congress
ALA	Arakan Liberation Army
ALP	Arakan Liberation Party
ANA	Arakan National Army
ANC	Arakan National Council
APODETI	Associacao Popular Democratica Timorense (Timorese Popular Democratic Association)
ARIF	Arakan Rohingya Islamic Front
ARNO	Arakan Rohingya National Organisation
BCIET	British Campaign for an Independent East Timor
BIA	Burma Independence Army
CBM	Confidence-Building Measures
CPA	Coalition Provisional Authority (in Iraq)
DFA	Department of Foreign Affairs
EC	European Community
EOKA	Ethnikí Orgánosi Kypríon Agonistón (National Organization of Cypriot Fighters)
ETIM	East Turkestan Islamic Movement
ETLO	East Turkestan Liberation Organization
EU	European Union
FCO	Foreign and Commonwealth Office
FRETILIN	Frente Revolucionaria do Timor-Leste Independente (Revolutionary Front for an Independent East Timor)
ICJ	International Court of Justice
ICRC	International Committee of the Red Cross
IGC	Interim Governing Council (in Iraq)
ISCI	Islamic Supreme Council of Iraq
ISF	Iraqi Security Forces
ITG	Iraqi Transitional Government
KLA	Kosovo Liberation Army
LTTE	Liberation Tigers of Tamil Eelam
MILF	Moro Islamic Liberation Front

NATO	North Atlantic Treaty Organization
NUPA	National United Party of Arakan
PAC	Pan Africanist Congress
PRC	People's Republic of China
RIF	Rohingya Independence Force
RPF	Rohingya Patriotic Front
RSO	Rohingya Solidarity Organisation
SCIRI	Supreme Council for the Islamic Revolution in Iraq
SFRY	Socialist Federative Republic of Yugoslavia
SLC	State of Law Coalition
TAPOL	British Campaign for the Release of Indonesian Political Prisoners
UDI	Unilateral Declaration of Independence
UDT	Uniao Democratica Timorense, (Timorese Democratic Union)
UIA	United Iraqi Alliance
UN	United Nations
UNFC	United Nationalities Federal Council
UNFICYP	United Nations Peacekeeping Force in Cyprus
UNGA	United Nations General Assembly
UNMIK	United Nations Mission in Kosovo
UNSC	United Nations Security Council
UNTEA	United Nations Temporary Executive Authority

Introduction
Territorial separatism in context

Damien Kingsbury and Costas Laoutides[1]

One of the most striking patterns in the study of contemporary international conflict, particularly since the end of the Cold War, is the increasing pervasiveness of territorial claims by minority groups as a means of dealing with perceived or real collective injustices. In addition, over the last three decades, the United States and the USSR/Russia have increasingly abandoned client states, thus the support mechanisms that were often available to regimes facing separatist dissent have been reduced or disappeared. This weakening of international support for governments of sometimes doubtful territorial legitimacy has given fresh impetus to the widespread and deepening challenge of separatism (Armitage 2007; Bartkus 1999; Bessinger 2002; Heraclides 1991; Horowitz 1985; Lake and Rothschild 1998; Spencer 1998). As a result, there are numerous separatist movements throughout the world, dozens of which remain engaged in armed conflict aiming at the creation of new, independent states.

While once predominant forms of warfare were interstate and then wars of decolonization, separatist wars have continued to devolve outstanding politico-spatial, ethnic, economic and historic grievances. Separatist wars are often bloody, usually protracted and exact a price from participants that, proportionally, is often well in excess of their potential benefit. Such wars are often considered as intrastate wars as they occur within internationally recognized states. Moreover, since not all separatist wars seek to change the government of the state, many may be considered as civil wars, particularly where such war is classified as being between two organized armies within the same state, with high levels of intensity, sustainability and organization. To illustrate, the American Civil War, the Nigerian Civil War and Sri Lanka's Eelam Wars can be considered as clear examples of separatist wars also being understood as civil wars. Yet, it is worth noting that whereas most civil wars intend to replace the central government, they can be limited in their aims to changing policies, such as determining the territory within the state.

Despite their violence, destructiveness and, commonly, lack of success, separatist wars not just continue, but multiply, presenting the greatest challenge to the post-World War II state system that has otherwise taken for granted the territorial integrity of states. The permanency of states, never an historical given, is under challenge once more, with the potential to redraw the boundaries as well as the economic and strategic interests of substantial parts of the world. However, states as we have come to understand them do appear to be a permanent feature of international relations; they are reified by the UN Charter (1945 art. 2, par. 4)[2] and, with very few exceptions, regard themselves not only as territorially sovereign, but, also, as exclusive and indivisible (Newton 2005).

The modern sense of sovereignty and indivisibility of states evolved historically in Europe, albeit not in a linear or causal fashion, through a gradual transformation of the notion of political community and its relation to territory (Hall 1999; Krasner 1993, 1995–6; Teschke 2003). Where once the distinction between polities had been fluid, changeable and often vague, modern state sovereignty was confirmed within hard, fixed and specific territorial borders (Elden 2013, pp. 279–321). In negotiating and defining such borders, the emerging national collective identity of the sovereign people problematized diverse notions of minority identity and, thus, numerous groups of people otherwise unaligned with the 'sovereign' were incorporated, willingly or unwillingly, within specific territorial demarcations (Hall 1999, pp. 132–171; Tilly 1993). This, of course, is not to say that European state borders remained permanently unaltered but rather that states were to be defined, in the first instance, by the institutionalization of sovereign authority, be that invested in their people or otherwise. In most cases the crystallization of statist national identities during the nineteenth and early twentieth centuries alleviated strong elements of difference within states. Statism contributed to the gradual establishment of common language groups and cultures, and a sense of identity increasingly defined as 'nation' emerged (Mann 1993, pp. 571–590). There was then, broadly, a confluence between the people as a bonded political group and the territory they claimed as representing their institutionalized interests. Such states were very largely inclusive; people and their territory were amalgamated in states often regardless of their preferences and the fact that once a people and their territory had been included within a state, almost by definition, the state worked to maintain its demographic and territorial coherence through exclusive sovereignty. The exclusivity of sovereignty is, however, qualified by the question of the legitimacy of the government or, in terms of separatist claims, the legitimacy of the state. By definition, separatist organizations do not regard the state from which they wish to separate as legitimate, either in total or in relation to the specific territory which they wish to establish as separate. Thus, the ground for regionalized dissent was established along with statism.

The normative basis for territorial separatism is the principle of self-determination which in essence reifies the division of the world into states whose peoples are characterized by an actual, a claimed or a constructed national identity. As a principle for world order, self-determination was the product of two competing agendas in the second half of the nineteenth century and again towards the end of World War I. Following the rise of nationalism in the nineteenth century, Bolshevik ideology promoted the notion of national self-determination as a right of secession from imperial rule intended to bolster the anti-imperialist left in Europe rather than the peoples of the colonies. On the other hand, the US President Woodrow Wilson (1918), coming from a liberal perspective, repeatedly talked about the need for a post-war settlement based on 'the consent of the people,' making the idea of self-determination relevant mainly to the defeated European powers (Manela 2007, pp. 127–128). Nevertheless, in the period following World War I, the rhetoric of self-determination was adopted by colonized peoples around the world whose growing national aspirations were formulated as claims against their rulers. The era of colonialism, largely concluding in the second half of the twentieth century, carved out territories across the globe that were to become independent modern states similar to those that evolved in Europe. Yet, as with and perhaps greater than Europe's experience, colonized peoples who felt a questionable sense of affinity with their colonial masters were subsequently included in the post-colonial states.

After the end of World War II the right to self-determination was incorporated in the UN Charter and became part of the international legal arsenal of the decolonization movement (Crawford 2006, pp. 107–131). But in former colonies, usually demarcated according to administrative convenience rather than based on local forms of group identity, under the principle of *uti possidetis*, peoples who had once had little to do with each other or who were, in some instances, historical enemies, found themselves as citizens of the same state (e.g., see Chapter 8 on Cyprus). The narrow interpretation of self-determination as a legal norm by the UN deprived several groups from pursuing their claims peacefully within the boundaries of international law and, thus, it laid the grounds for territorial separatism (Tomuschat 2006). The reluctance by international community to (re-)define the content of self-determination in a decolonized world led to a number of inconsistent and ad hoc interpretations of the principle generating legal and political confusion (Chapter 2 in this volume is an example of this phenomenon). Consequent separatist conflicts now constitute one of the biggest challenges to global peace and security. These conflicts frequently manifest as high levels of collective violence and human rights abuse, both by separatist organizations and, more commonly, the states that seek to oppress their claims (Caplan 2005; Doyle 2010; Pavković and Radan 2008; Roeder 2007; Walter 2009; Weller and Wolff 2005).

The direct claim to territorial control that separatist conflicts make is a *sine qua non* condition for existence and survival in international politics (Buzan 1991; Holsti 1996; Toft 2003). Usually cloaked under the discourse of nationalism and ethnic identity, separatist movements and states alike associate their identity with a particular territory or 'homeland' which secures their survival (Kubo 2011; Kingsbury 2007, pp. 36–77). This phenomenon echoes the way the international state system operates; by exercising control over territory states protect their people from coercion and foreign occupation. In order to address a grievance based on their collective identity and common territory political communities in many cases believe that they need to obtain the status of an independent state and enjoy recognition by the international community. There is, then, a paradox in the logic embedded in the current model of independent states: the state is designed to preserve its territorial integrity and hence oppose its break-up, but communities that seek to separate in turn wish to establish another sovereign state. Therefore, independence, territorial sovereignty and international recognition are seen to be the conditions that can overcome the shortcomings that the political community experiences under the pre-existing state.

Beyond the immediate issues of territorial cohesion, external involvement in separatist struggles has been common practice for separatist (and other violent non-state) organizations. Third party intervention can be multifaceted; separatist organizations commonly find shelter in, sponsorship, or other forms of support from neighboring countries, thus contributing to bilateral and regional instability. Indeed, some separatist organizations, although with legitimate claims of their own, are understood as proxies or otherwise in the service of larger strategic arrangements (e.g., the use of Kurdish guerillas in northern Iraq during the Iran–Iraq War, 1980–8). From the perspective of the host country, such organizations can be used as a buffer against an untrusted neighbor (e.g., Thailand's former covert support of Burmese Karen separatists), as part of a policy of destabilization (e.g., China's support for separatist organizations in north-east India), or in an effort to establish a more friendly regional government (e.g., India's intervention in Bangladesh). Even in cases where a separatist organization does not concur with the strategic interests of another state, if successful, the creation of a new, separate state alters regional strategic balance by pursuing its own set of interests rather than those of the 'parent' state. The creation of Bangladesh, Eritrea, South Sudan, Kosovo and Timor-Leste each have established new regional dynamics that have required neighboring states to adjust their strategic policy settings, not always in ways which are regionally benign. State creation as an outcome of secessionist struggle, however, is not always straightforward since exercising effective control over territory is a necessary but not sufficient condition for international legitimacy. Often new entities lack international recognition and the creation of de facto states, usually supported by neighboring patron states, adds another layer of perplexity to the regional security nexus (Caspersen 2012; see Chapter 6 in this volume on the importance of recognition as a political tool). In addition, claims to separatism are associated frequently with the development of organizations that have been characterized as 'terrorist' (Jackson 2007; Tuastad 2003; Zarakol 2011). In this case, non-state actors are usually viewed as illegitimate by the state in question and often by the international community, regardless of their methods or the basis for their claims (Chapter 7 in this volume illustrates this point). In some cases, such allegations against separatist organizations, based on trans-national associations, have some basis further highlighting the need for a framework to distinguish between terrorist and non-terrorist organizations.

As mentioned, separatist conflicts are characterized by extreme violence whilst their settlement usually comes at a high human, economic and political price, especially in cases where the logic of denial prevails by prioritizing military options (Walter 2009). Civilians are regularly displaced by such conflicts and often targeted by security forces for being sympathetic to separatist claims, while separatist organizations similarly target civilians who are not sympathetic or at least comply with their requirements, such as paying 'taxes' to fund their activities. What is certain, in such cases of military 'solutions', is the high number of casualties and the widespread gross violation of human rights that military engagement typically brings. Although military victory can have a significant impact on the dynamic of the conflict, it is uncertain whether it can end the conflict (Heraclides 1997). There are numerous examples of asymmetric warfare seeming to favor the larger military force but resulting in an effective stalemate, not least in separatist conflicts and especially where the separatist organization enjoys the popular support of the population it claims to represent. There are various estimates of the necessary ratio of military force required to win an asymmetric war, often cited at around 2:100 of the civilian population (Kozelka 2008) or 20:1 of the irregular military force. But the reality is that, no matter what the ratio between the forces is, a separatist organization able to draw on even a small group of committed militants with popular support can continue a struggle almost indefinitely.

Territorial separatism as a socio-political phenomenon stands at a crossroads of several lines of inquiry. As a field of study it is a contested terrain (Chapter 1 in this volume) which has become the focus of many disciplines requiring the division of labor among several branches of social sciences, political philosophy and law (international and constitutional law). However, the interdisciplinary character of territorial separatism is derived from the fact that the problem is fundamentally complex, calling for the integration of the contributions that the individual disciplines make (Repko 2012). Thus, understanding and analyzing separatist conflict and its potential for resolution must be an interdisciplinary exercise. The etiology for territorial separatism is subject to historical, ethnic, economic, political and structural factors (Toft 2012). Accordingly, separatism, as a complex social phenomenon, has to be analyzed from different perspectives in order for us to reach a holistic understanding of it. But this is not enough, since understanding is the first step towards an integrated approach that would seek to remedy separatist conflict and alleviate harm and suffering from both physical and non-physical violence. For all their successes and failures, separatist conflicts should not be seen only through the mono-dimensional ethnocentric lens which scholars, journalists, policy-makers and politicians have traditionally employed.

This book sets out to consider how and why separatism arises and, potentially, how its claims can be addressed. In doing so it covers a range of interdisciplinary perspectives and draws on a number of case studies that, between them, provide a reasonable sense of the breadth of the separatist spectrum. The volume brings together contributions on different themes within the broader literature on separatism, each with important implications for our understanding of the particular models that have been applied to the study of the various aspects of separatism and their limitations. The central argument and the key contributions of this book are twofold. First, it aims to situate the question of separatism within the broader socio-political context of the international system, arguing that a set of historical events as well as local, regional and global dynamics have converged to provide the catalysts that often trigger separatist conflicts. Second, this book situates progress towards a new conceptual framework. The argument here is that territorial separatism poses a very specific challenge to conventional wisdom concerning conflict analysis and resolution within the context of international relations including issues such as the role of democracy, humanitarian intervention and post-conflict peacebuilding. The chapters in this book argue collectively that approaches to tame separatism can only endure and bring about positive outcomes if they are developed organically from the bottom up and in isolation from ideological agendas. This is a basis from which international legitimacy and endurance can be generated, leading to an outlook for state formation that can transcend some of the exclusionary characteristics of the Westphalian model.

The interdisciplinary character of the field is reflected in the first section of the book, with the opening chapter by Pavković addressing the diversity of approaches to secession that have yielded different and sometimes incompatible definitions of the phenomenon. This, then, sets the parameters for the studies that follow. Pavković notes that James Crawford (2006) restricts the concept of secession only to the withdrawal of territory which is opposed by a functioning host state. Mutually agreed withdrawal of territory or a withdrawal which is opposed by a disintegrating state do not, in his view, count as secession. Hechter (1975, 1992), by way of comparison, restricts secession only to the cases in which the host state remains as it was before the territory was withdrawn, whereas for John Wood (1981) every case of secession is a case of state disintegration. This chapter understands separatism in the broader sense, including the actual or intended withdrawal of territory from an existing state which results, or is intended to result, in the creation of a new state.

Peter Radan follows this theme by addressing the key question as to whether there is a provision in international law for secession or whether it is simply a matter of whether such a claim is able to be asserted or denied. Radan suggests that international law is not clear as to whether there exists a limited right to unilateral secession or whether secession is purely a question of fact. Illustrating this point, Radan identifies the 1998 opinion in *Reference re: Secession of Quebec*, where the Supreme Court of Canada recognized that '[t]he process of recognition [of states], once considered to be an exercise of pure sovereign discretion, has come to be associated with legal norms' (Secession Reference 1998, p. 443). The issue explored by Radan in this chapter is the extent to which this statement pictures the situation with respect to statehood through secession. It has been argued that the right of peoples to self-determination grants a limited or 'remedial' right of secession. In 2010, the International Court of Justice, in its advisory opinion relating to Kosovo's secession from Serbia had, but declined to grasp, an opportunity to clarify international law in relation to secession. Thus, Radan argues, the question of secession in international law appears to remain open.

Damien Kingsbury's chapter on the failure of the state in relation to ethnic groupings returns to first principles, by proposing that the purpose of the state is

Introduction 7

to represent the interests of its citizens, which implies holding them in equal regard in relation to those benefits, opportunities or safeguards that the state is able to provide. To the extent that it has the capacity to do so, this implies that the state fulfills its basic civic function of existing on behalf of its citizens equally. His chapter further proposes that where states are challenged by separatist rebellions, this is primarily a consequence of the failure of the state to fulfill its basic functions to all its citizens equally, hence alienating geographically specific minority groups. While the potential pool of examples to draw on to help analyze the rationale for separatism is wide, Kingsbury's chapter compares five case studies with which he has direct experience; Sri Lanka, Aceh, West Papua, Mindanao and Timor-Leste.

Costas Laoutides follows by examining how sustainable peace can be pursued in separatist conflicts and what the challenges are for peacebuilding operations within this context. He argues that secessionist conflicts are a particular type of internal conflict that raises issues of territorial control and survival of the communities in question. However, he suggests that separatist conflicts appear to be more amenable to negotiated settlements than other types of internal conflict. A qualification to this, he says, is that the implementation of peace accords through peacebuilding operations face two key challenges: the need for establishing a common political foundation for the distinct community that will foster trustful relations, and the transition of former fighters to agents of peace through a paradigmatic departure from identity politics that implement the ethnic security dilemma.

Richard Jackson continues the conflict resolution theme by problematizing the dominant peacebuilding template which international institutions currently apply to societies emerging from separatist war, thereby opening up analytical and normative space for the consideration of radically alternative peacebuilding approaches. His chapter starts by outlining a constructivist model of separatist war initiation, arguing that, among others, discursive factors, social structures, histories, narratives, discursive practices, play a central role that is relatively under-valued in most quantitative and structurally-based approaches to separatist war explanation, as well as in most institutional understandings of the causes of separatist war. Jackson then offers a brief but sustained critique of contemporary post-civil war peacebuilding approaches, particularly in terms of their neglect of the discursive factors highlighted in the constructivist model, but also in terms of their links to neoliberal imperialism and governmentality. In the final part of his chapter, Jackson proposes a radically alternative approach to 'discursive peacebuilding' after separatist war, which encompasses conflict transformation, agonistic democracy and dialogic politics, and the demilitarization of politics and its replacement with nonviolent and pacifist politics. As such, he proposes a peacebuilding approach which takes a post-Weberian or post-state polity as its normative goal.

The second part of the book focuses on the dynamics of various case studies. Not intending to be exhaustive, the case studies are chosen as a broad representative group of different types and stages of separatist claims and conflicts.

Clinton Fernandes begins this section by considering the effect of international recognition of territorial integrity or annexation and incorporation, with particular reference to East Timor. Fernandes argues that when Indonesia invaded East Timor in 1975 and annexed it in 1976, it followed a precedent established in 1969 during the 'Act of Free Choice' in West Papua: it denied the population the opportunity to choose their political future. Instead, it chose a group of 'representatives' who would vote unanimously to join Indonesia. As Fernandes notes, Indonesia expected the international community to extend official recognition of the annexation of East Timor, as had occurred with West Papua. Such recognition, if repeated widely by other states, may have extinguished East Timor's bid for freedom. Yet Indonesia failed to obtain widespread *de jure* recognition of its takeover of East Timor, with Australia being the only Western state to recognize the annexation. In this contest of recognition, Fernandes explores the relationship between civil society groups and policy-makers over this question of recognition. He argues that political considerations were uppermost in the minds of policy-makers as they pondered the legal implications of that recognition, which was eventually overturned.

Terry Narramore takes a different approach to separatist claims, by considering how the policies of a government can actually exacerbate separatist tensions, in this case considering the case of Xinjiang in China's north-west. As he notes, violent resistance of Uyghurs to the Chinese Communist Party's rule in Xinjiang provides a stark reminder that while China's sovereignty over Xinjiang is not in jeopardy and its policies have contained separatist movements, it is these same policies continue to provoke separatist sentiment and Uyghur–Han (Chinese) tensions and violence. The July 2009 'riots' in Xinjiang's capital, Urumqi, were tragic demonstrations of this policy failure. Xinjiang thus remains an intractable case of the 'successful but not conclusive' (Heraclides 1997, p. 704) containment of separatism, while Uyghur resistance has entered a phase marked by more intense Uyghur–Han conflict.

The case of Cyprus presents a special conundrum within the separatism–unity paradigm, given that the state has been partitioned between approximately ethnic communities, each strongly supported by, or client of, an external state. As Michális Michael notes in Chapter 8, partition has always had an ominous presence in Cyprus's political discourse. If the history of the Cyprus conflict could be deduced to a single schema, he writes that it would be as the contradictory, often-violent, interplay between separatism/secession/division and unification/integration/reconciliation. By examining one of the world's most protracted international conflicts, Michael probes how attempts at reunification have fared, especially the ethical challenge of how to construct a legal-constitutional order that is dictated by a set of historical determinants. These are said to include the desire to rectify past injustices which reconciles human rights and group security with the expectation of upholding the fundamental precepts of liberal democracy, while at the same time fortifying the foundations for sequential integration/unification and negating the paradigm of secession, division and partition.

The war in Iraq, and its extended aftermath, have had a number of consequences, key among which is that as one of the arbitrarily constructed states that was a product of the Sykes–Picot Agreement of 1916, Iraq's loose sense of unity has begun to unravel, as discussed by Ben Isakhan in Chapter 9. In his chapter, Isakhan examines the calls by the Supreme Council for the Islamic Revolution in Iraq (SCIRI) for an autonomous Shia Islamic state in the south of Iraq. While such calls have deep historical roots and have long formed part of SCIRI's complex political and ideological history, they achieved a renewed momentum following the US attempt to bring a form of democracy to Iraq after the 2003 invasion. While the prospects for Shia secession in Iraq remain low, this chapter finds that it nonetheless forms an ongoing and central part of SCIRI's political agenda and thus constitutes a key element in the make-up of the fractured Iraqi state.

Returning to South-east Asia, Anthony Ware explores the secessionist aspects of Muslim–Buddhist communal violence in Rakhine State, Myanmar, that has accompanied that country's move away from overt authoritarianism. From one perspective, the secessionist struggle in Rakhine was largely won by the Burmese military in the 1950s–60s, when the major, separate armed rebellions by both Rakhine Buddhists and Rohingya Muslims was put down by the central government. Yet, despite being significantly weakened, four militant groups remain on the western Burmese border area, the Arakan Liberation Army and the Arakan Army, which is linked to the National United Party of Arakan (NUPA, one of only two of the United Nationalities Federal Council's (UNFC) 12 armed ethnic groups to have not entered peace talks with the government), and, on the Rohingya side, the Rohingya Solidarity Organisation (RSO) and the Arakan Rohingya National Organisation (ARNO). Underscoring anti-Muslim violence has been the failure of a transition from secessionist conflict into a positive peace, set against the secessionist and nationalist aspirations of many of both the Rakhine Buddhist and Rohingya Muslims. When added to the five decades of structural violence by a military-led government, particularly against the Rohingya minority, what has been commonly reported as simply 'Muslim–Buddhist communal violence' is better understood as a complex of factors coalescing to inform and perpetuate that violence.

The volume concludes with a critical summation of the key arguments and points the way towards both academic and policy explorations in this evolving field of critical research. Not only does the conclusion serve as a postscript to claims for separate identity and the civil, intrastate separatist wars they can engender, it highlights some of the most recent critical thinking on the intertwined issues of separatism, the state, political identity and the possibilities for the resolution of such conflicts.

Notes

1 We would like to acknowledge the two anonymous reviewers for their invaluable comments.
2 Interestingly, this is in contradiction with possible interpretation of Charter 1.2 concerning the 'self-determination of peoples'.

References

Armitage, D 2007, *The Declaration of Independence: A Global History*, Harvard University Press, Cambridge, MA.

Bartkus, V 1999, *Dynamic of Secession*, Cambridge University Press, Cambridge, UK.

Bessinger, M 2002, *Nationalist Mobilization and the Collapse of the Soviet State*, Cambridge University Press, Cambridge, UK.

Buzan, B 1991, *People, States and Fear*, Harvester Wheatsheaf, London.

Caplan, R 2005, *Europe and the Recognition of New States in Yugoslavia*, Cambridge University Press, Cambridge, UK.

Caspersen, N 2012, *Unrecognised States*, Polity Press, Cambridge.

Crawford, J 2006, *The Creation of States in International Law*, 2nd edn, Cambridge University Press, Cambridge, UK.

Doyle, DH 2010, *Secession as an International Phenomenon: From America's Civil War to Contemporary Separatist Movements*, University of Georgia Press, Athens, GA.

Elden, S 2013, *The Birth of Territory*, Chicago University Press, Chicago.

Hall, RB 1999, *National Collective Identity: Social Constructs and International Systems*, Columbia University Press, New York.

Hechter, M 1975, *Internal Colonialism: The Celtic Fringe in British National Development*, University of California Press, Berkeley, CA.

Hechter, M 1992, 'The Dynamics of Secession,' *Acta Sociologica*, vol. 35, pp. 267–283.

Heraclides, A 1991, *The Self-Determination of Minorities in International Politics*, Frank Cass, London.

Heraclides, A 1997, 'The Ending of Unending Conflicts: Separatist Wars,' *Millennium: Journal of International Studies*, vol. 26, no. 3, pp. 679–707.

Holsti, K 1996, *The State, War, and the State of War*, Cambridge University Press, Cambridge.

Horowitz, DL 1985, *Ethnic Groups in Conflict*, University of California Press, Berkeley, CA.

Jackson, R 2007, 'Constructing Enemies: "Islamic Terrorism" in Political and Academic Discourse,' *Government and Opposition*, vol. 42, no. 3, pp. 394–426.

Kingsbury, D 2007, *Political Development*, Routledge, London and New York.

Kozelka, G 2008, *Boots on the Ground: A Historical and Contemporary Analysis of Force Levels for Counterinsurgency Operations*, School of Advanced Military Studies, United States Army Command and General Staff College, Fort Leavenworth, Texas.

Krasner, SD 1993, 'Westphalia and All That,' in J Goldstein and RO Keohane (eds), *Ideas and Foreign Policy: Beliefs, Institutions, and Political Change*, Cornell University Press, Ithaca, NY, pp. 235–264.

Krasner, SD 1995–6, 'Compromising Westphalia,' *International Security*, vol. 20, no. 3, pp. 115–151.

Kubo, K 2011, 'Secession and Ethnic Conflict', in A Pavković and P Radan (eds), *The Ashgate Research Companion to Secession*, Ashgate, Aldershot, pp. 207–225.

Lake, D and D. Rothschild (eds) 1998, *The International Spread of Ethnic Conflict: Fear, Diffusion and Escalation*, Princeton University Press, Princeton, NJ.

Manela, E 2007, 'Dawn of a New Era: The "Wilsonian Moment" in Colonial Contexts and the Transformation of World Order, 1917–1920,' in S Conrad and D Sachsenmaier (eds), *Competing Visions of World Order: Global Moments and Movements, 1880s–1930s*, Palgrave Macmillan, Houndmills, UK, pp. 121–149.

Mann, M 1993, *The Sources of Social Power, vol. II: The Rise of Classes and Nation-States, 1760–1914*, Cambridge University Press, Cambridge, UK.

Newton, K 2005, *Foundations of Comparative Politics: Democracies of the Modern World*, Cambridge University Press, Cambridge, UK.

Pavković, A and Radan, P (eds) 2008, *On the Way to Statehood: Secession and Globalisation*, Ashgate, Aldershot.

Repko, A 2012, *Interdisciplinary Research: Process and Theory*, 2nd edn, Sage Publications, London.

Roeder, P 2007, *Where Nation-States Come From: Institutional Change in the Age of Nationalism*, Princeton University Press, Princeton, NJ.

Secession Reference 1998, *Reference re: Secession of Quebec* (1998) 161 *Dominion Law Reports*, 4th edn, pp. 385–449.

Spencer, M (ed.) 1998, *Separatism: Democracy and Disintegration*, Rowman & Littlefield, Lanham, MD.

Teschke, B 2003, *The Myth of 1648: Class, Geopolitics and the Making of Modern International Relations*, Verso, London.

Tilly, C 1993, 'National Self-Determination as a Problem for All of Us,' *Daedalus*, vol. 122, no. 3, pp. 29–36.

Toft, MD 2003, *The Geography of Ethnic Violence: Identity, Interests, and the Indivisibility of Territory*, Princeton University Press, Princeton, NJ.

Toft, MD 2012, 'Self-Determination, Secession and Civil War,' *Terrorism and Political Violence*, vol. 24, no. 4, pp. 581–600.

Tomuschat, C 2006, 'Secession and Self-Determination,' in MG Cohen (ed.), *Secession: International Law Perspectives*, Cambridge University Press, Cambridge, UK, pp. 23–45.

Tuastad, D 2003, 'Neo-Orientalism and the New Barbarism Thesis: Aspects of Symbolic Violence in the Middle East Conflict(s),' *Third World Quarterly*, vol. 24, no. 4, pp. 591–599.

United Nations Charter 1945, Section 2, par 4.

Walter, BF 2009, *Reputation and Civil War: Why Separatist Conflicts Are So Violent*, Cambridge University Press, Cambridge.

Weller, M and Wolff, S (eds) 2005, *Autonomy, Self-governance and Conflict Resolution*, Routledge, London.

Wilson, W 1918, 'A Program For Peace' (also known as the *Fourteen Points Speech*), US Congress Joint Session, January 8.

Wood, JR 1981, 'Secession: A Comparative Analytical Framework,' *Canadian Journal of Political Science*, vol. 14, pp. 109–135.

Zarakol, A 2011 'What Makes Terrorism Modern? Terrorism, Legitimacy, and the International System,' *RIS*, vol. 37, no. 5, pp. 2311–2336.

Part I
Territorial separatism in an interdisciplinary perspective

1 Secession

A much contested concept

Aleksandar Pavković

Definitions and their differences

When reading some scholarly works on secession, one may wonder whether the study of secession is a worthwhile scholarly activity at all. Some legal scholars and political scientists define secession so narrowly as to allow only a few cases of secession *stricto sensu* in the past century. These scholars seem to imply that since secession is such a rare phenomenon, there is no point in comparative study of secession; what may appear to be a comparative study of secessions is, in their view, a study of different phenomena – for example, dissolution of states, which do not require a comparative study of secessions. Moreover, these definitions suggest that there is no point in searching for general principles for moral or normative justification or assessment of secession. Why worry whether secession is morally justifiable when there are so few of them and it is not likely that there will be more of them in the future? In this chapter I argue that the restrictive definition of secession prevents us from exploring and understanding comparable political processes in different areas of the world, and from attempting to find the norms which could guide or justify a set of similar political actions which have caused considerable harm to large numbers of people (and thus stand in need of moral justification). While the more permissive definition certainly allows us to explore both these political processes and normative frameworks, a few highly permissive definitions of secession, I argue, are too broad to be useful for a comparative study of the secessionist phenomenon.

The definitions of secession discussed in this chapter focus on the withdrawal of territory and sovereignty from an internationally recognized state. This is, indeed, what *all* definitions of secession have in common: they agree that secession involves the withdrawal or detachment of territory and its population from the jurisdiction of an established state; in this process, it is generally agreed, the established state loses the sovereignty or the capacity to exercise its sovereignty over the detached territory. As we shall see, the definitions of secession to be discussed here differ in their views on:

1 The means which are employed to effect the withdrawal or detachment. The key difference is the use or the threat of use of force or its absence.

2   The effect of the withdrawal on the territorial integrity of the state from which the withdrawal is made. The difference here is between the detachments that breach the state's territorial integrity and the detachment of territories that are not considered to be part of the state's bounded territory.
3   The effect on the legal and political identity of the state from which the withdrawal is made. The difference is between those states which retain their previous legal/political identity after the withdrawal and those which change it and/or lose it altogether.

The UN Charter and all subsequent UN resolutions prohibit (1) the use of force in interstate relations, except in self-defense (the UN GA Resolution 1514 (1960) extended this to the cases of the defense of the right to self-determination of colonial peoples) and (2) any breaches of the territorial integrity and political unity of UN member states. The UN documents pointedly neither prohibit nor allow the use of force and the breach of territorial integrity for the purposes of secession (as distinct from decolonization); the word 'secession' and its possible cognates is simply absent from the UN documents. In the world in which secessions do happen, it has been left to scholars to debate what is secession and what means, usually prohibited by the UN, are allowed in various attempts at territorial detachment, and, if so, which type of territorial detachment qualifies for such exemptions. One way of addressing the latter question is to find classificatory concepts or categories other than secession and to subsume most territorial detachments under these non-secession categories. Thus, one can argue, as it has been in the case of former Yugoslavia, that the detachments in question were in fact part of the dissolution of a state which leads to the disappearance of states (see points 2 and 3 above). Any violent conflict occurring in the cases of alleged dissolution of states would be categorized as internal and not interstate use of force (see point 1 above). Neither the dissolution nor disappearance of states nor, of course, internal uses of force are barred by the UN Charter and other UN resolutions or conventions. The new UN doctrine of Responsibility to Protect (R2P) prohibits not intrastate wars but only certain types of internal violence against non-combatants. Another way of minimizing the occurrence of secession is to treat some detachments of territory (for example, that of East Timor from Indonesia) as instances of decolonization which do not threaten the territorial integrity of UN member states (point 2 above). Within the UN legal framework, decolonization is not secession but a legally required exercise of the right of self-determination of colonial peoples.

Instead of looking at secession as detachment of territories, let us focus on the phenomenon as a political process and as a political outcome. What do the supporters of secession want to achieve, apart from (or in addition to) the independence of the territory that they claim from the state in which they live at present, the state which we shall (without any prejudice) call their 'host state'? They want to be ruled or governed by a different group of people – usually those who belong to the same national group as they do. They may also want to have a different apparatus of government, including a different legal order, from that of the host state; the desired difference may be only in the nomenclature, institutional structure and staff of the new apparatus. Moreover, they want to have a different political life, the life from which the political parties and politicians from the host state will be excluded. In short, they want a different ruling elite and a different institutional and political regime. If so, they want to achieve a change of governing elite and a change of institutional political and legal system/regime by detaching the territory on which they live from the host state. Secession can be thus regarded as a process which, if successful, leads to the change of the governing elite and the political/legal regime similar to other processes which lead to such change *without* the detachment of territory. Viewing secession as a political process of this allows us to raise the following two related questions:

1 How are people mobilized to support or demand such a change?
2 How is the demand for this kind of change related to the demand for the detachment of territory?

It is quite possible that the demand for the detachment of the territory is an instrument for effecting the change of elites and regime, in particular when there is no other way of achieving the latter but by detaching the territory from the host state. In relation to that, one can also ask how one can effect the desired change of elites and regime *without* detaching the territory or at least without causing the harmful consequences that such a detachment often brings about. Legal scholars or normative theorists do not address questions of this kind; however, political scientists interested in comparative study of secessions do so. As I argue in the last section of the chapter, the difference in the questions they address about secession may, at least to some extent, explain the difference in their definitions of secession.

Definitions of secession: the contest

Restrictive approaches

Crawford's approach to secession is probably the best known example of a restrictive definition of secession: 'attempts at secession – which may be defined as the creation of a State by the use or threat of force without the consent of the former sovereign' (Crawford 2006, p. 375). Many others scholars, including social scientists, restrict secession to the detachment of territory 'without the consent' of the host state, i.e., the former sovereign (Anderson 2013). As Radan (2008) and Anderson (2013) note, the definition of secession here is made contingent on a specific process of detachment or withdrawal. There are a variety of reasons for taking such a restrictive approach. For Crawford, the cases in which the sovereign consents to a detachment of a territory are unproblematic from the point of international law and international practice of recognition of states: if and when the host state consents to such a withdrawal of territory, it recognizes the independence of the newly created state and other states are free to, and they do, follow suit. Likewise, the recognition by the host state appears to be necessary for the admission of a newly created state to the UN, the exclusive club of sovereign and independent states. In this sense, detachments of territory and creation of new states on these territories *with* the consent of the host state ('former sovereign') pose no problem for international law and practice and hence are not deemed to be secessions: secessions are only those problematic cases of detachments to which the host state at least initially does not consent. Political scientists such as Heraclides (1991) who offer similar definitions to Crawford's, probably find the above unproblematic detachments of territory lacking in many features of the 'abrupt and unilateral' separations which they prefer to study. The latter 'abrupt and unilateral', that is, non-consensual secessions, are characterized by a protracted political conflict often escalating to violence; Heraclides and many other social scientists are primarily interested in the political conflict that is at the core of non-consensual secession. Hence, in their view, only those 'abrupt and unilateral' qualify as secessions.

Indeed, the absence of consent of the host state is usually associated with the use or threat of force: in demanding or proclaiming independence, without the consent of the host state, the secessionists perceive any use of force against their emergent state as aggression *against which* the use of force is justified. In demanding or proclaiming independence, the secessionists are claiming the status of the sovereign state which thereby gains the right of self-defense against those who are challenging its sovereignty. In turn, in withholding consent from a detachment of territory, the host state, as a legal sovereign, is retaining the right to use force on that territory and to prevent its detachment. In granting consent to a detachment, the host state is giving up its sovereignty over the territory and thereby losing any right to use force on that territory. Granting consent to a detachment in this sense makes the detachment so unproblematic as to look like ceding or relinquishing of the territory; hence, one could indeed argue that such *voluntary* cessation of territory is categorically or conceptually different from its (*involuntary*) secession (Haverland 2000, p. 255).

Yet as Radan (Pavković with Radan 2007, p. 7) pointed out, divorce is a legal termination of a marriage, whether one or both partners consent to it. Why would the termination by mutual agreement or consent belong to a different category from the termination with only one partner consenting? The analogy of divorce, widely used in discussion of secession, is usually quite misleading (Aronovitch 2000). But in this case the analogy is not meant to tell us anything about secession itself but only about a restrictive approach to defining secession.

The absence of consent is not sufficient to conceptually differentiate a non-consensual detachment of territory leading to the creation of a new state, from a similar detachment which has, at some point prior to or after the formal proclamation of independence, gained the consent of the former host state. By asking whether a state has been created through secession we are not, *eo ipso*, asking *whether* its detachment has gained consent of the host state or not. Thus we are not making a conceptual or categorical mistake if we say that Montenegro or Iceland or Norway were created by way of secession (these cases involved a mutual agreement to the detachment of territory). By calling these three cases 'secessions', we are thereby *not* implying that the host state has withheld consent from the creation of the new state. The question of its consent would be, as it were, a question of *how* the secession took place and not *whether* it did.

Permissive approaches

Permissive definitions are often advanced in response to the restrictive ones and thus tend to be inclusive. Radan (2008, p. 18) defines secession as 'the creation of a new state upon territory previously forming part of, or being a colonial entity of, an existing state.' Anderson (2013, p. 344) defines it similarly as 'the withdrawal of territory (colonial or non-colonial) from part of an existing state to create a new state.'

Even more inclusive definitions of secessions are found in legal scholarly literature. Haverland has, for example, defined secession as 'the separation of part of the territory of a State carried out by the resident population with the aim of creating a new independent State or acceding to another existing state' (2000, p. 254). Accordingly, secession does not need to aim at the creation of a new state: a transfer of territory from one state to another, which is often called 'irredenta', also counts as secession (for a comprehensive list of the scholars who endorse this kind of definition see Anderson 2013, p. 371, note 148).

The aim of Haverland's inclusive definition is to differentiate detachments of territory in which the resident population is involved as an alleged agent of the detachment from those in which the resident population is not so involved. In this way the detachments of this kind are differentiated from various kinds of territorial annexation in which the population is not involved; such as, for example, cases of sovereign purchase of territory, practiced up until the late nineteenth century (e.g., of Alaska from Russia) or of border adjustment. In the latter cases, the former sovereign is relinquishing or *ceding* territory and the resident population is *not* an agent of this change.

Against so inclusive a definition one can advance at least the following three reasons. First, in the present state system, regulated by the UN, if a populated territory is withdrawn from the jurisdiction of a state – with or without the involvement of its population – the territory faces only the following two options: either a new state is created on this territory or the territory falls under the jurisdiction of another state. There is no third option allowing this territory to remain outside state jurisdiction: there is no option of *terra nullius* for territories with permanently resident populations. These two outcomes remain irrespective of the agent which allegedly carried out the withdrawal. In view of this, the agent of the withdrawal appears to be irrelevant to the determination of the legal category – secession or irredenta – to which a particular withdrawal belongs.

Second, the resident populations, the alleged agents of the withdrawal in the case of both secession and irredenta, appear to belong to two different types of agency. In order to withdraw territory from a state and *create* a new state, the resident population (or rather its representatives) do not need to seek approval or acceptance of any third party. If a resident population is to *transfer* its territory to another state, it needs to gain prior approval and acceptance of the receiving state. In the latter case the agency is *conceptually* constrained by a third party: no transfer of the territory (irredenta) can be made if the receiving state does not want to accept it.

Third, the two outcomes – the creation of a new state and the transfer of territory to another state – have hugely different legal and political consequences and are consequently regulated in fundamentally different ways. As Radan (2008, p. 22) notes, secession (as he defines it) involves only two parties while irredenta involves three. From a legal point of view this is a fundamental difference reflected in the different kind of legal prescriptions or reasoning relating to the two types of detachment of territory (Anderson 2013, p. 372). The creation of a new state introduces a new apparatus of government and a new, formally independent player in the international state system. Since the transfer of territory only changes the state jurisdiction over the territory, the only change, apart from the state jurisdiction, is the change of borders. This is the case whether the resident population is an agent of this change or not.

One way of approaching the agent of change issue would be to keep the term 'transfer of territory,' to cover any transfer of territory from one state to another irrespective of the agent of change. But if one needs to identify the agent of change or transfer, then one could distinguish transfer through *withdrawal* from transfer through *annexation*. The first would concern cases in which a residential population acts to detach their territory from their host state with the intent of transferring their territory to another state, that is, of joining another state (and not with the intent of creating a new state). This, one could argue, was the case of Crimea in March 2014, whose regional assembly first voted to withdraw from Ukraine and then its population voted in a referendum to join the Russian Federation. Such transfers through withdrawal can be called 'irredenta' to distinguish them from withdrawals with the intent of creating new states which we call 'secession'. The cases in which the residential populations did not act in any way would be classified as cases of transfers through annexation. Examples of this would include the annexation of the Portuguese-governed territories Goa, Damian and Diu in 1961 by India and of the Syrian territory of the Golan Heights by Israel in 1967. These annexations were carried out by military force of the annexing state without the participation of the resident populations. Both annexation and irredenta would come under the wider classification of transfer of territory; in the latter, but not the former, the resident population would be considered an agent of change. In any case, irredenta as a transfer of territory would be distinct from secession as a creation of a new state and would therefore not be included in a definition of secession.

For Radan and Anderson, whose definitions exclude irredenta, a key feature of the creation of a new state is another kind of transfer – the transfer of sovereignty from the previous host state to a new state. It is this transfer of sovereignty that in effect creates the new state. Their focus on the transfer of sovereignty and its outcome leads these two legal theorists to discount any other features of secession as irrelevant to the definition of secession. The transfer of sovereignty to a new state occurs both in the case of an overseas colony and in the case of a territory which forms a part of the bounded territory of state, thus secession includes decolonization.

Their view sharply differs from the doctrine of decolonization as stated in the UNGA Resolutions 1514 and 1515 and the subsequent UN conventions and resolutions. The UN doctrine limits the creation of new states *only* to the territories which are recognized as 'non self-governing territories' and which are, in fact, separated from the host state not only ethnically but geographically, that is, by a sea or ocean. Moreover, any withdrawal of territory which is part of the integral territory of a member state by force or by the threat thereof is explicitly prohibited by the UN Charter and the above resolutions. But as long as the outcome is the creation of a new state, neither the status nor the geographical position of the new state prior to its creation nor its impact on the territorial integrity of its previous host is of relevance to Radan's and Anderson's definitions of secession.

But if one focuses exclusively on the transfer of sovereignty to a new state, then a transfer of sovereignty to a new state resulting from *unification* of two or more states would also, paradoxically, count as secession. In contrast to irredenta which involve transfers of a *part* of a state, in the cases of unification *whole* states join together with other states. The result is either an amalgamation of one state into an existing state, such as that of the German Democratic Republic into the Federal Republic of Germany in 1991 or in a creation of a new state, such as the Kingdom of Italy in 1861 and the German Reich in 1871. Unification is thus conceptually distinct both from irredenta, transfer of territory, and from secession, creation of a new state by withdrawal or detachment of territory and its population.

According to Anderson's definition, decolonization is a case of secession in which sovereignty from one *part* of an existing state, a colony, is transferred to a new state formed on that very part. In the cases of unification leading to the creation of new states, sovereignty is transferred from the *whole* of a state to the new state which now encompasses the state from which the sovereignty is transferred. But the difference between the whole and a part of a state is in effect geographical: and geographical differences are of no consequence for Radan's and Anderson's definition of secession. For these two theorists, the geographical proximity of the seceding region to its host state is irrelevant. If the geographical distinction between the territories which are within the borders of the host state and its overseas territories plays no role in the definition of secession, why should the distinction between the whole and a part of the state play a key role in distinguishing unification from secession? Why should a mere geographical fact that the sovereignty is transferred from the whole and not from a part of the state exclude unification, as a transfer of sovereignty, from the definition of secession? Anderson and Radan offer no answer to these questions.

While excluding irredenta as a transfer of sovereignty, Anderson's and Radan's definition fails to exclude another kind of transfer of sovereignty, unification, which is, from a legal and from a political point of view, fundamentally different from secession.

Continuity versus fragmentation of the host state

Crawford's definition assumes that for secession to take place, it is necessary that the host state that opposes it continue to exist after the secessionists demand or proclaim their independence from it. If there is no sovereign host state at that time, the new state is created not through secession from, but through dissolution (fragmentation) of, the former host state. The demand for the continuity of the former host state greatly reduces the number of secessions: in many cases the end result of the detachment of one or more territorial units is the disappearance of the former host state and in all these cases, according to Crawford, there is no secession. For example, this happened not only in the case of the Socialist Federal Republic of Yugoslavia (SFRY) in 1991 but also in the case of the United Kingdoms of Sweden and Norway in 1905: as a result of the withdrawal of Norway, the former host state ceased to exist.

The requirement of the continuity of the host state is further restricted by the social scientist Michael Hechter. According to Hechter (1992, p. 277): 'Pure secession ... occurs when a highly effective state permits a secessionist territory to withdraw from its embrace.' This occurred only in the case of Norway in 1905 and of the Irish Free State in 1922. According to Hechter, in 1970/1 Pakistan was not a highly effective state and hence the detachment of Bangladesh was not pure secession. In this work Hechter advocates a rational choice theory of secessions: secessions are, according to his theory, outcomes of a rational choice both of the governments (rulers) and secessionist populations. Thus, the governments (rulers) of the host state need to have a choice of countering secessionist demands; only an effective state could provide such a choice. If a state is not effective, then the withdrawal of its territory is due not to the rational choice of the host state rulers and secessionist populations but to its weakness, that is, to its lack of capacity to counter secessionist demands. Detachment of territory from weak states may – and does – lead to their eventual disappearance (such as the USSR and SFRY). For Hechter, apart from the rare cases of rational choice, withdrawal of a territory is a result of the weakness or of fragmentation of the host state; the former may be called secession (but not pure!) while the latter is a mere fragmentation of the state.

In contrast to Crawford and Hechter, Radan and Anderson do not require the host state, let alone an effective host state, to continue as a state after its former territory became a new state. Radan (2008, p. 31) classifies the withdrawals of territory leading to dissolutions of the host state (such as those above) as 'dissolving secessions.' According to the social scientist Wood (1981, p. 112), secession 'involves the dismemberment of a territorial state' which results from the formal withdrawal of a member unit or units from the central political authority. In every case of secession, a '*dismemberment* of territorial state'[1] and its 'political disintegration' also involves a political detachment of 'loyalties, expectations, and political activities from a jurisdictional center' (Wood 1981, p. 111). Wood's definition combines territorial dismemberment with the political processes which are necessarily involved in the procedure of dismemberment. Since decolonization of overseas territories does not involve the dismemberment of state's territory, decolonization does not, necessarily, count as secession. In all other respects, the scope of Wood's definition appears to be equivalent to Radan's and Anderson's definitions.

How many secessions are there?

Restrictive definitions, as we have seen, minimize the number of secessions: according to Crawford, the only post-1945 secession is the one of Bangladesh from Pakistan which was both opposed by the host state (continuing to exist after secession) and effected by the use of force (that is, by the Indian military). For Hechter, this does not count as pure secession since the only two pure secessions are those of Norway and of the Irish Free State. For Crawford the former does not count as secession because it was at the end mutually agreed and the latter was regarded at the time as a form of decolonization.

According to Radan, Anderson and Wood, these three cases and all the other cases involving the creation of new states *all* count as secession. According to Wood, the detachment of the Irish Free State would be classified as secession or as decolonization and possibly as both. This case involved a territorial dismemberment of the United Kingdom of Great Britain and Ireland (secession) but the legal status of the new state, that of British dominion, was that of a former British colony (decolonization).

All of the definitions of secession discussed here, except Wood's, emphasize one of the following features which serves as the distinguishing mark of secession: the use or threat of use of force, or the opposition of the host state (Crawford), the territory's population as the agent of its withdrawal from the host state (Haverland), the transfer of sovereignty to the new state (Radan, Anderson) and the rational choice of the rulers to let the territory go (Hechter). Only Wood's definition, apart from requiring territorial dismemberment, lists several political processes involved in secession – some of which are also found in other non-secessionist contexts. This is what one would expect from a definition which forms the basis for an analytical framework for *comparative* study of secession as a political phenomenon. Unlike legal regulation, comparative study of secession as does not require the exclusion of all non-secession cases from its field of inquiry; it allows some cases to be studied under the classification of secessions and/or under a different classification.

Although Wood does not discuss decolonization, there are significant differences between the political processes involved in decolonization and those in secession. Colonies are generally not regarded as part of the 'sacralized' national territory nor are their inhabitants regarded as equal citizens of the host state; hence, unlike secessionists, the inhabitants of colonies do not and cannot participate in the political life of the metropolis/host state on equal footing. In advocating decolonization, inhabitants of a colony cannot be accused of attempting to break up their 'motherland' or 'fatherland' – as secessionists often are.

The detachment of Bangladesh from Pakistan in 1970 illustrates how postcolonial secession differs from decolonization from a European metropolis – although some scholars, such as Islam (1985), still regard it as a case of decolonization. In spite of the widespread discrimination against them prior to 1970, Bengalis, the natives of East Pakistan, served, as Pakistani citizens, in high administrative and military offices in Pakistan and participated in Pakistani political life. Once the main Bengali party gained a majority in all-Pakistan elections in 1970, its leader became a prime minister designate with a mandate to form a government of all Pakistan. Once he was prevented from doing so, his Bengali party proceeded to declare the independence of Bangladesh (East Pakistan) of which he later became the first prime minister. In contrast, no native politician in the pre-1947 British Raj (to which Pakistan belonged) could ever aspire to become the prime minister of the UK, its metropolis. Colonial political parties neither aimed to take power in its colonial metropolis nor could their political leaders aspire to the highest offices in the metropolitan states.

A comparative study of secessions (as territorial dismemberments) and decolonization would be likely to discover more differences – and perhaps some similarities – between the two but would probably not throw much light on processes of secessions outside the colonial context. It is no surprise that there have been no comparative studies of decolonization and secession as political processes.[2]

How do the definitions of secession affect their normative assessment?

The definitions of secession discussed above were not offered within, or in support of, a normative moral or political assessment of secession. In spite of that, they unintentionally influence our moral appraisal of the value and consequences of secession. Here we shall attempt to identify only some aspects of this impact.

In a secessionist conflict, supporters of the host state would often point out the following *negative* moral consequences of secession:

1   In the process of secession populations claiming secession renounce their allegiance to the state in which they live. As a betrayal of one's motherland/fatherland, this is, according to the supporters of the host state, intrinsically wrong. Moreover, it creates hostility among individuals and groups which felt no such hostility before and thus have morally negative consequences.
2   Secession leads to the loss of territory, resources and population and the weakening of the host state. This is an undeserved harm inflicted on the population of the host state.
3   Secessions often (but not always) lead to the (undeserved) loss of property, power and status of those who belong to the majority group in the host state.
4   Secession often (but not always) leads to violence, loss of life and forced eviction of people who did not do anything to deserve this fate.

In this chapter we are not assessing any of those normative claims. All of them are contested in one way or another, and in response to any of the above, advocates of secession can respond that their goal is to gain freedom and to exercise their fundamental right to self-determination. Freedom from an alien state and the exercise of this right, they believe, trumps any harmful consequences including those listed above (some of which are, in their view, avoidable). The restrictive definitions of secession imply that harmful secessions are an exception and therefore a normative assessment of them is an idle and unnecessary exercise. For Crawford there is only one secession, that of Bangaladesh, in the post-1945 period. All other violent and non-violent withdrawals of territory are not secessions. Since secessions are so rare, there is no point in attempting to articulate normative rules for secessions in contrast to other violent processes. Similarly, for Hechter pure secessions are those in which the rulers of the host state are able to assess the costs and benefits of secession of a part of their territory. In this way they rationally tend to minimize harm both to their populations and to the populations of the secessionist territory. The harm from other violent detachments are, according to Hechter, not consequences of rational choices but of political processes which the rulers and participants do not fully control. There is no need for normative assessment of (the very few) pure secessions and of many other forms of state fragmentation: the former are already governed by the rule of harm minimization and the latter are not within the control of its participants or decision-makers.

The permissive and inclusive legal definitions (such as Anderson's and Radan's) appear to imply, similarly, that harmful consequences, whatever they may be, are not consequences of secessions, as defined, but of the means that participants in secessionist processes choose to use to effect secessions. In consensual or negotiated secessions both sides choose to use peaceful methods and both the emerging state and the previous host state agree that there is nothing wrong in renouncing allegiance to the previous host state and the loss of its territory. In many cases of decolonization and 'dissolution secessions' the same peaceful methods were used and harmful consequences avoided. From this one can conclude that it is not secession, defined as a transfer of sovereignty and the creation of a new state, that raises any ethical questions. It is the methods that are used by political movements to pursue secession and the methods that host states use to counter them that cause harm and thus raise ethical questions. According to the permissive definitions, secessions are in fact morally neutral acts.

In short, both restrictive and permissive definitions of secession (except Wood's) tend to minimize or deny the need for normative assessment of secessions and shift the normative assessment either to territorial detachments or dissolutions which are not defined as secessions or to the ways secessions are carried out.

According to Wood, secession is defined in terms of several political processes which indeed may have harmful consequences and which may be evaluated from different moral points of view, some of which may regard these processes as intrinsically wrong. Unlike other permissive definitions, Wood's definition leaves open the possibility both of moral assessment of some secessions and of moral neutrality of others (for a similar view see Pavković 2011).

Normative theorists of secession, who are attempting to elaborate a set of moral norms for normative assessment of secessions within a philosophical framework, generally pay no attention to the debates about the definition of secession among legal theorists and social scientists. In the first ever outline of a normative theory of secession in contemporary philosophy, Beran (1984, p. 21) defines secession as follows: 'the withdrawal, from an existing state and its central government, of part of this state, the withdrawing part consisting of citizens and the territory they occupy.'

There is no mention of the use of force or threat thereof, of the continuity of the host state following secession, of rational choice or of overseas territories of existing states. Decolonization for Beran is only a peripheral problem and his discussion is restricted to secessions from 'unified' states; further, by comparing secession to a divorce between two persons, Beran effectively excludes irredenta whose result, the transfer of one entity to another, is not comparable to divorce. In short, Beran appears to offer a permissive definition similar in scope to Wood's. Later normative theorists offer no definition of secession of their own but appear to assume a permissive definition similar to that of Beran, while at the same time they reject Beran's normative theory of the right to secession (Dietrich 2011). Thus both Buchanan (1991) and Wellman (2005), who offer diametrically opposite normative theories of the right of secession, assume that secession involves the creation of new states, the break-up (Wood's 'dismemberment') of existing states and the consequent changes in their political boundaries.

Normative theorists search for *universal* moral norms that could justify the creation of new states through the process of territorial dismemberment. Were they to assume any of the restrictions on secession proposed by the above restrictive definitions, they would undermine the universality of the principles they propose. But given that decolonization affects the existing states in a morally and politically different way than secession does, they usually do not include decolonization within their conception of secession.

Why define secession?

Legal scholars appear to differ in their views on the possibility of legal *regulation* of secession. Crawford does not believe that international law can or should regulate the creation of new states by secession out of existing states. Radan and Anderson, as well as many others, believe that there is an emergent legal prescription in international law and practice which may in time come to legally regulate secession. Their views are reflected in their definitions of secession. One could perhaps argue that their definitions are constructed so as to provide support for their views on the regulation of secession.

In contrast, political scientists aim to explain why and how secession happens; in short, they search for explanatory theories of secession. As we have seen, their choice of explanatory theory may be reflected in their definition of secession. Hechter's preference for rational choice explanation leads him to a highly restrictive definition of secession. Wood's preference for a dynamic explanatory theory, in which explanatory variables are allowed to interact in a variety of ways, leads him to propose one of the most permissive definitions of secession. Like normative theorists, many social scientists do not explicitly discuss definitions of secession; those who, like Wood, espouse dynamic explanatory theories which allow for multi-path interactions of variables, assume a permissive definition similar to his (indicatively see Horowitz 1985 and Siroky 2011). The advocates of dynamic theories obviously have no reason to think that secession needs to be defined in terms of a single set of characteristics or variables which would categorically differentiate it from any other political process. As Wood has emphasized, secessionist movements' professed aims often oscillate between separatism, the striving for an increased autonomy from the political center, and secessionism. Hence secessionism cannot, in practice, be sharply differentiated from various forms of political separatism. And, taking this observation further, those who study secession from a historical perspective often adopt an even more permissive definition than Wood's and, like Radan and Anderson, include decolonization under secession (Coggins 2011).

The common ground between the legal, normative and political science definitions of secession is thus to be found in a permissive or inclusive approach to such a definition. In any case, the definition of secession is currently a topic of debate neither in political science nor in normative theory of secession. But as part of their ongoing debate regarding the legal regulation of secession, legal scholars are still debating the question of what secession is. And as they differ in their views as to how to regulate secession, they will probably continue to differ in their definition of secession. Their debate may perhaps come to an end if and when secession comes to be regulated by positive international law; such law would need to *define* what secession is, and then legal scholars may be left only with the task of interpreting positive international law and its definition of secession.

Notes

1 This obviously rules out unification of states.
2 Even Hechter (1975), who uses the concept of 'internal colonialism' in his study, excludes decolonization from his definition of secession.

References

Anderson, G 2013, 'Secession In International Law: What Are We Talking About?' *Loyola of Los Angeles International and Comparative Law Journal*, vol. 35, no. 3, pp. 343–389.

Aronovitch, H 2000, 'Why Secession is Unlike Divorce,' *Public Affairs Quarterly*, vol. 14, no. 1, pp. 27–39.

Beran, H 1984, 'A Liberal Theory of Secession,' *Political Studies*, vol. 32, pp. 21–31.

Buchanan, A 1991, *Secession: The Morality of Political Divorce from Fort Sumter to Lithuania and Quebec*, Westview Press, Boulder, CO.

Coggins, BL 2011, 'History of Secessions: an Overview,' in A Pavković and P Radan (eds), *The Ashgate Companion to Secession*, Ashgate, Aldershot, pp. 23–44.

Crawford, J 2006, *The Creation of States in International Law*, 2nd edn, Oxford University Press, Oxford.

Dietrich, F 2011, 'Changing Borders by Secession: Normative Assessment of Secession,' in A Pavković and P Radan (eds), *The Ashgate Companion to Secession*, Ashagte, Aldershot, pp. 81–98.

Haverland, C 2000, 'Secession,' in R Bernhardt (ed.), *Encyclopedia of Public International Law*, Vol. IV, North-Holland, Amsterdam, London and New York, pp. 354–356.

Hechter, M 1975, *Internal Colonialism: The Celtic Fringe in British National Development*, University of California Press, Berkeley, CA.

Hechter, M 1992, 'The Dynamics of Secession,' *Acta Sociologica*, vol. 35, pp. 267–283.

Heraclides, A 1991, *The Self-Determination of Minorities in International Politics*, Frank Cass, London.

Horowitz, DL 1985, *Ethnic Groups in Conflict*, Berkeley, University of California Press.

Islam, R 1985, 'Secessionist Self-Determination: Some Lessons from Katanga, Biafra and Bangaladesh,' *Journal of Peace Research*, vol. 22, no. 4, pp. 217–227.

Pavković, A 2011, 'The Right to Secede: Do We Really Need It?' in A Pavković and P Radan (eds), *The Ashgate Companion to Secession*, Ashgate, Aldershot, pp. 439–452.

Pavković, A with Radan, P 2007, *Creating New States: Theory and Practice of Secession*, Ashgate, Aldershot.

Radan, P 2008, 'Secession: A Word in Search of a Meaning,' in A Pavković and P Radan (eds), *On the Way to Statehood: Secession and Globalization*, Ashgate, Aldershot, pp. 17–32.

Siroky, DS 2011 'Explaining Secession,' in A Pavković and P Radan (eds), *The Ashgate Research Companion to Secession*, Ashgate, Farnham, pp. 45–80.

Wellman, CH 2005, *A Theory of Secession: The Case for Political Self-Determination*, Cambridge University Press, Cambridge, UK.

Wood, JR 1981, 'Secession: A Comparative Analytical Framework,' *Canadian Journal of Political Science*, vol. 14, pp. 109–135.

2 Secession

A question of law or fact?

Peter Radan

Introduction

In its 1998 opinion in *Reference re: Secession of Quebec*, the Supreme Court of Canada recognized that 'the process of recognition (of states), once considered to be an exercise of pure sovereign discretion, has come to be associated with legal norms' (Secession Reference 1998, p. 443). The issue to be explored in this chapter is the extent to which this statement pictures the situation with respect to statehood through secession. The eminent Australian international lawyer and scholar, James Crawford, maintains that 'secession is neither legal nor illegal in international law, but a neutral act the consequences of which are regulated internationally' (Crawford 2006, p. 390). If there is any move towards secession being regulated by international law, the source of such law is to be found in the right of peoples to self-determination which is one of the few peremptory and non-derogable norms of international law (*jus cogens*).[1] Indeed, the International Court of Justice (ICJ) has ruled that the right of self-determination was an essential principle of contemporary international law and an *erga omnes* obligation (East Timor Case 1995, p. 243).[2] If the right of a people to self-determination does ground a right of secession then, according to Crawford, 'it is probably the case that the use of force by a non-State entity in the exercise of self-determination is legally neutral, that is, not regulated by international law at all (though the rules of international humanitarian law may well apply)' (Crawford 2006, pp. 134–135).

If, as Crawford maintains, secession is neither legal nor illegal in international law, the resolution of secessionist disputes is ultimately dependant upon the use and preponderance of force. In this respect, Steven Ratner has observed that 'international law declares the lack of either a blanket right to, or prohibition against, secession and seemingly relegates its achievement to a pure power calculus' (Ratner 1996, p. 590). This sentiment aligns itself with the Realist school of thought in international relations theory. For Realists, international law merely reflects the interests of the powerful states with the consequence that the success of any secession attempt is ultimately dependent upon the recognition of statehood by powerful states. The importance of recognition is reflected in the fact that its achievement is the major foreign policy goal of any secessionist movement. Although recognition is not necessary to achieve statehood, in the context of secession 'the viability of a would-be state in the international community depends, as a practical matter, upon recognition by other states' (Secession Reference 1998, p. 443). Without such recognition the seceding entity cannot be regarded as a member of the international community, and the secession will most likely end in failure. The importance of recognition in secessionist conflicts can be illustrated by a number of examples. The recognition of the independence of the Spanish American states by the United States in 1822 was described by Samuel Flagg Bemis, the noted American scholar of diplomatic history, as 'the greatest assistance rendered by any foreign power to the independence of Latin America' (Gleijeses 1992, p. 487). The recognition by India, a significant regional power, of Bangladesh in 1971 was a key to the success of the Bangladesh secession from Pakistan (Crawford 2006, p. 141). That is not to say that an unrecognized or de facto state cannot exist if there is support for it by a sufficiently powerful state, a prime example of such being Turkey's continued support of the Turkish Republic of Northern Cyprus.

On the other hand, the failure to gain international recognition has been a major contributing factor to the failure of various secessions. In the case of the ultimately unsuccessful secession from the United States in the early 1860s of 11 southern states that constituted the Confederate States, the major foreign policy goal of the United States was to prevent international recognition of the southern Confederacy. President Abraham Lincoln was prepared to risk war with Great Britain over this issue. For the Confederacy international recognition was the single most important diplomatic goal (Taylor 1991, pp. 177–179). Lincoln's strategy succeeded (Jones 1995, p. 52). However, had Great Britain and the rest of Europe recognized the Confederacy it is arguable that the latter's secession from the United States would have succeeded. Widespread international condemnation of the secessions of Katanga from the Congo in 1960 and Biafra from Nigeria in 1967 doomed them to eventual failure. The fact that only Turkey has recognized the 1983 secession of the Turkish Republic of Northern Cyprus means that the latter's secession has not, at least to date, been successful (Jennings and Watts 1992, p. 130).

The right of self-determination and secession

On 24 October 1970 the UNGA adopted Resolution 2625 known as the Declaration on 'Principles of International Law Concerning Friendly Relations and Co-operation Among States in Accordance With the Charter of the United Nations' (Declaration on Friendly Relations). As its title indicates, the Declaration on Friendly Relations expounds a number of principles relating to friendly relations and co-operation among states. One such principle is 'the principle of equal rights and self-determination of peoples' (Principle 5) enshrined in the UN Charter. Principle 5 and its elaboration reads as follows:

The principle of equal rights and self-determination of peoples

[1] By virtue of the principle of equal rights and self-determination of peoples enshrined in the Charter of the United Nations, all peoples have the right

freely to determine, without external interference, their political status and to pursue their economic, social and cultural development, and every State has the duty to respect this right in accordance with the provisions of the Charter.

[2] Every State has the duty to promote, through joint and separate action, realization of the principle of equal rights and self-determination of peoples, in accordance with the provisions of the Charter, and to render assistance to the United Nations in carrying out the responsibilities entrusted to it by the Charter regarding the implementation of the principle, in order:

(a) to promote friendly relations and co-operation among states; and
(b) to bring a speedy end to colonialism, having due regard to the freely expressed will of the peoples concerned;

and bearing in mind that subjection of peoples to alien subjugation, domination and exploitation constitutes a violation of the principle, as well as a denial of fundamental human rights, and is contrary to the Charter.

[3] Every State has a duty to promote through joint and several action universal respect for and observance of human rights and fundamental freedoms in accordance with the Charter.

[4] The establishment of a sovereign and independent State, the free association or integration with an independent State or the emergence into any other political status freely determined by a people constitute modes of implementing the right of self-determination by that people.

[5] Every State has a duty to refrain from any forcible action which deprives peoples referred to above in the elaboration of the present principle of their right to self-determination and freedom and independence. In actions against, and resistance to, such forcible action in pursuit of the exercise of their right to self-determination, such peoples are entitled to seek and receive support in accordance with the purposes and principles of the Charter.

[6] The territory of a colony or other non-self-governing territory has, under the Charter, a status separate and distinct from the territory of the State administering it; and such separate and distinct status under the Charter shall exist until the people of the colony or non-self-governing territory have exercised their right of self-determination in accordance with the Charter, and particularly its purposes and principles.

[7] Nothing in the foregoing paragraphs shall be construed as authorizing or encouraging any action which would dismember or impair, totally or in part, the territorial integrity or political unity of sovereign and independent States conducting themselves in compliance with the principle of equal rights and self-determination of peoples as described above and thus possessed of a government representing the whole people belonging to the territory without distinction as to race, creed or colour.

[8] Every State shall refrain from any action aimed at the partial or total disruption of the national unity and territorial integrity of any other State or country.[3]

The crucial part of Principle 5 is the so-called 'safeguard clause' in paragraph 7. The very essence of this clause is that a state's territorial integrity is assured only under certain conditions.

In construing the meaning of the safeguard clause, it is clear that it protects the territorial integrity of a state that conducts itself 'in compliance with the principle of equal rights and self-determination of peoples.' In paragraph 1 of Principle 5 it is stated that by virtue of the principle of equal rights and self-determination of peoples 'all peoples have the right freely to determine, without external interference, their political status and to pursue their economic, social and cultural development, and *every State* has the duty to respect this right' (emphasis added). Thus, a state's conduct is bound by a principle that requires it to allow 'all peoples' the right to freely determine their political status and pursue their economic, social and cultural development. It was not until the adoption of the Declaration on Friendly Relations that it was clear that states had 'an affirmative duty to promote the realization of the right [of self-determination]' (Rosenstock 1971, p. 731). Antonio Cassese refers to this as an obligation to provide 'equal access to government' (Cassese 1995, p. 114). If a state does not so conduct itself with respect to all its population, its territorial integrity is not guaranteed. Crawford (2006, p. 418) accurately summarizes the meaning of the safeguard clause as follows:

> A State whose government represents the whole people of its territory on the basis of equality complies with the principle of self-determination in respect of all of its people and is entitled to the protection of its territorial integrity. The people of such a State exercise the right of self-determination on the basis of equality. The correlative is that a State which is governed democratically and respects the human rights of its people is entitled to respect for its territorial integrity.

The clear implication (not explicitly noted by Crawford) of the safeguard clause is the existence of an implied right of secession. The scope for secession within the safeguard clause, whilst noted by some commentators, has more often than not been overlooked or downplayed and occasionally denied (Radan 2002, pp. 54–55). However, many others do recognize the significance of the undoubted scope for its implied right of secession. For example, Dugard concludes that 'a Government that denies equal rights and self-determination to a people ... forfeits the right to respect for its territorial integrity. That is, in the final resort, a people so treated may exercise a remedial right of secession' (Dugard 2013, pp. 145–146). Kooijmans notes that:

> the right of secession is not a normal emanation of the right to self-determination, but an *ultimum remedium*, to be resorted to only if all efforts to find a solution within the State structure have been to no avail and if local and international remedies have turned out to be fruitless.
>
> (Kooijmans 1996, p. 216)

The right to secede implied by the safeguard clause is unaffected by paragraph 8 of Principle 5. Paragraph 8 protects a state's territorial integrity from the actions of other *states* (emphasis added). As White has observed, there is no prohibition in paragraph 8 against a people seeking self-determination either by secession or by replacement of an unrepresentative government (White 1981, p. 159).

On the preceding analysis, the right to secede pursuant to the safeguard clause rests with 'a people.' However, after stipulating that nothing can affect the territorial integrity of a state which conducts itself in accordance with the principle of equal rights and self-determination of peoples, the safeguard clause further stipulates that a state which does so conduct itself is 'possessed of a government representing the whole population belonging to the territory *without distinction as to race, creed or colour*' (emphasis added). The only inference that can be drawn from the 'without distinction' provision is that the right to secede is open only to groups defined in terms of 'race, creed or colour.'

There is debate over the extent to which the 'without distinction' qualification limits the implied right of secession set out in the safeguard clause (Cassese 1995, pp. 112–115; Radan 2002, pp. 57–60). However, whatever the merits of the debate may be, the issue would now appear to be an academic question in the light of the adoption by the UNGA, on October 24 1995, of the Declaration on the Occasion of the Fiftieth Anniversary of the United Nations (Fiftieth Anniversary Declaration). By Article 1, the General Assembly declared that it would, *inter alia*:

> Continue to reaffirm the right of self-determination of all peoples, taking into account the particular situation of peoples under colonial or other forms of alien domination or foreign occupation, and recognize the right of peoples to take legitimate action in accordance with the Charter of the United Nations to realize their inalienable right of self-determination. This shall not be construed as authorizing or encouraging any action that would dismember or impair, totally or in part, the territorial integrity or political unity of sovereign and independent States conducting themselves in compliance with the principle of equal rights and self-determination of peoples and thus possessed of a Government representing the whole people belonging to the territory without distinction of any kind.[4]

As can be seen from its wording, Article 1 has similarities to Principle 5 of the Declaration on Friendly Relations, in particular to the latter's safeguard clause. The critical difference between Article 1 and the safeguard clause is the qualification at the end of both provisions. The safeguard clause speaks in terms of representative government 'without distinction as to race, creed or colour,' whereas Article 1 is unlimited in scope, speaking of representative government 'without distinction of any kind.' Whatever doubts may have existed on the limits to the implied right to secession contained in the limiting words of the safeguard clause are removed by Article 1. Any group within an unrepresentative or discriminatory state has a prima facie right to secede (Sharma 1997, p. 226).

The potential impact of the safeguard clause was confirmed soon after its adoption in the context of the secession of Bangladesh from Pakistan in 1971. An International Commission of Jurists observed, in a 1972 study entitled *The Events in East Pakistan, 1971*, that the right to self-determination and the principle of territorial integrity were conflicting principles, and that the safeguard clause gave primacy to the principle of territorial integrity. However, the Commission also noted:

> It is submitted, however, that this principle is subject to the requirement that the government does comply with the principle of equal rights and does represent the whole people without distinction. If one of the constituent peoples of a state is denied equal rights and is discriminated against, it is submitted that their full right of self-determination will revive.
> (International Commission of Jurists 1972, p. 119)

Thus, according to the Commission, if the circumstances are present, as indeed they were with the Bangladesh situation, secession as the exercise of a people's right to self-determination is permissible.

Furthermore, the Supreme Court of Canada recognized that there was an arguable case that international law recognized such an implied right of secession. In *Reference re: Secession of Quebec*, the Court said:

> The international law right to self-determination only generates, at best, a right to external self-determination in situations of former colonies; where a people is oppressed, as for example under foreign military occupation; or *where a definable group is denied meaningful access to government to pursue their political, economic, social and cultural development*. In all three situations, the people in question are entitled to a right to external self-determination because they have been denied the ability to exert internally their right to self-determination.
> (Secession Reference 1998, p. 442; emphasis added)

The case of Kosovo

In 2010, in the context of Kosovo's declaration of independence from Serbia, the ICJ had before it the opportunity to clarify the extent, if any, to which the right of peoples to self-determination contained a legal right of secession.

The first significant demands for secession in Kosovo from Yugoslavia, as it then was, were made in 1981. This resulted in the Yugoslav National Army intervening to suppress Kosovo Albanian nationalism, and ultimately to limitations on its autonomy with the amendments to the Serbian Constitution in 1989. The Slovenian and Croatian declarations of independence from Yugoslavia in June 1991 triggered further demands for Kosovo's independence by its predominantly Albanian population. An independence referendum in September 1991 was followed by a declaration of independence in October 1991. Albania was the only state to then recognize Kosovo, as Kosovo's application to the European Union for recognition was rejected on account of it not being a Yugoslav republic (Radan 2002, pp. 196–201).

During most of the 1990s the situation in Kosovo was tense, with periodic outbursts of violence and civil unrest. Serbia's attempts to assert control over the province were then met with passive resistance, until the emergence of the militant Kosovo Liberation Army (KLA) forces in the late 1990s. The most significant factor leading to the emergence of the KLA was the failure to consider Kosovo's status at the Dayton negotiations in 1995 that brought about a conclusion to the hostilities in Croatia and Bosnia-Herzegovina. This failure led many Kosovo Albanians to conclude that the policy of passive resistance was a failure and to shift support to the more militant KLA. The breakdown of order in neighbouring Albania at that time came at a propitious time as it led to a flood of military equipment into the hands of the KLA.

The emergence of the KLA led to a dramatic escalation of violence in Kosovo. Although the United States had listed the KLA as a terrorist organization, in early 1998 it was de-listed. Following secret meetings between Richard Holbrooke, the key figure in the design of American policy towards the region at that time, and KLA representatives, in June 1998, Holbrooke told KLA representatives that Kosovo's independence would be achieved within five years. From that point on the United States resolutely pursued a policy consistent with that goal (Henriksen 2007, pp. 141–142). The Rambouillet Peace Conference in early 1999 presented Serbia with an ultimatum that it could not accept, and still maintain a claim to be a sovereign state. Indeed the terms of the Rambouillet document went further in that direction than did the Austro-Hungarian ultimatum presented to Serbia in July 1914. Just as in 1914, Serbia's refusal to accede to the ultimatum led to war.

Following the 78-day NATO military intervention against Serbia, Kosovo became an international protectorate, and although Serbia's sovereignty and territorial integrity were confirmed by the UN Security Council's Resolution 1244 (UNSCR 1244) which was adopted on June 10 1999, to all intents and purposes Kosovo ceased to be part of Serbia. The negotiations, envisaged by UNSC Resolution 1244, relating to a resolution agreeable to both the Serbs and Kosovo Albanians over the future status of Kosovo, proved to be fruitless (Trbovich 2008, pp. 121–170; Weller 2009, pp. 179–258). The Kosovo Albanians, knowing that the United States would never accede to Kosovo remaining within Serbia, simply rejected out of hand Serbia's offer of complete autonomy. The one possible means of reaching a negotiated solution, namely, partition of Kosovo, was, in the words of Hurst Hannum, 'inexplicably rejected' by the international community (Hannum 2007).

Following Kosovo's declaration of independence from Serbia that was proclaimed on February 17 2008, the UN General Assembly sought an advisory opinion from the ICJ on the question: 'Is the unilateral declaration of independence by the Provisional Institutions of Self-Government of Kosovo in accordance with international law?'

In *Accordance With International Law of the Unilateral Declaration of Independence in Respect of Kosovo (Advisory Opinion)* (the *Kosovo Advisory Opinion*) handed down on July 22 2010, the ICJ had, but did not grasp, the opportunity to provide an authoritative statement on the existence and extent of any legal right to secession in international law.

The ICJ's majority opinion looked at the question posed to it by the General Assembly in two parts. First, there was the issue of whether the declaration of independence was in accordance with general principles of international law. Second, there was the question of whether it was in accordance with the special law applying to Kosovo (*lex specialis*) that flowed from UNSCR 1244 and the institutional and constitutional framework for the administration of Kosovo pursuant to that resolution.

In relation to the first of these two parts, the ICJ said that it was asked to decide 'whether or not the applicable international law prohibited the declaration of independence' (Kosovo Advisory Opinion 2010, pp. 29–30). In construing the question, the ICJ's majority opinion took a technical and legalistic approach, ruling that the question was narrow and specific. It made a distinction between, on the one hand, the proclamation of a declaration of independence and, on the other hand, whether such a proclamation constituted the exercise of a right conferred by international law. In determining that the question put to it by the UN General Assembly raised only the first point and not the second, the majority opinion said:

> The task which the Court is called upon to perform is to determine whether or not the declaration of independence was adopted in violation of international law. The Court is not required by the question ... to take a position on whether international law conferred a positive entitlement on Kosovo unilaterally to declare its independence or, *a fortiori*, on whether international law generally confers an entitlement on entities situated within a State unilaterally to break away from it.
>
> (Kosovo Advisory Opinion 2010, p. 30)

It thus logically followed that the Court's ruling that the question demanded no decision on 'whether or not Kosovo has achieved statehood' nor on the 'legal effects of the recognition of Kosovo by those States which have recognized it as an independent State' nor as to 'whether or not the declaration has led to the creation of a State' (Kosovo Advisory Opinion 2010, p. 27). Indeed, the Court repeated on a number of occasions that such issues were not the subject of the advisory opinion and that it made no comment on them.

In substance the ICJ's majority opinion adopted the argument put forward by James Crawford, who appeared before the Court as counsel for the United Kingdom and who opened his oral arguments to the Court as follows:

> Mr. President, Members of the Court, I am a devoted but disgruntled South Australian. 'I hereby declare the independence of South Australia.' What

has happened? Precisely nothing. Have I committed an internationally wrongful act in your presence? Of course not. Have I committed an ineffective act? Very likely.... The reason is simple. A declaration issued by persons within a State is a collection of words writ in water; it is the sound of one hand clapping.

(Kosovo Advisory Opinion Oral Submissions 2009, p. 47)

Furthermore, the majority opinion rejected arguments that Kosovo's declaration of independence was illegal on the basis of previous Security Council resolutions that had condemned the declarations of independence relating to Southern Rhodesia, Turkish Northern Cyprus and Republika Srpska. In this respect the Court's majority said:

In all of those instances the Security Council was making a determination as regards the concrete situation existing at the time that those declarations of independence were made; the illegality attached to the declarations of independence thus stemmed not from the unilateral character of these declarations as such, but from the fact that they were, or would have been, connected with the unlawful use of force or other egregious violations of norms of general international law, in particular those of a peremptory character (*jus cogens*). In the context of Kosovo, the Security Council has never taken this position. The exceptional character of the resolutions enumerated above appears to the Court to confirm that no general prohibition against unilateral declarations of independence may be inferred from the practice of the Security Council.

(Kosovo Advisory Opinion 2010, p. 41)

As to whether the Kosovo Declaration of Independence breached the 'local law' created by and pursuant to UNSCR 1244, the majority opinion avoided the issue by ruling that the declaration was not made by any of the Provisional Institutions of Self-Government of Kosovo set up pursuant to UNSCR 1244. Rather, the majority opinion ruled that the declaration was made by the individuals who signed the Declaration and not the Kosovo Assembly (one of the Provisional Institutions of Self-Government of Kosovo) and that, as such, these individuals were not bound by the institutional framework established by UNSCR 1244. Had it been a declaration proclaimed by the Kosovo Assembly there would have been a violation of the international law set up pursuant to UNSCR 1244.

Although the majority opinion of the ICJ did not discuss the substantive question of the right of secession in international law, some of its judges did so in separate opinions. Thus, Judge Yusuf observed that there was no right of unilateral secession simply because a racially or ethnically distinct group within a state wished to secede. However, His Excellency went on to say:

[W]here the State not only denies [such a group] the exercise of their internal right of self-determination (as described above), but also subjects them to discrimination, persecution and egregious violations of human rights or humanitarian law ... the right of peoples to self-determination may support a claim to separate statehood provided it meets the conditions prescribed by international law, in a specific situation, taking into account the historical context. Such conditions may be gleaned from various instruments, including the Declaration on [Friendly Relations] ... [The safeguard clause of this Declaration] makes it clear that so long as a sovereign and independent State complies with the principle of equal rights and self-determination of peoples, its territorial integrity and national unity should neither be impaired nor infringed upon. It therefore primarily protects, and gives priority to, the territorial preservation of States and seeks to avoid their fragmentation or disintegration due to separatist forces. However, the ... clause in its latter part implies that if a State fails to comport itself in accordance with the principle of equal rights and self-determination of peoples, an exceptional situation may arise whereby the ethnically or racially distinct group denied internal self-determination may claim a right of external self-determination or separation from the State which could effectively put into question the State's territorial unity and sovereignty.... To determine whether a specific situation constitutes an exceptional case which may legitimize a claim to external self-determination, certain criteria have to be considered, such as the existence of discrimination against a people, its persecution due to its racial or ethnic characteristics, and the denial of autonomous political structures and access to government.... All possible remedies for the realization of internal self-determination must be exhausted before the issue is removed from the domestic jurisdiction of the State which had hitherto exercised sovereignty over the territory inhabited by the people making the claim. In this context, the role of the international community, and in particular of the Security Council and the General Assembly, is of paramount importance.

(Kosovo Advisory Opinion 2010, pp. 223–225)

In his separate opinion, Judge Cancado Trindade, on the basis of similar reasoning, reached the same conclusion (Kosovo Advisory Opinion 2010, pp. 195–197).

On the other hand, in his dissenting opinion, Judge Koroma ruled that there was no right of secession in international law. In support of his contention (Kosovo Advisory Opinion 2010, p. 80), Judge Koroma cited that part of the safeguard clause of the Declaration on Friendly Relations which stipulates as follows:

Nothing in the foregoing Paragraphs shall be construed as authorizing or encouraging any action which would dismember or impair, totally or in part, the territorial integrity or political unity of sovereign and independent States.

However, His Excellency omitted the crucial remaining words of the safeguard clause which stipulate as follows:

conducting themselves in compliance with the principle of equal rights and self-determination of peoples as described above and thus possessed of a government representing the whole people belonging to the territory without distinction as to race, creed or colour.

The failure to take into account the latter part of the safeguard clause highlights the difference in approaches taken by, on the one hand, Judge Koroma, and on the other hand, by Judges Yusuf and Cancado Trindade, as it was this very part of the safeguard clause upon which the latter based the existence of a qualified right of unilateral secession.

Reflections on the 'Kosovo Advisory Opinion'

There is widespread recognition that the international law rules relating to the regulation of secession need to be clarified as a means of facilitating the resolution of secessionist claims. From that perspective the ICJ's Kosovo Advisory Opinion is undoubtedly a disappointment.[5] A consequence of the Court's refusal to broach the broad question of when secession could be considered legal points to the Court preferring to see secession as a factual, rather than a legal, question, at least until such time as there is some clarification of legal issues through the process of UN declarations, conventions and other pronouncements. This process is unlikely to achieve such a goal. This stems from the essentially political nature of the UN. In this respect David Sloss makes the following comment:

> UN Declarations are an imperfect tool for clarifying the law because such declarations are the product of a negotiation process that necessarily involves compromise among states with competing interests. Insofar as states disagree about how best to reconcile the competing norms of self-determination and territorial integrity, use of ambiguous language helps to facilitate agreement on a final document that allows all competing factions to declare victory. Indeed, this appears to offer at least a partial explanation for the tortured language quoted above from the 1970 Declaration. In sum, the process of compromise undermines the utility of UN Declarations as a tool for clarification of legal principles.
> (Sloss 2002, pp. 361–362)

Andrew Coleman has argued that ICJ advisory opinions could make a contribution to facilitating peaceful resolution of secessionist claims in that such a process would develop preconditions governing the legitimacy of secessionist claims. He then suggests that the preconditions could be that the secessionist group: (1) demonstrate respect for international law; (2) accept the inviolability of international borders; (3) demonstrate popular support for independence through a supervised referendum; (4) demonstrate that they have been denied democratic governance; (5) demonstrate that the secessionist group has been subject to foreign or alien subjugation; and (6) establish that they are capable of forming a state as defined by international law (Coleman 2010).

Sloss also argues that ICJ adjudication of secessionist claims through the use of advisory opinions would be extremely useful in resolving secessionist claims, and suggests two major benefits that would flow from such a process. First, 'case-by-case adjudication ... is likely to be a better mechanism than adoption of United Nations Declarations or conventions', and second, 'international adjudication may, in some cases, facilitate political resolution of secessionist disputes' (Sloss 2002, p. 358).

The approach taken by the ICJ in the Kosovo Advisory Opinion lends support to Sloss' second point, in the sense that the Court's opinion has done little if anything to resolve the Kosovo situation. At the time of the ICJ decision on July 22 2010, 71 of the 193 member states of the UN had recognized Kosovo's independence. Despite the predictions of many commentators that the ICJ decision would lead to a swag of recognitions, this has not been the case. As of the time of writing this chapter (April 2014), only 37 additional states recognized Kosovo – all of them being relatively minor states in terms of international power and influence.[6] Meetings, discussions and political posturing continue over the issue, with media reports in recent times dealing with whether partitioning Kosovo is a possible pathway forward. Arguably, a clear statement from the ICJ on the question of whether Kosovo's secession was legally justified, rather than whether the issuance of mere declaration of independence was legal, would have led, one way or the other, to a resolution of the final status of Kosovo.

It could be asked what the reasons were for the ICJ adopting a very narrow and technical construction of the question posed by the UN General Assembly and then giving the answer that it did. It is submitted that the Court was reluctant to approve any, even limited or qualified, legal right of secession that would undermine the principle of the territorial integrity of states. However, to so rule would have upheld Serbia's territorial integrity at the expense of Kosovo's independence, a position that the Court's judges found to be unpalatable. However, by interpreting the question before it as, in effect, a 'free speech' issue, the Court was able to maintain the legality of the declaring of independence. In effect the Court ruled that secession is a matter of fact and left it to the political process to determine Kosovo's fate, guessing that, in the long run, Kosovo will eventually gain its independence and admission to the UN. However, this approach has arguably provided no assistance in relation to the myriad of other secessionist claims around the world, which will continue to be determined by violence and power politics, much as has always been the case.

Conclusion

Whether the right of peoples to self-determination grants a legal right of unilateral secession from an existing independent state is still an unresolved issue. It may be that international law is moving slowly towards the recognition of a 'remedial' right of secession along the lines suggested by Judges Yusuf and

Cancado Trindade in Kosovo Advisory Opinion, a right which Dugard regards as 'not only necessary for justice but also for peace' (Dugard 2013, p. 278). However, in the meantime, as is suggested by the ICJ majority decision in Kosovo Advisory Opinion, secession is still, ultimately, a question of fact.

The current position is perhaps best summarized by Brad Roth who, in the light of analyzing the safeguard clause of the Declaration on Friendly Relation, writes:

> Where a government manifestly fails to 'represent the whole people belonging to a territory without distinction', as by the conduct of ethnic cleansing, the imperatives of 'territorial integrity' and 'political unity' lose their rationale. Arguably, being subject to gross and systematic discrimination reveals a minority group (whether marked by ethnic or other characteristics) to be a 'people' with its own right of self-determination – though no minority group in the non-colonial context has ever been authoritatively declared to be a 'people'. More likely, patterns of extreme discrimination are now seen as justifying the international community – especially collectively, through Security Council action under Chapter VII of the Charter – in derogating from the system's ordinary respect for territorial integrity and political unity.
>
> (Roth 2008, pp. 136–137)

Notes

1 In a study prepared by the Special Rapporteur of the Sub-Committee on Prevention of Discrimination and Protection of Minorities, it was stated that 'no one can challenge the fact that, in the light of contemporary international relations, the principle of self-determination necessarily possesses the character of *jus cogens*': E/CN.4/Sub.2/405/Rev.1, at 12.
2 *Erga omnes* obligations have been defined as 'obligations of a State towards the international community as a whole ... In view of the importance of the rights involved, all States can be held to have a legal interest in their protection; they are obligations *erga omnes*' (Barcelona Traction Case 1970, p. 32).
3 The numbering of the paragraphs in Principle 5 does not appear in the original text and is inserted here for convenience in relation to the discussion of Principle 5.
4 At the second World Conference on Human Rights organized by the United Nations and held in Vienna in June 1993, the more than 180 states adopted, on 25 June 1993, by consensus, the Vienna Declaration and Programme of Action. The declaration in Article 2, paragraph 1 reaffirmed the right of all peoples to self-determination in terms identical to Article 1 of the two international covenants of 1966, and in Article 2, paragraph 3 stated in identical terms the last sentence of Article 1 of the Fiftieth Anniversary Declaration: The Vienna Declaration and Programme of Action, United Nations Department of Public Information, Doc. DPI/1395–39399, August, 1993.
5 '[T]he [ICJ] ... largely failed to seize [an] opportunity' (Burri 2010, p. 882). '[T]he Advisory Opinion will have minimal legal significance either for the status of Kosovo or for our understanding of state formation and self-determination in the twenty-first century' (Hannum 2011, p. 159). 'We are no further towards a real settlement of the Kosovo dispute than we were before the ICJ opinion' (Ker-Lindsay 2011, p. 8). '[T]he court adopted a very narrow interpretation of the question put to it by the General

Assembly. In doing so, the court avoided confronting a number of legal issues that would have benefited from authoritative statements of law in order to dispel many of the uncertainties that still affect the Kosovo conflict' (Tricot and Sander 2011, p. 361). '[T]he Court adopted a fallacious line of reasoning on the legality of UDIs under international law, guided by the image of the disgruntled South Australian, which allowed it to avoid pronouncing on rules governing the secession of States' (Dugard 2013, p. 239).

6 For a list of states that have recognized Kosovo see: 'Who Recognized Kosova as an Independent State?' available online at: www.kosovothanksyou.com/. Major international states such as China, Russia, India, Spain, Argentina and Brazil have not recognized Kosovo.

References

Barcelona Traction Case 1970, *Barcelona Traction, Light, & Power Co* (*Belgium v Spain*) [1970] *International Court of Justice Reports* 3.

Burri, T 2010, 'The Kosovo Opinion and Secession: The Sounds of Silence and Missing Links,' *German Law Journal*, vol. 11, no. 8, pp. 881–889.

Cassese, A 1995, *Self-Determination of Peoples: A Legal Appraisal*, Cambridge University Press, Cambridge, UK.

Coleman, A 2010, 'Determining the Legitimacy of Claims for Self-Determination: A Role for the International Court of Justice and the Use of Preconditions,' *St Antony's International Review*, vol. 6, no. 1, pp. 57–78.

Crawford, J 2006, *The Creation of States in International Law*, 2nd edn, Oxford University Press, Oxford.

Dugard, J 2013, *The Secession of States and Their Recognition in the Wake of Kosovo*, AIL-Pocket, The Hague.

East Timor Case 1995, *Case Concerning East Timor (Portugal v Australia)* [1995] 105 *International Law Reports*, pp. 227–417.

Gleijeses, P 1992, 'The Limits of Sympathy: The United States and the Independence of Spanish America,' *Journal of Latin American Studies*, vol. 24, no. 3, pp. 481–505.

Hannum, H 2007, 'A Better Plan for Kosovo: Independence Sets a Bad Precedent, Partition is Better,' *Christian Science Monitor*, May 7.

Hannum, H 2011, 'The Advisory Opinion on Kosovo: An Opportunity Lost, or a Poisoned Chalice Refused?' *Leiden Journal of International Law*, vol. 24, no. 1, pp. 155–161.

Henriksen, D 2007, *NATO's Gamble, Combining Diplomacy and Airpower in the Kosovo Crisis 1998–1999*, Naval Institute Press, Annapolis, MD.

International Commission of Jurists 1972, 'East Pakistan Staff Study,' *The Review*, vol. 8, pp. 23–62.

Jennings, R and Watts, A 1992, *Oppenheim's International Law, Volume I, Peace*, 9th edn, Longman, London.

Jones, H 1995, 'History and Mythology: The Crisis Over British Intervention in the Civil War,' in RE May (ed.), *The Union, the Confederacy, and the Atlantic Rim*, Purdue University Press, West Lafayette, IN, pp. 29–67.

Ker-Lindsay, J 2011, 'Not Such a "*Sui Generis*" Case After All: Assessing the ICJ Opinion on Kosovo,' *Nationalities Papers*, vol. 39, no. 1, pp. 1–11.

Kooijmans, PH 1996, 'Tolerance, Sovereignty and Self-Determination,' *Netherlands International Law Review*, vol. 43, no. 2, pp. 211–217.

Kosovo Advisory Opinion 2010, *Accordance With International Law of the Unilateral*

Declaration of Independence in Respect of Kosovo (Advisory Opinion) [2010] 150 *International Law Reports*, pp. 1–227.

Kosovo Advisory Opinion Oral Submissions 2009, 'Verbatim Record of Oral Submissions on 9 December 2009,' retrieved 25 April 2014, www.icj-cij.org/docket/files/141/15734.pdf.

Radan, P 2002, *The Break-up of Yugoslavia and International Law*, Routledge, London.

Ratner, SR 1996 'Drawing a Better Line: *Uti Possidetis* and the Borders of New States,' *American Journal of International Law*, vol. 90, no. 4, pp. 590–624.

Rosenstock, R 1971, 'The Declaration of International Law Concerning Friendly Relations: A Survey,' *American Journal of International Law*, vol. 65, no. 4, pp. 713–735.

Roth, BR 2008, 'State Sovereignty, International Legality and Moral Disagreement,' in T Broude and Y Shany (eds), *The Shifting Allocation of Authority in International Law*, Hart Publishing, Oxford, pp. 123–161.

Secession Reference 1998, *Reference re: Secession of Quebec* (1998) 161 *Dominion Law Reports*, 4th edn, pp. 385–449.

Sharma, SP 1997, *Territorial Acquisition, Disputes and International Law*, Martinus Nijhoff Publishers, The Hague.

Sloss, DJ 2002 'Using International Court of Justice Advisory Opinions to Adjudicate Secessionist Claims,' *Santa Clara Law Review*, vol. 42, no. 2, pp. 357–389.

Taylor, JM 1991, *William Henry Seward, Lincoln's Right Hand*, HarperCollins, New York.

Trbovich, AS 2008, *A Legal Geography of Yugoslavia's Disintegration*, Oxford University Press, New York.

Tricot, R and Sander, B 2011, 'The Broader Consequences of the International Court of Justice's Advisory Opinion on the Unilateral Declaration of Independence in Respect of Kosovo,' *Columbia Journal of Transnational Law*, vol. 49, no. 2, pp. 321–363.

Weller, M 2009, *Contested Statehood, Kosovo's Struggle for Independence*, Oxford University Press, Oxford.

White, RCA 1981, 'Self-Determination: Time for a Re-assessment?' *Netherlands International Law Review*, vol. 28, no. 2, pp. 147–170.

3 Vertical distinction as civic failure
State–nation disjuncture

Damien Kingsbury

In 2009 on a remote beach in north-east Sri Lanka, the Liberation Tigers of Tamil Eelam (LTTE) made their last stand against the army of the government of Sri Lanka. The Tamil Tigers had been fighting a war of liberation for the previous 26 years, but the weight of population and economic resources told against them as the government of Sri Lanka engaged in total war to finally destroy the LTTE. To many outside Sri Lanka, the question arose as to what pushed the LTTE into such a position? More to the point, given the general tendency towards failure, what is it that compels groups to arm themselves against the state and to seek separate statehood?

This chapter proposes that the principle purpose of the state is to fulfill its basic civic function of existing on behalf of its citizens equally. Where states are challenged by separatist rebellions, this is primarily a consequence of the failure of the state to fulfill its basic functions to all its citizens equally, privileging some groups over others and hence alienating other, usually minority, groups. While the potential pool of examples to draw on to help analyze the rationale for separatism is wide, this chapter draws on five case studies with which the author has direct experience.

The case studies for this analysis are Sri Lanka, Aceh, West Papua, Mindanao and Timor-Leste. Of the case studies, Sri Lanka ended a 26-year war with the complete destruction of the separatist LTTE in 2009. In Aceh, Indonesia, a peace agreement was achieved in 2005, ending 29 years of war and resulting in an autonomous province with a relatively free and fair democratic process. In West Papua, at the other end of the Indonesian archipelago from Aceh, an unresolved low level insurgency marked by a high level of human rights abuses has been underway since Indonesia took control of the territory from Dutch administration in 1963. After separatist fighting starting in the late 1960s, in Mindanao, the Philippines, peace talks between the government and separatist Moro Islamic Liberation Front (MILF) began in 2005 with a ceasefire agreement over that period broken by occasional violence. Although progress has been slow, there have been solid steps towards a long-term resolution of this conflict, with renewed government commitment to finding a lasting settlement based on the idea of an autonomous Muslim region in Mindanao. Timor-Leste, meanwhile, freed itself from 24 years of Indonesian incorporation through a UN supervised vote in 1999 and achieved formal independence in 2002. While each of these separatist claims has to date had different outcomes, there has been much that identified them in common in support of their original claims. In seeking to understand why bonded groups of people decide to try to separate from the state, it is necessary to understand how they understand themselves and what it is, normatively, that they are choosing to separate from.

What is 'nation'?

There are competing definitions of what comprises a 'nation', but perhaps a bonded political group within a broadly defined territory fits with a broadly agreed definition. The term 'nation' is sometimes used where what is meant is the 'state'. In this, a 'state' may be confluent with, but is functionally and analytically distinct from, 'nation'. The order, method and sequencing of constituting the nation and constructing the state contributes directly to the relationships that exist between the constituent members of each. Where nations exist they may aspire to statehood; where states are established without a pre-existing national base, they will commonly seek to develop a coherent constituent political society.

The idea of what constitutes a nation combines a number of criteria that overlap with other forms of social formation but which are, for the purpose of the exercise, understood differently. A 'nation' is often understood as often related to but distinct from an ethnic group, which similarly overlaps with the idea of a tribe. The latter being more than a band of people but not yet constituting a nation relies on two general criteria. First, a tribe is usually based on a kinship group in which members have a relatively close familial or social link to each other (Fried 1975). Second, the tribe may have minimal social institutions and the tribe's association with a given territory is usually not formally delineated and may shift depending on prevailing conditions.

Precursor groups to nations tend to cohere out of mutual necessity, either through defense or protection of a particular social group or through shared exchange and/or mutual assistance. As societies become more complex, nations also cohere around cultural and religious institutions and around forms of political authority, such as a local chief or lord and, eventually, a greater regional ruler. From this point of local to wider and more formal organization, there are, broadly, three theoretical approaches to understanding nation formation.

The first theory of nation formation can be categorized as 'primordialist,' reflecting an emphasis on ascriptive criteria of nation formation (Gellner 1983; Horowitz 1985; Petersen 2002; Smith 1986, pp. 22–46). According to this approach, a people will cohere around a common language as a means of communication on mutually relevant issues. This bond will be especially powerful if it occurs within a largely contiguous and spatially compact territory which can further enhance the sense of local relevance and, in the case of pre-modern language formation, help ensure the consistency of the language that is available to the community. The linguistic commonality shared by the community frames the conceptual space available to them (Nuyts and Pederson 2000), helping to shape its shared worldview, which may include coherence around a common religious belief system. This, in turn, helps create a 'natural' or 'organic' bond within the group.

There is little doubt that sharing a common language and culture within a common geographic are powerful influences on social coherence and that, at one level, they could constitute or contribute to the idea of 'nation.' This would be especially true if the term was understood in its original, Greek sense of ethnicity (*ethnos*) which is usually translated as 'nation' and which, in the commonly cited passage from Herodotus (8.144.2), means 'the community of blood and language' and of 'the common way of life' (Roisman and Worthington 2010). However, the term 'nation' (*natio* – to be born of) did not come into use until the medieval period, at universities to distinguish groups of students, by which time it was beginning to take on a more complex meaning, in particular in relation to an expectation of being ruled by a familiar law, implying institutionalist function.

This association with law then leads to a more 'instrumentalist' understanding of the meaning of 'nation' (Smith 2001; Taras and Ganguly 2010). Institutions can also have an informal quality, particularly in political processes but also in more generalized notions of social interaction including manners or other unenforced social codes of conduct. An instrumentalist understanding of nation might, then, also include civic values and institutions, codes or rule of law and, under this, notions of equity and civic equality, and social institutions reflecting the formation of civil society, such as castes, interest groups, political parties, guilds or unions.

The idea of territorial contiguity may also be included under the idea of instrumentalism in that it requires an element of institutional coherence in order to maintain its conventional claim to sovereignty. However, the association with territory also links back to primordialist notions of nation, such as ancestor worship, father/motherland and so on. It may also include claims that are the consequence of a specific nationalist political program leading to the idea of the nation as constructed, in which national identity is, to a considerable degree, manufactured (Anderson 1983; Bremmer and Taras 1997, p. 687; Hobsbawm 1999, ch. 3; Hobsbawm and Ranger 1983). Elements of a constructed national identity may include the standardization or imposition of language, the formalization of history and the embellishment of mythology by way of explaining a common and usually glorious past, along with other markers or symbols of cohesive identity including a flag, a national song or anthem, and other symbols and rituals that are designed to bond a people around a common idea of loyalty.

All three of these elements are emphasized and contribute to retreat to unity or a coalescing in the face of adversity and in particular that of war. A common threat or enemy draws on and enhances primordial sensibilities, requires a high degree of social and institutional organization and compels a relatively high degree of uniformity with strong emphasis on myth and symbols and narrowly delineated loyalty (Erikson 1968; Kingsbury 2007, pp. 51–53; May 2002).

Elements of each of these explanatory factors are found in the formation of most contemporary nations. Where these factors are not in relative balance or where one or more factors are missing, there is a correspondingly high likelihood of dysfunction in national cohesion. It is also worth noting that group or national identity is dynamic and reshapes according to changing circumstances and needs, both reflecting internal group considerations, such as what works well or what are the agreed group values, as well as externally imposed considerations such as challenge or threat or shifting material or economic circumstances.

Moreover, new groups can come into being, cohering around a new or previously unarticulated agenda. This was the case of a cohering Tamil identity, as well as in Mindanao around the organizing principle of Islam, although there is a case to suggest that Acehnese national identity had existed in one form or another for several hundred years. In West Papua there are elements of national identity based on a common Melanesian heritage, although tribal and specific ethnic identities also remain strong, while in Timor-Leste a national consciousness begun developing in the early 1970s but strengthened considerably following the Indonesian invasion of 1975. In each case, there is an element of conscious construction of the idea of 'nation' through an overt nationalist program.

Where one or more of the three basic elements of nation formation are diminished or missing, problems of unity may occur. These include, in the case of arbitrary state creation, for example based on a post-independence imperial colony, that there might not be a well developed sense of primordialism and indeed, where previously mutually hostile groups have been compelled to come together under colonial rule. This can be seen to be the case in Sri Lanka, where once mutually hostile kingdoms were subsumed under Portuguese, Dutch and then English colonial polities and then granted independence as a unitary state, and in Indonesia where numerous pre-colonial polities (e.g., Aceh pre-1873) or politically unorganized territories (e.g., West Papua) were brought together under Dutch colonialism, with the post-colonial invasion and incorporation of then Portuguese Timor into the Indonesian unitary state. The Philippines was a collection of polities and locally ruled territories until the Spanish occupation, although Mindanao was not subsumed and incorporated until the arrival of the US military following the 1898 Treaty of Paris and even then strongly resisted.

The meaning of the state

Most nations, or at least nations of size and organization sufficient to assert themselves, seek to manifest themselves through the creation of an institutional entity that covers the occupied territory. That is, given the opportunity, nations generally seek to have their interests manifested in and represented by a state. In such an arrangement, both the state and the citizens have a reciprocal duty; the state to protect and promote citizens' interests, in return for citizens' duties and obligations to the state. Such arrangements are most successful, and most fully comply with a sense of justice, when they are entered into and maintained on a voluntary basis which implies some continuing degree of commitment to it.

The state, as it is generally understood in the contemporary sense, refers to a demarcated area in which a government exercises political and judicial authority including a monopoly over the legitimate use of force (Smith 1986, p. 235). Within a given territory, the state can be identified by the presence and activities of its institutions, which define its functional capacity. That is, the area of the state defines the functional sovereign reach and integration of its embedded, 'explicit, complex and formal' agencies (Krader 1976, p. 13; Evans 1995). As a key part of the sovereignty of the state, it has as a central function its own institutional coherence and continuation; the state must continue to exist. States therefore almost always oppose any internal or external challenge to their existence. Finally, international recognition is a common criterion for achieving statehood. Not only must the state have a capacity to enter into international relations with other states, such other states must also recognize its right to exist. Importantly, in cases where assertions to national identity also seek to establish a state, their success or failure often hinges on the support or otherwise they receive from other states. However, except where external states have an interest in the diminution of another state, they generally support the state system status quo.

While a state claims authority within its borders, it normatively does this on behalf of its citizens, as a manifestation of their political will. This implies a social contract between the state and its citizens, in which the state can expect, and compel, compliance, or a duty to comply, while citizens can expect that the state will reflect and represent their interests. In reality, however, such social contracts that exist between developing states and their citizens are frequently undermined, compromised or arbitrarily changed to suit the needs and interests of ruling elites. Such has been the case in Sri Lanka in relation to both the division between its privileged elite and much of its peasantry and urban labor and workers and between its Sinhalese ethnic elite and its Tamil minority. Indonesia's political and economic elite has historically focused the political and economic resources of the state in among a small section of the population of Jakarta, with local elites linked into this centralized network. This has led to regional disaffection, not least in Aceh and West Papua, as well as the method of the latter's incorporation, as with that of Timor-Leste. So, too, the political and economic elite of the Philippines has plundered the state to its own benefit, perhaps most arbitrarily in the plundering of lands occupied by the Muslim population of Mindanao as a mechanism to ease population and economic pressures elsewhere.

Where states have low levels of institutional capacity, they have a tendency to fail to deliver services on behalf of their citizens on one hand while on the other tend to resort to basic forms of compulsion in order to retain state control in the face of consequent dissent.

Civic opportunity

'Civic opportunity' might be described as the opportunity that a state has to implement functions that result in fulfilling its civic obligation to its citizens.

This might be most reasonably achieved through a state that encourages, or at least allows, participation in political processes, representation of constituent state members in decision-making bodies such as a parliament or other forms of legislature and executive, and a relatively high degree of transparency and accountability, all functioning under equal and consistent rule of law.

Civic opportunity may, however, initially be limited by the widespread negative effects of war, the flight of capital that usually accompanies war, the damage to infrastructure, the reduced institutional capacity of the successor regime and, in some cases, being required to accept debts that the colonial power had accrued (as was the case of Indonesia). By way of contrast, the regimes and political elites of many post-colonial states often come to power promising 'liberation' and improvement in living conditions with the removal of exploitative colonialism. Allied with the often common struggle for independence, immediate post-colonial regimes often enjoy a 'honeymoon' period in which the constituent members of the state not only welcome the new regime but are often prepared to give it time to get in order the affairs of the state. In the case studies, however, there was no 'honeymoon' period in relation to their disaffected minorities; in each case disaffection existed either prior to the establishment of the post-colonial state or almost immediately following the establishment of that state.

There are, broadly, three theoretical approaches to understanding civic opportunity. These might be characterised as comprising modernism, transitions and mechanisms. Each of these seeks to provide a causal explanation for how civic opportunity might present itself or be developed. In each case that civic opportunity is equated with democratization or democratic opportunity, with this chapter employing that rationale without seeking the further debate of democratic types, failures of democracy and so on.

Following the beginning of post-World War II decolonization, the idea of 'modernism' was deeply influential, drawing as it did on the economic, political and social experience of the developed West and, if not explicitly, the mechanistic logic of Marxist political economy (even if development modernists would be unlikely to accept the association). The basic principles of modernist development theory are that development is driven by economic capacity, which in turn proceeds according to a particular linear path. According to Rostow (1960, ch. 2), traditional or pre-colonial societies are based on subsistence agriculture, the development of extractive industries and savings and investment, increases in productivity and the creation of surpluses, industrialization initially linked with primary industries along with further savings and investment, technological progress and then, with 'take off,' the increasing diversification of industry into manufacturing and service sectors along with high levels of production and consumption. As the society in question progressed along this linear path, it would be assisted by an increasing emphasis on literacy, rule of law and, eventually, democratic processes underpinned by a sizeable middle class (Acemoglu and Robinson 2006, ch. 3; Huntington 1968).

While some states were successful in developing along these lines, they were few and appeared to respond to specific circumstances:

The assumptions of modernization theory that liberal democratic regimes would be inexorably produced by the process of industrialization was replaced by a new preoccupation with the ways in which the state apparatus might become a central instrument for both the repression of subordinate classes and the reorientation of the process of industrial development.

(Stepan 1985, p. 317)

None of the case study states developed along this linear modernist path and in large part the failure of the political outcome of 'modernization' contributed directly to the related failure to implement equitable mechanisms of social organization. Recognition of this non-linear character of development led to further analysis of processes leading to civic outcomes, in particular that of political 'transitions' from authoritarian forms of government to more representative and accountable forms.

The transition period is characterized by both opportunity and threat. Where there is opportunity, it is often understood in terms of the resolution of a negative (usually associated with the end of a chaotic or dysfunctional government or dictatorship). Sometimes, however, this change may be towards a more closed or authoritarian political model. Even where new forms of government may have the external characteristics of democracy (e.g., the Philippines in 1986, or Indonesia in 1998), there may be hidden components that fundamentally compromise the capacity of the general population to meaningfully participate in political affairs (O'Donnell 1996, pp. 34–51). That is, democratic transition is often procedural rather than substantive. Beyond this, regime change is not by definition towards a more desirable/participatory outcome. Although the current tendency has been for regime change to move away from authoritarian models, it can also impose non-democratic or authoritarian rule. Recent examples of this negative form of regime change, between 1999 and 2006, include Pakistan, the Central African Republic, Sao Tome and Principe, Guinea-Bissau, Haiti, Mauritania, Nepal and Thailand.

Assuming that much regime change will be opposed, and that transitions especially from authoritarian to democratic models require a shift in allegiance of the military, the military itself will often be politicized and divided between those who support regime change and those who oppose it. O'Donnell and Schmitter (1986, pp. 15–17) characterize such military factions as 'hardliners' and 'softliners.' As these terms imply, hardliners oppose change, while softliners facilitate change, usually cautiously. Examples of successfully facilitated change by softliners who have taken advantage of 'the military moment' (O'Donnell and Schmitter 1986, p. 39) include Portugal and Greece in 1974, the Philippines in 1986, and Indonesia in 1998, although there are also numerous examples in Latin America. Moreover, limited liberalization away from a direct military rule while retaining a capacity for existing elite control or liberalization without introducing democracy may also be facilitated by such a softline military approach (e.g., Indonesia 1986–91). Softliners, however, sometimes overestimate their popular support, and may engender a backlash which sets back movement towards liberalization (O'Donnell and

Schmitter 1986, p. 8). For example, in Indonesia, President Habibie's decision to allow East Timor to vote on independence in 1999 resulted in his own political denouement, with his liberal successor being ousted halfway through his presidential term.

As Dahl (1971, p. 208) noted, a state is unlikely to quickly develop a democratic political system if it has had little or no experience of public contestation and competition, and lacks a tradition of tolerance towards political opposition. That is, regime change in such a state is at least as likely to default to an alternative authoritarian government, or to partially do so. Similarly, although cautioning against political expectations arising out of such structural preconditions, Di Palma (1991, p. 3) noted that economic instability, a hegemonic nationalist culture and the absence of a strong, independent middle class all impede transition from an authoritarian political model towards one that is more democratic. These qualities all affected each of the case study countries, if at differing times.

In considering transitions from authoritarian to democratic models, there are a range of conditions that might be claimed to be essential for successful regime change. As noted by Dahl (1989, p. 111), these include the institutional capacity issues of control of the military and police by elected civilian officials; democratic beliefs and culture and no strong interference by foreign powers that are hostile to democracy. Further, Dahl (2000, p. 147) identified conditions that were not absolutely necessary, but which were favorable for the establishment of democracy, including a modern market economy and society, and weak subcultural pluralism.

The incompletion of regime change can be demonstrated in the Philippines where, in 1986, the dictator Ferdinand Marcos lost the support of his US backers and, eventually, the country's oligarchic elite and sections of the military. In this respect, there appeared to have been an elite pact for careful change in the Philippines (O'Donnell and Schmitter 1986, pp. 40–45). Capitalizing on the 'political moment,' elites, with the support of mass mobilization, developed or reasserted political parties and organized political constituencies under a 'grand coalition.' In Indonesia in 1998, this also occurred, although rather than reflecting a more gradual economic decline and a sudden political incident, there was a more gradual political decline and a sudden economic incident, or 'economic moment' (O'Donnell and Schmitter 1986, pp. 45–7), the collapse of the Indonesian currency, followed by a sudden 'political moment,' the resignation of President Suharto after more than three decades in power. In the case of a sudden economic crisis, such as the 1997–8 financial collapse in Indonesia, there is an implied socio-economic pact between those who are most disaffected or economically disadvantaged and those appear to be able to assume responsibility for alleviating the crisis. In what Dahl (1970) has referred to 'the democratic bargain' of trust, fairness and compromise, this pact normatively corresponds to a type of social contract.

The evolution of political forms from absolute autocratic rule towards civil participatory/representative government, require a type of social contract between citizens and its government. Accordingly, the government accedes authority to the population, mediated by an independent authority in return for right to rule. This occurs on a sliding scale of a balance of authority until it is agreed that authority is ultimately vested in the citizens, is only held by the political leader or government on behalf of the citizens, and is able to be rescinded by the citizens in an agreed and orderly manner.

In this, it is important that elites who intend to continue or expand their political rule are able to satisfy, or be seen to address, most outstanding demands while at the same time avoiding the strongest dissatisfactions from manifesting into collective action. As O'Donnell and Schmitter note (1986, p. 70), transitional regimes from authoritarianism tend to be smoother and more successful if they promote essentially conservative or right-wing political outcomes, as this is seen as less threatening to outgoing authoritarian elites. Democratic 'idealists,' usually on the left/center-left, are only given the opportunity to engage in transitional processes if elite survivors from the previous regime are willing to negotiate a mutually satisfactory set of rules of the new game. Where such negotiations fail, more active, usually leftist, political actors may be rapidly marginalized, as occurred in post-1986 Philippines and in post-1998 Indonesia. In the latter case, those demanding total reform of the political system were quickly marginalized, resulting in the fragmentation of the reform movement. The consequence of this leftist marginalization and fragmentation was that the political agenda quickly reverted to control by conservative elites, while the election as president of the reformist cleric Abdurrahman Wahid by an oppositional if conservative coalition resulted in his own ouster by those same elites less than two years later.

In the case of the Philippines, public protest against then President Marcos and the blatant falsification of election results, backed by sections of the military, led to his ouster and replacement by his electoral opponent, Corazon Aquino, the widow of Marcos' murdered former opponent, Senator Benigno Aquino. While Corazon Aquino came to power on the back of a popular protest movement, she in fact ushered in elite rule mirroring that of the oligarchic pre-dictatorship era. Under Aquino, the Philippines' elite structurally excluded genuine open participation in politics, despite it formally being an open electoral contest, and returned to squabbling over the spoils of state between them. In Indonesia, by comparison, the resignation of Suharto in 1998 and the weakening of the highly centralized state apparatus he and the military had constructed, led to a rash of genuine political reforms under his immediate successor, Habibie. A reconsolidating status quo elite and destabilization of the state under the reformist presidency of Abdurrahman Wahid partly contributed towards his ouster and replacement by pro-status quo elite/pro-military Megawati Sukarnoputri in mid-2001. Of particular transitional note, however, was the role played by military 'softliner,' Susilo Bambang Yudhoyono, first as the leader of the reform faction of the Indonesian military in the early 1990s, following from dissent towards the then president and then as a political actor and finally as president himself.

As noted, not all regime changes are towards democracy. Some changes may be partial or lead to conflict while others simply revert from one type of authoritarianism to another. These different experiences of regime change invariably reflect competing views of what constitutes political progress; what is to some fairness is to others interference; what to some is freedom is to others disorder depending on how one views the basic concepts of freedom and equality.

A third approach to understanding opportunities for civic change is through 'causal mechanisms,' which examines processes and episodes, or the 'cogs and wheels' of causal processes (Hedstrom and Ylikoski 2010). This approach does not suggest a particular mechanism but rather locates mechanisms of change within context, examining the relationships between participating entities and their relevant properties. The questions that are asked in such an analysis is how those properties interact, how they are organized and what influences them? As an explanatory method, the causal mechanisms approach offers some useful insights in specific cases, but it is probably inadequate for constructing a consistent theoretical model for understanding the process of achieving civic opportunity.

However, what does appear to be consistent across case studies is a tendency in post-colonial societies towards a manifest lack of and hence heightened competition for resources, a high and often increasing degree of patron-clientism and a tendency to respond disproportionately to expressions of concern or protest, often expressed as violent attacks on the state as opposed to raising concerns about individual behavior.

Civic failure

While there is a significant body of literature on the subject, the circumstances which lead to civic failure and violent social divisions remain incompletely understood (Chandler 2010; Richmond 2011). Kaufmann *et al.* (2010) chart indicators of political stability and the absence of violence as part of a larger governance project, relying on secondary data. However, they do not chart the factors that lead to such instability and violence or its absence. Moreover, most of the causal research to date has focused on sub-Saharan Africa. Collier and Sambanis (2007), for example, lump South and South-east Asia under the term 'Other Regions.'

Despite this somewhat dismissive reference to the region of the case study countries, arguably foremost in this field is Collier's work on the 'conflict trap' (Collier 2009). Collier draws heavily on statistical data to establish a link between per capita GDP and propensity to conflict. However, Collier's quantitative reliance is limiting, which he acknowledges by having to guess about causal relationships. Importantly, too, his brief references to countries in South and South-east Asia area are limited and, in some cases, inaccurate, notably in relation to Timor-Leste, where he incorrectly claimed army protesters attempted a 'coup' and described Sri Lanka's 2002 ceasefire as being a 'peace settlement' (Collier 2009, pp. 74, 79).

Also widely employed, Berdal and Malone's (2000) 'greed and grievance' thesis provides a causal relationship between overt economic motives and intrastate instability and, again, focusing primarily on Africa (Bodea and Elbadawi

2007; Collier and Hoeffler 2000). Collier *et al.* (2003, p. 53) provide a wider study on propensity and duration of civil war, but again return to the central idea that 'poverty increases the chances of civil war,' noting that civil war increases poverty and hence creates a greater likelihood of a return to civil war. Overlapping with some of the case studies (East Timor, Aceh, West Papua), Braithwaite's 20-year comparative 'Peacebuilding Compared' (2010a, 2010b, 2010c) demonstrates a link between low levels of economic development and low levels of political development, in which notions of state responsibility and civic duty are, at best, poorly understood.

Not all social division is, however, negative. A modernist approach to social division sees as healthy the organization of social forces within an agreed, non-violent framework based on interest. Industrialization, urbanization, class formation and democratic contest within an agreed civic model are part of what can be called horizontal distinction. In this, socio-economic groups band together into generally representative blocs, usually according to economic rather than ethnic interest. As a result, while there are social divisions, rather than being primordial in character, they tend to be between what might roughly be termed richer and poorer, with each group advocating policies best suited to their own interests and arguing in favor of those policies as the most economically sustainable. Competition between these groups, usually divided into two broad sets of agendas, is commonly marked by the institution civic codes of mediation, such as elections, to avoid the alternative of class war in which, in most cases, both parties end up losing.

There are, however, cases where horizontal difference is not mediated through an agreed civic code of mediation, which in the case study countries has led to high levels of civil violence. Sri Lanka has seen two class-based rebellions against its government, in response to what was seen as a legacy of colonial privilege by a ruling elite at the expense of the country's vast majority of poor. The first rebellion was in 1971 (Cooke 2011, ch. 4), with a second in 1987, even though its proponents have claimed that on the first occasion the rebellion was prompted by a government attempt to suppress the Janatha Vimukthi Peramuna (JVP – Peoples' Liberation Front). The rebellions left around 15,000 and 50,000 people dead respectively and the imposition of emergency rule (Cooke 2011, pp. 365–367). Instead of addressing poorer people's needs, the Sri Lanka government became more entrenched as a vehicle for the interests of the upper class.

In the Philippines, an entrenched ruling elite has dominated the Philippines' political and economic life since the colonial period, alienating a largely landless or otherwise marginalized peasantry and a smaller urban working class or underclass. Although the Philippines had an electoral system, this has been rigged through violence, vote-buying and electoral fraud to ensure no effective voice for the country's poor. The Philippines' first rebellion, the communist 'Hukbalahap Rebellion' (1946–54), was initiated against Japanese invaders during World War II, but extended into the post-war period in the face of political manipulation and failed economic reforms. Although defeated by a combination of limited reforms and an extensive military campaign, the corrupt and iniquitous political and economic system led the Communist Party to re-launch a rebellion in 1969, continuing through various phases and still active at the time of writing. In both the case of Sri Lanka and the Philippines, what could be categorized as radical horizontalism was based on a failed civic model. Unsurprisingly, with civic failure alienating constituent members of the state based on class, with a high level of patron–client relations and ethnic preference, it was unsurprising that both countries also underwent significant ethnic rebellions, reflecting a failure to address vertical or ethnic distinction.

Lack of institutional capacity is a major contributing factor for state fragility, state failure and conflict recurrence in post-conflict societies in Africa (Collier and Sambanis 2007). This is especially the case in multi-ethnic states and where an ethnic group with access to power and resources privileges its own to the exclusion of other, usually ethnic, groups. Where lack of access to economic opportunity is the driving force for grievance, redressing economic inequality can be an important factor in promoting ethnic conflict (Berdal and Malone 2000; Collier and Hoeffler 2000). Bodea and Elbadawi (2007) and Collier et al. (2003) provide a wider study on propensity and duration of civil war, but again return to the central idea that 'poverty increases the chances of civil war,' noting that civil war increases poverty and hence creates a greater likelihood of a return to civil war (Collier 2009, p. 53).

Most of the research done in this field has been based on studies in Africa. However, there is considerable evidence from the case study countries that similar circumstances also apply. Sri Lanka's slide into ethnic civil war was a direct result of the disenfranchisement of the Tamil minority and the discriminatory and often aggressively chauvinist policies of the Sinhalese-dominated government while separatist conflict in Mindanao stems directly from the Philippines' 'Homestead' program (1903–1970s), described by the Philippines government as a 'mode of acquiring alienable and disposable lands of the public domain for agricultural purposes' (GRP 2003). Under this program, landless Christians were given land in what was then predominantly Muslim Mindanao and in so doing disenfranchising the pre-existing Muslim 'Moros' who commonly did not have formal titles of land ownership. It was not until 1997 that the Philippines' government passed an Indigenous Peoples' Rights Act which helped traditional landowners secure formal title to their land, by which stage the depth of disillusionment with the Philippines government by Moro separatists was entrenched.

Similarly, Acehnese felt aggrieved that not only was a promise of special autonomy following the early Darul Islam rebellion of the 1950s and early 1960s never fulfilled but that, under the New Order, Acehnese were displaced by predominantly Javanese transmigrants as well as being denied economic opportunities from the exploitation of natural resources within Acehnese territory. In West Papua, indigenous Melanesians have consistently been denied equality of access to state resources, have frequently been removed from their traditional lands to make way for resource extraction or migration from western Indonesian islands, have suffered extensive human rights abuses with claims of loss of lives in the many tens of thousands and have otherwise been profoundly discriminated against by ethnic Malays and consistently have the lowest human development indicators in Indonesia. A low-level rebellion against the central government has been underway since soon after Indonesian occupation in 1963 (Fernandes 2006).

East Timor faced a double problem of an Indonesian invasion in 1975 and 29 years of brutal occupation and the directly related deaths of over a quarter of the pre-invasion population and then, after achieving independence, coming to the brink of civil war over political and ethnic loyalties in 2006. In particular, East Timor reflected a clear case of failure of the state, or its mentor, the UN, to build sufficient capacity to address the needs of the state's constituents. As a result of the breakdown of state order, the UN was compelled to return, maintaining a substantial presence for the following six years (Kingsbury 2009, ch. 6).

In each of the case studies, a lack of state capacity aligned with repression and/or economic exploitation of minority peoples led directly to grievances that manifested in rebellion. Resistance to unequal incorporation into the state was heightened rather than assuaged by a high degree of state constructivism, compelled upon minority populations in each of the case studies. Also, the state's ideological program of 'nationalism' was alien to the disenfranchised minority, requiring learning a new, foreign language that represented exploitation and repression, along with a functional agreement by the alienated minority to accept the idea of the incorporating state as constituting a bonded national entity, in which dissonance between state requirements and national claims is subsumed until it is no longer able to be maintained. At this point, the build-up of such dissonance can manifest in group violence against the state, its representatives and symbols.

In each of the case studies, vertical division or division between major ethnic groups has been the result of a series of factors that militate against the formation of a bonded political identity. The pre-existence of tribalism or clan loyalty highlights primordial ethnic distinctions and relatively closed social systems based on loyalty and patronage. This tends to breed patron-clientism, in which benefits accrue on the basis of favors and loyalty to a powerful tribal figure rather than on the basis of non-ethnic equity. It is an essentially non-participatory decision-making process and has low or non-existent levels of civic inclusion. This process consolidates the ethnic group and, by so doing, militates against more regularized civic methods of social organization.

In cases where the opportunity for a transition to a civic model presents itself, this may fail in cases where there is inadequate preparation and/or a lack of prior institutional capacity. Moreover, even where there may be sufficient preparation and institutional capacity to initiate a transition to a civic structure, it may still fail through inadequate habituation, being unable to cohere around institutional structures.

Mechanisms towards civic order work where there is a coherent pre-industrial multi-ethnicity based on functional rule of law, equity and civic equality. The common alternative is that there is an incoherent pre-industrial multi-ethnicity based on civic failure, leading to a state retreat to compulsion/use of force (reflecting what is available, what is known/familiar), consequent illegitimacy in the eyes of the compelled community, disjuncture between state illegitimacy and vertical political loyalty and, finally, alienation, a retreat to the ethnic or vertical with consequent calls for the establishment of a new state that more accurately reflects the coherence of the geographically specific ethnic group. This, then, reflects the logic of the claim to a geo-institutional manifestation by the 'nation,' moves towards establishing a separate state. In this, it may be possible to establish ethnic unity, but there is no guarantee that a state can or will move to establish a viable sense of civic unity. However, failure to establish civic unity in a multi-ethnic state can and often does lead to state fragility/failure and claims to further devolution, thus recreating the cycle of compulsion and violence.

References

Acemoglu, D and Robinson, J 2006, *Economic Origins of Dictatorship and Democracy*, Cambridge University Press, New York.

Anderson, B 1983, *Imagined Communities*, Verso, New York.

Berdal, M and Malone, D (eds) 2000, *Greed & Grievance: Economic Agendas in Civil Wars*, Lynne Rienner, Boulder, CO.

Bodea, C and Elbadawi, I 2007, *Riots, Coups and Civil War: Revisiting the Greed and Grievance Debate* (Policy Research Working Paper 4397), The World Bank, Washington, DC.

Bremmer, I and Taras, R (eds) 1997, *New States, New Politics*, Cambridge University Press, Cambridge, UK.

Braithwaite, J 2010a, *Pillars and Shadows: Statebuilding as Peacebuilding in Solomon Islands*, ANU E-Press, Canberra.

Braithwaite, J 2010b, *Reconciliation and Architectures of Commitment: Sequencing Peace in Bougainville*, ANU E-Press, Canberra.

Braithwaite, J 2010c, *Anomie and Violence: Non-truth and Reconciliation in Indonesian Peacebuilding*, ANU E-Press, Canberra.

Chandler, D 2010, *International State-building: The Rise of Post-Liberal Governance*, Routledge, London.

Collier, P 2009, *Wars, Guns and Votes: Democracy in Dangerous Places*, HarperCollins, New York.

Collier, P and Hoeffler, A 2000, *Greed and Grievance in Civil War* (Policy Research Working Paper 2355), The World Bank, Washington, DC.

Collier, P and Sambanis, N 2007, *Understanding Civil War*, 2 vols, The World Bank, Washington, DC.

Collier, P, Elliot, L, Hegre, H, Hoeffler, A, Reynal-Querol, M and Sambanis, N 2003, *Breaking the Conflict Trap: Civil War and Development Policy*, The World Bank and Oxford University Press, Washington, DC and Oxford.

Cooke, M 2011, *The Lionel Bopage Story: Rebellion, Repression and the Struggle for Justice in Sri Lanka*, Agahas Publishers, Colombo.

Dahl, R 1970, *After the Revolution: Authority in Good Society*, Yale University Press, New Haven.

Dahl, R 1971, *Polyarchy and Opposition: Participation and Opposition*, Yale University Press, New Haven.

Dahl, R 1989, *Democracy and its Critics*, Yale University Press, New Haven.
Dahl, R 2000, *On Democracy*, Yale University Press, New Haven.
Di Palma, G 1991, *To Craft Democracies: An Essay in Democratic Transition*, University of California Press, Berkeley, CA.
Erikson, E 1968, *Identity: Youth and Crisis*, Faber & Faber, London.
Evans, P 1995, *Embedded Autonomy*, Princeton University Press, Princeton, NJ.
Fernandes, C 2006, *Reluctant Indonesians*, Scribe Publications, Melbourne, Victoria.
Fried, M 1975, *The Notion of Tribe*, Cummings Publishing Company, Boston.
Gellner, E 1983, *Nations and Nationalism*, Cornell University Press, Ithaca, NY.
Government of the Republic of the Philippines 2003, *Commonwealth Act No 456 ('Public Land Act'), 1903, amended 1939*, GRP, Manila.
Hedstrom, P and Ylikoski, P 2010, 'Causal Mechanisms in the Social Sciences,' *Annual Review of Sociology*, vol. 36, pp. 49–67.
Hobsbawm, E 1999, *Nations and Nationalism Since 1870: Programme, Myth, Reality*, Cambridge University Press, Cambridge, UK.
Hobsbawm, E and Ranger, T (eds) 1983, *The Invention of Tradition*, Cambridge University Press, Cambridge, UK.
Horowitz, D 1985, *Ethnic Groups in Conflict*, University of California Press, Berkeley, CA.
Huntington, S 1968, *Political Order in Changing Societies*, Yale University Press, New Haven.
Kaufmann, D, Kraay, A and Mastruzzi, M 2010, *Political Stability and Absence of Violence*, Worldwide Governance Indicators, retrieved July 24 2014, http://info.worldbank.org/governance/wgi/index.aspx#home.
Kingsbury, D 2007, *Political Development*, Routledge, London.
Kingsbury, D 2009 *East Timor: The Price of Liberty*, Palgrave Macmillan, London.
Krader, L 1976, *Dialectic of Civil Society*, Prometheus Books, New York.
May, R 2002, 'The Moro Conflict and the Philippine Experience with Muslim Autonomy,' paper presented at the Asia-Pacific Workshop, Canberra.
Nuyts, J and Pederson, E 2000, *Language and Conceptualisation*, Cambridge University Press, Cambridge, UK.
O'Donnell, G 1996, 'Illusions about Consolidation,' *Journal of Democracy*, vol. 7, no. 2, pp. 34–51.
O'Donnell, G and Schmitter, P 1986, *Transitions from Authoritarian Rule: Tentative Conclusions about Uncertain Democracies*, Johns Hopkins University Press, Baltimore, MD.
Petersen, R 2002, *Understanding Ethnic Violence*, Cambridge University Press, Cambridge, UK.
Richmond, O 2011, *A Post-Liberal Peace*, Routledge, London.
Roisman, J and Worthington, I (eds) 2010, *A Companion to Ancient Macedonia*, John Wiley, Chichester, UK.
Rostow, W 1960, *The Stages of Economic Growth: A Non-Communist Manifesto*, Cambridge University Press, Cambridge, UK.
Smith, A 1986, *The Ethnic Origins of Nations*, Blackwell Publishers, Oxford.
Smith, A 2001, *Nationalism: Theory, Ideology, History*, Polity Press, Cambridge, UK.
Stepan, A 1985, 'State Power and the Strength of Civil Society in the Southern Cone of Latin America,' in P Evans, D Rueschemeyer and T Skocpol (eds), *Bringing the State Back IN*, Cambridge University Press, Cambridge, UK, pp. 317–344.
Taras, R and Ganguly, R 2010, *Understanding Ethnic Conflict*, 4th edn, Pearson, Boston.

4 Negotiating sustainable peace in separatist context

Costas Laoutides

Introduction

Building peaceful, stable and legitimate states in the aftermath of conflict and war constitutes one of the most challenging questions in several fields of social science such as development studies, political science and international relations. In recent times there has been a change of focus in the international scene with internal asymmetric conflicts becoming one of the new security challenges for the international community. The fall of the Berlin Wall and the end of bipolarity in tandem with the resurgence of nationalism allowed room for territorial separatism to be (re-)discovered and take centre stage in international politics. The gradual fragmentation of Yugoslavia and the Soviet Union along with the independence of Eritrea and Timor-Leste at the dawn of the twenty-first century strengthen further the interdisciplinary research agenda that led to several studies on separatist conflicts (Gurr 1993; Gurr and Harff 1994; Hale 2008; Pavković and Radan 2007).

During the same period the world witnessed an unprecedented 'outbreak of peace' as a result of the conception of the new world order. Peace operations ranging from provision of good offices to full scale military intervention took place in a number of internal conflicts (including secessionist ones). The challenge of establishing peace in post-war/post-conflict scenarios obtained currency and unpacked a series of questions related to the 'task list' of such operations. Peacebuilding became synonymous with state-building and nation-building, a conceptual melange that added to the complexity around the task of when and how peace can be achieved and sustained (Fukuyama 2004, p. 50; Ignatieff 2003; Newman *et al.* 2009).

This chapter focuses on the role of peacebuilding in secessionist conflicts as a particular category in the typology of internal conflicts. They are particular because the potential political outcome of such conflicts is the creation of new states and hence a question to ask is whether the task of peacebuilding in this type of conflict is the same as the one of reconstructing a country torn by civil or ethnic conflict that lack the territorial/secessionist dimension (Kubo 2011). Control of territory is associated with survival in international politics; it is a *sine qua non* condition for the existence of a state and its political community

(Buzan 1991, pp. 65–92; Toft 2006, pp. 17–33). In this context, territory is seen as an undivided value that makes separatist conflicts highly intractable. Two reasons may account for such a view, first ethnicity is often employed as the main narrative for survival in international relations, thus for both the separatist and the host state territory is invested with an identity/moral value that make their claim to territory legitimate, imperative and non-negotiable. Second, the current conception of world order with its emphasis on territorial sovereignty has been crystallized in international law through the UN Charter that protects the territorial integrity of member states, thus offering an advantage against any challenge to the boundaries of existing states, especially outside the colonial context (Crawford 2006, pp. 388–418).

These observations constitute the point of departure for this chapter which is in three parts. Part one explores how separatist conflict resolution was shaped in the post-Cold War era; in particular I revisit the discussion on how separatist wars end, highlighting an undercurrent in support of negotiated settlements in separatist scenarios. Part two examines how negotiated settlements in secessionist conflicts were implemented through international peacebuilding operations. The final part highlights two key challenges for sustainable peace in separatist scenarios, namely the need for a coherent and legitimate political community over the territory in question, and the transition of fighters to political agents of peace away from models of exclusionary politics.

The ending of secessionist conflicts

The question of how separatist conflicts end, if ever, is often subsumed under larger studies on the termination of ethnic conflicts and civil wars. A major dichotomy that dominates the literature is between violent and non-violent ways of ending internal/civil wars (including separatist wars) (Hartzell and Hoddie 2007; Licklider 1993; Luttwak 1999; Stedman *et al.* 2002; Toft 2010a; Walter 2002). Over the past 20 years major peacebuilding efforts in secessionist scenarios have taken place in cases where there was an escalation to war. In what follows I revisit the debate over the dilemma 'military victory or negotiated settlement', highlighting also those studies that focus particularly on separatism as their findings deviate from the conclusions of wider studies on civil wars.

The idea that the way a civil war ends may determine the post-war outcome has become prominent in the study of internal conflicts. Large-scale studies on civil war have concluded that outright military victory by one side is the most likely outcome. According to Licklider (1995, p. 684) out of 57 civil war endings during the second half of the twentieth century, 43 ended by military victory and only 14 by negotiated settlement. Licklider also found that military victory leads to more stable outcomes than negotiated settlements. Renewal of violence occurred in 15 percent of the internal wars that concluded with military victory and in as much as half of the cases of negotiated settlement. However, in those endings that broke down after a while, the negotiated settlements lasted longer than the military victories. In a similar fashion, Toft (2010b) argues that rebel victory decreases the likelihood of war recurrence. These studies could lend quantitative support to a wider argument which was lucidly encapsulated in Luttwak's article entitled 'Give War a Chance' (1999). According to this view external intervention blocks the transformative effects of decisive victory and exhaustion, and thus increases the probability of war to recur. Negotiated settlements brokered by international efforts may produce political arrangements that do not reflect the social and political patterns on the ground, thus maintaining unstable distributions of power which may reignite hostilities after the departure of international agents (Atzili 2006–7; Weinstein 2005). Therefore, the best option is allowing belligerents to continue fighting until one side achieves military victory (Herbst 1996–7). Outright victory enhances the likelihood of a durable peace and effective post-war reconstruction because the loser's capacity to resort to war should be low (Pillar 1983; Wagner 1993). The critical point for territorial separatism in this approach is the undogmatic take on the territorial integrity of the state, especially in cases where there is an evident state collapse (Englebert and Tull 2008; Johnson 2008). The redrawing of territorial boundaries may be desirable if it reflects the new political arrangements on the ground and further restores physical control and order in the region (Englebert 2009; Herbst 2003, pp. 314–316; Kraxberger 2012).

Although the view that civil wars rarely end in settlement constitutes a near-orthodoxy in the literature, studying separatist conflicts as a distinctive subgroup of internal conflict/war provides quantitatively an interesting alternative to the military victory argument and potentially unpacks a number of questions when dealing with conflicts of this type. In two separate studies Heraclides (1997) and Ayres (2000) provide evidence that separatist conflicts are more amenable to negotiated settlement than civil wars in general. Heraclides found that out of 77 ended conflicts the total number of military victories (31 percent) is not overwhelmingly more than the total number of negotiated settlements (26 percent). Similarly, Ayres established that out of 50 cases in his study there were 22 defeat endings, 22 agreement endings, four ceasefires and two inaction endings. These findings make a case in favor of negotiated settlements as, at least, an equally possible option for resolving separatist conflicts, an argument that is in tune with what policy-makers, and many scholars, saw as a priority vis-à-vis internal wars (including secessionist wars) in the post-Cold War environment. The employment of a wide range of options in the form of economic incentives, diplomatic support and good offices was seen as the avenue to cease violence and protect the populations at risk. This option was also underpinned by the post-World War II normative environment where the use of military violence was restricted for purposes of self-defense. A number of developments may account for the 'resort to peace' argument that was supported in the new era.

The trend of negotiated settlements has been promoted in cases of territorial separatism which have been characterized by their unending fashion. The fact that various devolution options short of independence have been successful, mainly in democratic countries, preventing the recurrence of violence supported the case for negotiated settlement with the aim of progressive devolution (Guelke

2012; Sisk 1996; Wolff and Yakinthou 2011). Conversely, strategies of physical extermination of opponents, such as ethnic cleansing or genocide, and mass abuse of human or minority rights are more likely to follow outright military victory than a negotiated settlement. However, in the last 20 years the growing importance of democracy and human rights as conditions for the international legitimacy of states made the concept of 'smite to unite' increasingly untenable, thus lending further advantage to negotiated settlements as the appropriate path to resolve separatist conflicts.[1] This approach was further enhanced by a shift in the way the international community was dealing with the principle of self-determination. Gradually claims to self-determination have been seen in a more positive light, albeit with several ad hoc provisos that protect the principle of territorial integrity, especially for groups with no realistic prospect for accommodation and autonomy. States that seek political solutions through negotiated settlements or through peaceful partition tend to be less criticized.

As the victor of the Cold War and the only superpower the United States came under increasing pressure to take moral responsibility for the world's ongoing civil wars (Kaplan 1994). There was a widely shared conviction that political and economic liberalism, the winning model of the Cold War, offered a key to solving a broad range of social, political and economic problems including violent conflict. A broad ideological shift took place in a number of countries and leading international organizations, there was a move towards liberal forms of government based on the idea of elections, constitutional limits on governmental powers, and respect for civil and political rights. Such changes reflected the spirit of liberal triumphalism perhaps best symbolized by the claim that humankind had reached the (liberal) endpoint in its ideological evolution (Fukuyama 1989). The euphoria of the time also influenced the field of separatist movements where as early as 1992 the suggested criteria for transition to independent statehood were underpinned by the liberal paradigm incorporating provisos such as the creation of constitutional democracies with market economies and protection of civil, political and minority rights (Carley 1997; Halperin *et al.* 1992, pp. 84–93).

Similarly, the UN 'revolution' on peacemaking and peacebuilding signaled a major turn in the way the international community was approaching the quest for peace. Several different flows of reflection and agency-based research came together in order to establish what might be called the state-building paradigm. In the aftermath of the Cold War Helman and Ratner (1992–3) argued that internal conflict leading to state collapse was the emerging international security challenge and they called the international community to consider a novel and multilateral effort to undertake nation-saving responsibilities. The then UN Secretary-General Boutros-Ghali interpreted the collapse of communism in 1989 as resulting in the dissolution of the classical realist distinction between external security policies and internal stability and peace. The first major report that flagged up the UN's role in the post-Cold War order was Ghali's 1992 'An Agenda for Peace,' followed by a number of publications that ultimately led to the UN Peacebuilding Commission in 2006. The Agenda and the consecutive publications refashioned the traditional doctrine of the UN which sought to expand its role in creating and maintaining world order by increasing the importance of peacekeeping and peacebuilding operations. Stabilizing and pacifying weak or failed states became a security issue in its own right, a necessary precondition for a more stable and peaceful international environment. This resulted in the UN deploying a number of operations in countries shattered by internal armed conflict, including some separatist cases. The conceptual base for these operations was that rapid liberalization in all sectors of the society would create the conditions for long-lasting peace and stability. It was believed that negotiated settlements based on democracy and market economy were the sound foundations for an open and peaceful society, which, once established, can be self-perpetuating (Peceny and Stanley 2001).

The unfolding of peacebuilding in separatist scenarios

Although external involvement in separatist conflict has attracted the attention of scholarly work (Heraclides 1990, 1991; Saideman 2001, 2007), very often separatist cases are part of wider studies on ethnic conflict and/or civil war where the emphasis is placed mainly on providing an exegesis of the causes that lead to international involvement (Findley and Teo 2006; Khosla 1999; Mullenbach 2005; Rost and Greig 2011; Saideman 2002). Equally there is a growing literature on the relationship between involvement that leads to negotiated settlement and sustainable peace outcomes in civil wars at large (Bell 2000; Hartzell and Hoddie 2007; Hoddie and Hartzell 2010; Walter 2002). Despite the widespread support among experts and policy-makers of non-violent solutions of internal conflict, a key issue that negotiated settlements in separatist scenarios face is the possibility the peace accords be simply used as a stepping stone towards another round of violence that could end in further territorial fragmentation. This 'slippery slope' fear is also enhanced by the strong international normative framework in favor of the territorial integrity of the state that depicts secession as anathema. However, no guarantees could be provided that a peaceful agreement would not lead to future secessionist attempts. A negotiated settlement has to be tried out in order to test how it works and whether the disputants are committed to a peace process that is seen as advantageous. In the new international environment that fostered an alternative agenda for the UN, peacebuilding operations were seen as a means for consolidating the achieved negotiated settlements. Involvement in separatist conflicts did not deviate from the trend of peacebuilding and its mainstream liberal premises. However, secessionist conflicts are particular in the sense that their ending may entail the creation of new territorial units in the international system, thus posing specific challenges for the international community. In fact, the majority of secessionist cases with international peacebuilding operations after 1989 were marked by the creation of a new state (Bosnia, Kosovo and East Timor) (Paris and Sisk 2009, p. 2).[2]

Democratization and marketization were the diptych that underpinned the general strategy to promote peace in secessionist conflicts. Planning for elections was a primary task in all operations and in most cases it happened within a three-year time frame (Paris 2004, p. 19). The liberal premises of peacebuilding operations prioritized early democratic consolidation as the analysis departed from a substantive understanding of democracy and moved towards a procedural model of democratization, thus shifting the emphasis from the outcomes to the rules and procedures that govern politics. In this line of thought a society qualifies as democratic when it has the proper procedures and institutions regardless of their quality and the political outcome they deliver (Mainwaring 1992; O'Donnell 1992). Peace was understood in procedural terms rather than substantive terms, strong democratic rules that govern politics constitute the framework for peaceful relations. An immediate effect of this distinction was an increase in the number of procedural models and institutional arrangements designed to minimize the occurrence of populism by increasing the cost of authoritarian rule. The transition from authoritarianism to democracy as a result of well-designed institutions became part of the international toolkit of democratization in the new world order. The transitional democracy paradigm was further supported by the underlying assumption that the democratization process is shaped by political elites and the local communities were excluded from active political participation. Accordingly, early elections were imperative in order to legitimize the entire process, thus making space for the elites to proceed with the implementation of institutions as the paramount factor for effective state-building and long-term peace (Berman 2007; Carothers 2002, 2007; Fukuyama 2007; Mansfield and Snyder 2007). Fast-track democratization worked in parallel with economic reforms. There was a call for rapid transformation of the economic structures that would lead to the development of free-market economies. This strategy was pursued through the elimination of barriers in the flow of capital and goods within and across the country's borders but also with the stimulation of private enterprise and the reduction of the state's role in the economy.

However, the limitations of liberalization strategies gradually posed significant challenges to peacebuilding efforts. The urge for swift democratic transition and rapid economic reforms did not address the root causes of the conflict, which in some cases led to destabilizing results. The secessionist conflicts in Bosnia and Kosovo were prominent examples of these limitations. The signing of the Dayton Agreement in 1995 ended the war in Bosnia and raised the hopes that active international engagement in internal conflict could make the post-Cold War world a better place. The Agreement attempted to make Bosnia a liberal democracy, assuming that such a transformation would, by definition, reduce the possibility of violence recurring. The new constitution of Bosnia and Herzegovina confirmed this direction both in the political and economic spheres. The Agreement also prescribed quick elections with the aim of initiating the integration process of the physically and ethnically separated communities of the country, it was a priority to reconstitute the state's political institutions with representation from all three communities (Paris 2004, p. 100). The elections, however, reaffirmed the power of the hardliners who were least committed to pursuing inter-ethnic reconciliation. After the first two rounds of elections in

1996 and 1998 the wartime nationalists were further reinforced, solidifying the dichotomies among the ethnic communities. Despite several attempts by the international community to promote moderate voices that could foster reconciliation and integration, the situation did not alter in the 2006 and 2010 general elections. The protagonists of the military clash were kept in their places and they consolidated further their political power as international agencies through their actions supported the dysfunctional structures that emerged from the war. Instead of designing an electoral system that would encourage compromise and genuine political participation, international peacebuilders focused on quick 'free and fair' elections which brought adverse results, questioning the viability of Bosnia as a unified state which is sustained more by international pressure than the will of its people to live together (Coakley 2010, p. 202). The perplexed political environment in post-war Bosnia also had serious shortcomings with regard to the economic liberalization efforts. Although emphasis was placed on repairing war-damaged infrastructure and the establishment of institutional structures able to manage an open market economy, the acute institutional and political vacuum generated adverse results as the internationally-mandated privatization reinforced shadow markets and enriched the extremist groups. Bosnia's cumbersome institutional structures with complex bureaucracy and the long-standing problems with organized crime and corruption have hampered the country's economic growth (Pugh 2005).

Similar problems have been prominent in post-intervention Kosovo. After the end of NATO's military operations in 1999 the UN undertook the task to govern Kosovo through an interim administration mission (UNMIK). UNMIK's mandate was based on the UNSC Resolution 1244 which paved the way to Kosovo's multi-level transition to peace. The Resolution was underpinned by the liberal paradigm of peacebuilding that combines security with normative, institutional, social and economic considerations. Thus UNMIK's mission included the promotion of electoral democracy that would produce democratic practices and lead to self-sustained peace, developing the rule of law and power-sharing mechanisms in governance to promote ethnic reconciliation, supporting civil society in support of human rights and social inclusion, and, finally, establishing an open market economy that would achieve economic growth and prosperity (Del Castillo 2008, p. 140). The broad and open-ended mandate of UNMIK created significant tensions between the mission and the nascent Kosovo authorities. The Kosovars who had experience in civil government due to their past autonomous status in federal Yugoslavia began to provide some civil functions, an urge that could also indicate their readiness to be actively involved in the exercise of political power in the emerging entity (Crocker 2004, pp. 194–196). UNMIK, pegged to the liberal peacebuilding imperative for swift procedural democracy, held elections for the Kosovo assembly in 2001. The result reflected a sharp ethnic division between Kosovar Serbs and Kosovar Albanians but also highlighted a divide within the ranks of the latter. The prolonged political infighting that followed delayed the formation of the government that participated in the Provisional Institutions of Self-Government, an institution designed to share responsibility for administering Kosovo with UNMIK. In addition, although local policy and legal institutions were democratically elected with the responsibility to co-administer Kosovo, UNMIK retained executive power to overrule their decisions, thus undermining their legitimacy and weakening their capacity for valid administration. There were voices from the local community that UNMIK did not consult with them sufficiently, and ignored the local NGO community that was becoming increasingly vibrant. The peacebuilding agents through their actions reinforced the extremist elements of the society and marginalized moderate voices, thus damaging their capacity (Richmond 2007, p. 166; Richmond 2011).

Similarly, the formation and consolidation of parallel structures of government in areas dominated by Serbs were tolerated by UNMIK in the initial period of UN administration until 2008, which paved the way for the current situation characterized by the ongoing Serbian interference, the divided loyalties and an overall undermining of any effort for the integration of the distinct communities into a coherent Kosovar political society. Also, there was slow progress in developing an effective and cohesive rule of law sector. The lack of vital reforms in the justice and governance sectors has offered the perfect conditions for corruption to flourish and become a permanent structural impediment in the political and economic progress of the new entity. Especially in the economic sector the uncertainty over property rights, the parallel structures in the North, and the misguided policies made Kosovo aid-dependent with high unemployment and corruption which undermine any attempt for progress towards self-sustainability and development (Del Castillo 2008, pp. 157–160). The current situation in Kosovo is characterized by uncertainty about its status as an independent state. Despite the recognition that it has received from a number of states after 2008, Kosovo continues to face multiple challenges to its sovereignty that may pose a direct threat to the stability of the new state and the region. The inefficient institutions, the weak economy and the parallel/separate structures in the Serbian areas indicate the difficult way ahead. Like in Bosnia, Kosovo is sustained more because of the international presence than the will of its people.

The experience of peacebuilding operations in separatist scenarios such as those in Bosnia and Kosovo is characterized by ebb and flow. War recurrence has been avoided in all cases and the new entities that have been created enjoy some form of stability marked by the absence of large-scale violence for a long period. However, as we saw in the discussion above, a number of factors contributed to the wider problems that peacebuilding faces in separatist scenarios. The newly emerged independent polities have to deal with a number of challenges in order to complete a successful transition towards a meaningful peace that goes beyond the mere achievement of a ceasefire, and co-existence of distinct communities under an assertive international presence. In the next section I discuss two interrelated issues which, although they can occur in non-separatist cases as well, constitute significant challenges in the separatist context as they are directly associated with the creation of a new state and the claim to territorial control as a means of survival in international politics.

Two challenges for sustainable peace in separatist conflicts

Separatism, peacebuilding and the background condition

Secessionist conflicts are underpinned by a real or perceived sense of injustice and grievance by a distinct society that is territorially concentrated within a larger state. Territorial separatism can be seen as political disintegration, which, drawing on the classic definition by Haas (1968, p. 16), is 'the process whereby political actors in several distinct political systems are persuaded to shift their loyalties, expectations, and political activities toward a new centre, the institutions of which possess or demand jurisdiction over the pre-existing sub-system.' Thus separatism entails the move of loyalties and allegiances by members of the distinct community from the jurisdictional state core towards new centers of legitimate political organization usually associated with the creation of new states (Bartkus 1999). Legitimacy of the new territorial entity is crucial in this process. Holsti (1996, pp. 82–98) offers a useful schema as he distinguishes state legitimacy into two categories which present distinct challenges for the emerging states. Vertical legitimacy refers to the way the state functions in an appropriate way towards all of its citizens. Thus a state that promotes the interests of the society, regulates, intervenes and promotes civic opportunities in an undifferentiated fashion, achieves high levels of vertical legitimacy. Horizontal legitimacy, on the other hand, refers to the differentiated perceptions of social groups about one another and their relation to the state. If there is a low level of tolerance and acceptance between social groups and/or one social group regards the state as legitimate whereas another group rejects such legitimacy then the degree of horizontal legitimacy is low. This form of horizontal legitimacy harks back to nineteenth-century discussion on the relation between democracy and national groups as depicted by John Stuart Mill (1951, pp. 487–490), but it also alludes to the modernization paradigm. Rustow (1970), for example, argued that the transition to democracy can be fruitless unless the background condition is satisfied. This entails the unreserved realization by the vast majority of the citizens within a prospective democracy that they belong to the same political community. The background condition represents the level of horizontal legitimacy in any given state but also it defines the boundaries and identities of the state, and the political community it represents. Horizontal legitimacy is a key factor for exclusionary conduct, especially in separatist peacebuilding scenarios where the creation of a new state does not necessarily entail the existence of a unified political community that fulfills the background condition. Defining the political community and its boundaries is an issue of cardinal importance for separatism as the emerging state has to maintain the perception that it acts in a way that keeps at bay all exclusionary tendencies against groups that were involved in the prior armed conflict.

For peacebuilding operations the horizontal legitimacy between different groups attracted less attention than vertical legitimacy since liberal thought sees the individual as the primary agent of the society and the focus was on the relation between the individual and the state. Thus the focus was on vertical legitimacy with the prevailing assumption that the liberal state remains unaffected by identity allegiances and maintains equal treatment for all of its citizens. Hence, the degree of social cohesion among the groups, how they relate and interact under the same state, appeared to be a secondary issue for peacebuilders (Call 2012, pp. 44–46). This was evident in the belief that swift electoral processes could secure and embed the legitimacy of the new state across the population. Although elections may provide a certain degree of legitimacy for the population, they may simultaneously alienate social groups that perceive the post-election environment as one of exclusion and marginalization. The emphasis on vertical legitimacy through elections seemed to neglect the 'political sociology of the locality,' thus ignoring the nexus of identity, ideas and history and their amalgamation in contemporary interests of the political society in question (Jabri 2010, p. 49). Peacebuilders believed in a strong pedagogical element of procedural democracy which would have the capacity in an almost automated fashion, like an invisible hand, to alleviate deeply rooted divisions and bring about a political community anew, fulfilling the background condition. Instead procedural democracy strengthened the extremist elements which became powerful in the new political space of the emerging states. This tendency was exemplified in the quick transition of former combatants to parliamentarians in an instrumental fashion that did not reflect any change in the values and ideas of the opposing social groups. The latter point leads to the second undercurrent about the 'embracing the reviled' phenomenon as an outcome of negotiated settlements (Call 2012, p. 227).

Rebel transition and peacebuilding

The secessionist struggle is an organized one; voicing the grievances and taking action to remedy them can happen only through political organizations who act in the name of the distinct community (Bartkus 1999; Heraclides 1991). Self-determination movements question, at a very fundamental level, the monopoly of violence and its legitimacy claimed by the host state. It is a struggle of redefining the boundaries of political authority but also the extent of its recognition by the distinct community. In secessionist scenarios the question of legitimacy is of particular importance as the resolution of the conflict may lead to the establishment of a new territorial unit and hence there is a need for legitimate rule. Creating a new state implies primarily the construction and legitimacy of a monopoly of violence that can bring about and maintain social order, the latter understood as the protection of persons, property and promises (Lake 2010, p. 37; Orr 2002). Therefore one of the main aims of peacebuilding operations was to embrace former rebels and facilitate their transition from warriors to peaceful political agents through power-sharing mechanisms. The aim was threefold: first, former warring parties were integrated into the new institutions of government thus rendering them legitimate paragons of the new political system; second, their forces were gradually integrated into the new post-war society, and third there was a systematic legitimization of the new post-war political order. This transition was also a challenge for the military groups themselves as a dramatic change of context from war to peace will induce an adaptation to the new conditions if the organization was to maintain its dynamic in the emerging post-war environment (Lyons 2010, p. 152).

Incorporating opposing groups into the political system constitutes a major step towards self-sustaining peace in the post-conflict transition as violence becomes obsolete and the conflicts are kept within the realm of politics (Lyons 2010, p. 147). One of the strategies to incorporate paramilitaries into the new political society was by severing the military links between ex-combatants, a process usually taking place within a wider program of demobilization (Schulhofer-Wohl and Sambanis 2010). It was assumed that such a strategy would reduce the ability of ex-combatants to use organized violence to pursue their interests in the post-conflict society. However, severing the links was not seen necessarily as a panacea for a successful transition since no measure could guarantee that ex-combatants would not return to violence (Knight and Özerdem 2004, p. 508; SIDDR 2006, p. 24). Eliminating the influence that armed groups exercise through organized violence must be coupled with establishing new forms of political influence, thus the transformation of armed groups into political parties and the allocation of specific institution positions to their leaders within the new power-sharing structures have been seen as potential avenues of peaceful transition (Torjesen 2006). These types of incorporation encouraged former paramilitaries to operate within the political system and become pivotal stakeholders. In essence peacebuilding operations attempted to alter the perception of ex-combatants and civilians of governance processes.

The transition of armed groups to political parties was also supported by a wider effort to legitimize the emerging political system. This was pursued through the development of the passive participation of ex-combatants and civilians alike in the new polity (Schulhofer-Wohl and Sambanis 2010, p. 16). The emphasis on a procedural understanding of democracy by the peacebuilders seemed to confirm subsequent approaches in the literature suggesting that fair procedures create the legitimacy that forms the basis for individual non-instrumental compliance (Tyler 2006, p. 392). Thus it was believed that peacebuilding operations should encourage procedural justice, which in turn would enhance the legitimacy of the government and its acceptance by former warriors. To this end there was focus on increasing participation on policy-making by facilitating the creation of social networks and institutions organized around peacetime agendas steering away from the wartime polarization and entrenchment. Former warriors would have to adjust and express their will through transparent and just procedures rather than the use of violence.

This perspective relied on the procedural understanding of democratization that was embraced by liberal peacebuilding and it assumed that rebels could easily adjust to the new open political environment, which differed significantly from wartime. The emphasis on vertical legitimacy by the peacebuilders distracted them from considering elements of horizontal legitimacy among the different groups in the emerging new state. What peacebuilders took for granted was that although wartime separatist organizations may vary significantly in structure and values from peacetime democratic political parties that compete for political power, the adjustment to the new post-war reality could take place in a rather causal fashion as a result of the implementation of procedural justice in the electoral process. However, the monolithic character of these organizations, necessary for the war effort, deprived their members of developing background knowledge, skills and practices necessary for peacetime political parties. The swift transition from rebels to parliamentarians did not facilitate the peacebuilding process as it generated further ethno-political polarization that paralyzed any attempt at societal and economic transformation towards a meaningful peace (Aitken 2007). Newly established parties campaigned in their constituencies by promising to defend the interests of their nation while simultaneously signaling the danger of supporting multi-ethnic parties. In this climate former military leaders appeared as the most appropriate candidates to promote peace. What early elections were able to do was to confirm, through vote counting, the power that these groups had on the ground as a result of their military might (Lyons 2010, p. 149). As Sandole (2010, p. 95) pointed out for the dire situation in Bosnia, von Clausewitz's dictum turned upside down into 'politics is war by other means.'

Concluding thoughts

Territorial separatism is a type of asymmetric conflict highly associated with the Westphalian model of world politics based on the concept of national sovereign territorial states. Control of territory becomes an undivided value between parties in secessionist conflicts and often leads to circles of violence and destruction. The implementation of negotiated settlements through peacebuilding operations in separatist scenarios has limited war recurrence setting the scene for a more stable environment. However, there are several challenges for the move towards the establishment of cultures of peace. Creating a legitimate political foundation that embraces the distinct community and encourages all of its members in building trustful and inclusive relations is an important priority. This implies a renegotiation of the relation between the distinct society and the territory it inhabits; it is a call of abandoning identity discourses that are based on exclusion and marginalization. To this end the transition of former fighters to agents of peace presupposes a departure from identity politics that build on the ethnic security dilemma.

Notes

1 A prominent exception was the 2009 end of the Sri Lankan separatist war.
2 I refer here to operations with more than 200 personnel that attempted to crucially shape the post-conflict peace environment.

References

Aitken, R 2007, 'Cementing Divisions? An Assessment of the Impact of International Interventions and Peace-Building Policies on Ethnic Identities and Divisions,' *Policy Studies*, vol. 28, no. 3, pp. 247–267.

Atzili, B 2006–7, 'When Good Fences Make Bad Neighbours: Fixed Borders, State Weakness, and International Conflict,' *International Security*, vol. 31, no. 3, pp. 139–173.

Ayres, RW 2000, 'A World Flying Apart? Violent Nationalist Conflict and the End of the Cold War,' *Journal of Peace Research*, vol. 37, no. 1, pp. 107–117.

Bartkus, V 1999, *The Dynamic of Secession*, Cambridge University Press, Cambridge, UK.

Bell, C 2000, *Peace Agreements and Human Rights*, Oxford University Press, Oxford.

Berman, S 2007, 'The Vain Hope for "Correct" Timing,' *Journal of Democracy*, vol. 18, no. 3, pp. 14–17.

Buzan, B 1991, *People, States and Fear*, Harvester Wheatsheaf, London.

Call, C 2012, *Why Peace Fails: The Causes and Prevention of Civil War Recurrence*, Georgetown University Press, Washington, DC.

Carley, P 1997, 'U.S. Response to Self-Determination Movements: Strategies for Nonviolent Outcomes and Alternatives to Secession,' *Peaceworks*, no. 16, United States Institute of Peace.

Carothers, T 2002, 'The End of Transition Paradigm,' *Journal of Democracy*, vol. 13, no. 1, pp. 5–21.

Carothers, T 2007, 'The Sequencing Fallacy,' *Journal of Democracy*, vol. 18, no. 1, pp. 12–27.

Coakley, J 2010, 'Ethnic Conflict Resolution: Routes towards Settlement,' in J Coakley (ed.), *Pathways from Ethnic Conflict: Institutional Redesign in Divided Societies*, Routledge, Abingdon, UK, pp. 201–222.

Crawford, J 2006, *The Creation of States in International Law*, 2nd edn, Oxford University Press, Oxford, UK.

Crocker, BN 2004, 'Kosovo: Learning to Leverage "Liberator" Status,' in RC Orr (ed.), *Winning the Peace: An American Strategy for Post-Conflict Reconstruction*, Significant Issues Series, vol. 26, no. 7, Centre for Strategic and International Studies, pp. 193–209.

Del Castillo, G 2008, *Rebuilding War-Torn States: The Challenge for Post-Conflict Economic Reconstruction*, Oxford University Press, New York.

Englebert, P 2009, *Africa: Unity, Sovereignty, and Sorrow*, Lynne Rienner, Boulder, CO.

Englebert, P and Tull, DM 2008, 'Post-Conflict Reconstruction in Africa: Flawed Ideas about Failed States,' *International Security*, vol. 32, no. 4, pp. 106–139.

Findley, MG and Teo, TK 2006, 'Rethinking Third-Party Interventions into Civil Wars: An Actor-Centric Approach,' *The Journal of Politics*, vol. 68, no. 4, pp. 828–837.

Fukuyama, F 1989, 'The End of History?' *The National Interest*, Summer.

Fukuyama, F 2004, *State-Building: Governance and World Order in the 21st Century*, Cornell University Press, Ithaca, NY.

Fukuyama, F 2007, 'Liberalism Versus State-building,' *Journal of Democracy*, vol. 18, no. 3, pp. 10–13.

Guelke, A 2012, *Politics in Deeply Divided Societies*, Polity Press, Cambridge, UK.

Gurr, TR 1993, *Minorities at Risk: A Global View of Ethnopolitical Conflict*, The United States Institute of Peace Press, Washington, DC.

Gurr, T and Harff, B 1994, *Ethnic Conflict in World Politics*, Westview Press, Boulder, CO.

Haas, E 1968, *The Uniting of Europe*, Stanford University Press, Stanford, CA.

Hale, H 2008, *The Foundations of Ethnic Politics*, Cambridge University Press, New York.

Halperin, M, Scheffer, DJ and Small, PL 1992, *Self-Determination in the New World Order*, Carnegie Endowment for International Peace, Washington, DC.

Hartzell, CA and Hoddie, M 2007, *Crafting the Peace: Power-Sharing Institutions and the Negotiated Settlement of Civil Wars*, The Pennsylvania State University Press, University Park, PA.

Helman, GB and Ratner, SR 1992–3, 'Saving Failed States,' *Foreign Policy*, vol. 89, pp. 3–20.

Heraclides, A 1990, 'Secessionist Minorities and External Involvement,' *International Organization*, vol. 44, no. 3, pp. 341–378.

Heraclides, A 1991, *The Self-Determination of Minorities in International Politics*, Frank Cass, London.

Heraclides, A 1997 'The Ending of Unending Conflicts: Separatist Wars,' *Millennium: Journal of International Studies*, vol. 26, no. 3, pp. 679–707.

Herbst, J 1996–7, 'Responding to State Failure in Africa,' *International Security*, vol. 21, no. 3, pp. 120–144.

Herbst, J 2003, 'Let Them Fail: State Failure in Theory and Practice,' in RI Rotberg (ed.), *When States Fail: Causes and Consequences*, Princeton University Press, Princeton, NJ, pp. 302–318.

Hoddie, M and Hartzell, CA 2010, *Strengthening Peace in Post-Civil War States*, Chicago University Press, Chicago.

Holsti, K 1996, *The State, War, and the State of War*, Cambridge University Press, Cambridge, UK.

Ignatieff, M 2003, *Empire Lite: Nation Building in Bosnia, Kosovo and Afghanistan*, Vintage Publishing, London.

Jabri, V 2010, 'War, Government, Politics: A Critical Response to the Hegemony of the Liberal Peace,' in O Richmond (ed.), *Peacebuilding: Critical Developments and Approaches*, Palgrave Macmillan, Houndmills, UK, pp. 41–57.

Johnson, C 2008, 'Partitioning to Peace: Sovereignty, Demography, and Ethnic Civil Wars,' *International Security*, vol. 32, no. 4, pp. 140–170.

Kaplan, RD 1994, 'The Coming Anarchy,' *Atlantic Monthly*, vol. 273, no. 2, pp. 44–76.

Khosla, D 1999, 'Third World States as Intervenors in Ethnic Conflicts,' *Third World Quarterly*, vol. 20, no. 6, pp. 1143–1156.

Knight, M and Özerdem, A 2004, 'Guns, Camps and Cash: Disarmament, Demobilization and Reinsertion of Former Combatants in Transition from War to Peace,' *Journal of Peace Research*, vol. 41, no. 4, pp. 499–516.

Kraxberger, BM 2012, 'Rethinking Response to State Failure, with Special Reference to Africa,' *Progress in Development Studies*, vol. 12, no. 2–3, pp. 99–111.

Kubo, K 2011, 'Secession and Ethnic Conflict,' in A Pavković and P Radan (eds), *The Ashgate Research Companion to Secession*, Ashgate, Aldershot.

Lake, DA 2010, 'Building Legitimate States after Civil Wars,' in M Hoddie and CA Hartzell (eds), *Strengthening Peace in Post-Civil Wars States: Transforming Spoilers into Stakeholders*, Chicago University Press, Chicago, pp. 29–51.

Licklider, R (ed) 1993, *Stopping the Killing: How Civil Wars End*, New York University Press, New York.

Licklider, R 1995, 'The Consequences of Negotiated Settlements in Civil Wars: 1945–1993,' *The American Political Science Review*, vol. 89, no. 3, pp. 681–690.
Luttwak, E 1999, 'Give War a Chance,' *Foreign Affairs*, vol. 78, no. 4, pp. 36–44.
Lyons, T 2010, 'Soft Intervention and the Transformation of Militias into Political Parties,' in M Hoddie and CA Hartzell (eds), *Strengthening Peace in Post-Civil Wars States: Transforming Spoilers into Stakeholders*, Chicago University Press, Chicago, pp. 145–162.
Mainwaring, S 1992, 'Transition to Democracy and Democratic Consolidation: Theoretical and Comparative Issues,' in S Mainwaring, G O'Donnell and JS Velenzuela (eds), *Issues in Democratic Consolidation: The New South American Democracies in Comparative Perspective*, Notre Dame University Press, Indiana, pp. 294–341.
Mansfield, E and Snyder, J 2007, 'The Sequencing "Fallacy",' *Journal of Democracy*, vol. 18, no. 3, pp. 5–12.
Mill, JS 1951, *Utilitarianism, Liberty and Representative Government*, E.P. Dutton and Co, New York.
Mullenbach, MJ 2005, 'Deciding to Keep Peace: An Analysis of International Influences on the Establishment of Third-Party Peacekeeping Missions,' *International Studies Quarterly*, vol. 49, no. 3, pp. 529–556.
Newman, E, Paris, R and Richmond, O (eds) 2009, *New Perspectives on Liberal Peacebuilding*, United Nations University Press, Tokyo.
O'Donnell, G 1992, 'Transitions, Continuities and Paradoxes,' in S Mainwaring, G O'Donnell and JS Velenzuela (eds), *Issues in Democratic Consolidation: The New South American Democracies in Comparative Perspective*, Notre Dame University Press, Indiana, pp. 17–56.
Orr, R 2002, 'Governing When Chaos Rules,' *Washington Quarterly*, vol. 25, no. 4, pp. 139–152.
Paris, R 2004, *At War's End: Building Peace after Civil Conflict*, Cambridge University Press, Cambridge, UK.
Paris, R and Sisk, T (eds) 2009, *The Dilemmas of Statebuilding: Confronting the Contradictions of Postwar Peace Operations*, Routledge, London.
Pavković, A and Radan, P 2007, *Creating New States: Theory and Practice of Secession*, Ashgate, Aldershot.
Peceny, M and Stanley, W 2001, 'Liberal Social Reconstruction and the Resolution of Civil Wars in Central America,' *International Organization*, vol. 55, no. 1, pp. 149–182.
Pillar, PR 1983, *Negotiating Peace: War Termination as a Bargaining Process*, Princeton University Press, Princeton, NJ.
Pugh, M 2005, 'Transformation in the Political Economy of Bosnia Herzegovina since Dayton,' *International Peacekeeping*, vol. 12, no. 3, pp. 448–462.
Richmond, O 2007, *The Transformation of Peace*, Routledge, London.
Richmond, O 2011, *A Post-Liberal Peace*, Routledge, London.
Rost, N and Greig, JM 2011, 'Taking Matters into Their Own Hands: An Analysis of the Determinants of State-Conducted Peacekeeping in Civil Wars,' *Journal of Peace Research*, vol. 48, no. 2, pp. 171–184.
Rustow, DA 1970, 'Transitions to Democracy: Toward a Dynamic Model,' *Comparative Politics*, vol. 2/3, pp. 337–363.
Saideman, SM 2001, *The Ties that Divide: Ethnic Politics, Foreign Policy, and International Conflict*, Columbia University Press, New York.
Saideman, SM 2002, 'Discrimination in International Relations: Analyzing External Support for Ethnic Groups,' *Journal of Peace Research*, vol. 39, no. 1, pp. 27–50.

Saideman, SM 2007, 'Ties Versus Institutions: Revisiting Foreign Interventions and Secessionist Movements,' *Canadian Journal of Political Science*, vol. 40, no. 3, pp. 733–747.

Sandole, D 2010, *Peacebuilding*, Polity Press, Cambridge.

Schulhofer-Wohl, J and Sambanis, N 2010, *Disarmament, Demobilization, and Reintegration Programs: An Assessment* (Research Report), The Folke Bernadotte Academy Publications.

Sisk, T 1996, *Power Sharing and International Mediation in Ethnic Conflicts*, United States Institute of Peace, Washington, DC.

Stedman, SI, Rothchild, D and Cousens, EM (eds) 2002, *Ending Civil Wars: The Implementation of Peace Agreements*, Lynne Rienner, Boulder, CO.

Stockholm Initiative on Disarmament, Demobilization and Re-Integration (SIDDR) 2006, *Final Report*, Swedish Ministry of Foreign Affairs, Stockholm.

Toft, M 2006, *The Geography of Ethnic Violence*, Princeton University Press, Princeton, NJ.

Toft, M 2010a, *Securing the Peace: The Durable Settlement of Civil Wars*, Princeton University Press, Princeton, NJ.

Toft, M 2010b, 'Ending Civil Wars: A Case for Rebel Victory?' *International Security*, vol. 34, no. 4, pp. 7–36.

Torjesen, S 2006, *The Political Economy of Disarmament, Demobilization and Reintegration (DDR)* (Paper no. 709), Norwegian Institute of International Affairs, Oslo.

Tyler, TR 2006, 'Psychological Perspectives on Legitimacy and Legitimation,' *Annual Review of Psychology*, vol. 57, pp. 375–400.

Wagner, RH 1993, 'The Causes of Peace,' in R Licklider (ed.), *Stopping the Killing: How Civil Wars End*, New York University Press, New York, pp. 235–268.

Walter, BF 2002, *Committing to Peace: The Successful Settlement of Civil Wars*, Princeton University Press, Princeton, NJ.

Weinstein, J 2005, *Autonomous Recovery and International Intervention in Comparative Perspective* (Working Paper no. 57), Centre for Global Development, Washington, DC.

Wolff, S and Yakinthou, C (eds) 2011, *Conflict Management in Divided Societies*, Routledge, London.

5 Discursive peacebuilding and conflict transformation after separatist wars

A radical proposition

Richard Jackson

Introduction

The general puzzle I am concerned with in this chapter, why post-conflict peacebuilding has had limited success over the past few decades, particularly in the case of intrastate wars, including separatist wars, and how it might be made more successful, derives from both intellectual and normative sources. On the one hand, I have long been interested in the causal processes, and resolution of, political violence (Bercovitch and Jackson 2009; Jackson 2005, 2009a; Jackson and Dexter 2014); on the other, I am a pacifist and critical peace researcher concerned to apply immanent critique in the ongoing struggle for emancipation (McDonald 2009) and a world free from militarism and all forms of structural and direct violence.

Intellectually, the puzzle emerges from a number of key empirical observations about intrastate wars, political violence and peacebuilding. First, it is well-established that bouts of sustained political violence are highly correlated with, and strong predictors of, future bouts of violence (Walter 2004). Second, as a growing body of recent research has demonstrated, violent political transformations tend to produce states characterized by further violence and political instability, widespread human rights abuses and lack of democratic consolidation (Celestino and Gleditsch 2013; Stephan and Chenoweth 2008). These correlations provide strong evidence of the means–ends relationship in political transformations (Schock 2013, p. 279), whereby the use of violence appears to precondition actors to future uses of violence. Lastly, no one doubts that the empirical record of peacebuilding is one of rare successes; most peacebuilding missions have failed to prevent violent domestic orders continuing in the post-conflict period, further instances of major violence and instability, repression and failures of democratic consolidation, and in some cases, external war with neighboring states. In short, as both theory and practice, peacebuilding has been quite unsuccessful in its first few decades.

The aim of this chapter is to point to one particular peacebuilding failure, namely, the failure to deal with the discursive elements of intrastate war, particularly narratives of legitimate political violence, and then to suggest a radical solution to it: discursive peacebuilding and conflict transformation based on an open commitment to principled nonviolence. In the next section, I briefly outline a constructivist model of the 'causes' of sustained political violence, noting the key role played by discourses which legitimize the use of violence for political goals. In the following section, I briefly review some of the main criticisms of the dominant peacebuilding paradigm, including its state-building orientation, before focusing specifically on its failure to address the discursive structures, narratives and discourses that make political violence possible. In the final section, I make the case for discursive peacebuilding within a conflict transformation approach as a radical alternative to the current model. More importantly, I argue that discursive peacebuilding ought to be rooted in pacifist theory and practice, including the construction of non-militarized, post-Weberian political communities.

In short, my central critique and argument suggests that the continued use of political violence, even in the name of noble causes such as 'peace, freedom, and liberty,' or in contemporary terms, 'humanitarian intervention, stabilization and peacebuilding,' does not ultimately lead to peace and stability. Rather, it results in succeeding and quite predictable episodes of political violence throughout the ages in the name of various political 'goods.' The reason for this is that once violence has been legitimized as an acceptable tool of politics, and a socially-accepted mythology persists that it can be employed to positive ends (the myth of redemptive violence), it remains a constant temptation for elites and groups, a final resort for actors in the event of political deadlock. That is, as with any kind of discursive social practice, it is constitutive in its effects, constructing and sustaining a form of politics in which the resort to violence remains the final (legitimate) arbiter of power struggles.

The solution to this conundrum, how to build a peaceful political community in which violence is no longer employed as a political tool when creating such a state involves violent intervention and the state itself as an institution is based on the monopoly of legitimate violence, involves the discursive deconstruction of narratives and discourses of violence, or, the de-legitimization of all forms and recourse to political violence, and the conscious decision to construct pacifist political institutions and discourses. In other words, my radical proposition here is that the only way to create positively peaceful political communities is to move beyond the Weberian state itself and construct other forms of nonviolent, locally appropriate political institutions and processes. Theoretically and empirically, there are a number of resources which can be drawn upon for thinking about the contours of such a reformulation of contemporary political forms.

A constructivist model of the causal processes of intrastate war

This section briefly outlines a constructivist model of intrastate war initiation, or, a model of the social construction of sustained political violence (Demmers 2012; Jackson 2004, 2006, 2009b; Jackson and Dexter 2014). I will argue that, among others, discursive factors, such as social structures, histories, narratives, discursive practices, play a central role that is relatively under-valued in most quantitative and structurally-based approaches to intrastate war explanation, as well as in most institutional understandings of the causes of intrastate war. More specifically, the constructivist model outlined here suggests that intrastate wars (and other forms of organized political violence) occur in the confluence between a conflict-generating set of a material and social structures, willing and capable conflict agents, and a series of conflict-enabling discourses and discursive practices.

All three elements are assumed to be necessary to precipitate the outbreak of organized violence, which helps greatly in explaining the historically and spatially contingent nature of intrastate wars. In other words, the confluence of these three elements helps us to understand why campaigns of organized political violence occur when they do, and not earlier or later, why they occur in some places and not others (Kaufman 2001), especially when both places share similar conflict-prone characteristics, and why wars sometimes fail to occur when they might reasonably be expected to.

For example, in some cases a state may have all the structural conditions highly correlated with intrastate war outbreak, such as extreme levels of poverty and inequality, unconsolidated democratic institutions, high levels of repression and grievance, ethnic dominance of one group over another, high levels of militarization, culturally accepted discourses of hostility and victimhood, and the like, but because there are no willing and capable agents prepared to actively promote and precipitate violent conflict, no large-scale, organized outbreak of violence occurs. Similarly, in other states there may be elites intent on generating intercommunal or inter-ethnic conflict, but because the structural conditions are unpropitious to organized violence – the state is characterized by consolidated democracy, high levels of economic development, an equitable social structure, a culture of tolerance and the like – their efforts ultimately fail to generate the social consensus required to undertake organized political violence. Finally, states may have both the structural conditions necessary for conflict and agents determined to ignite it, but the actions of the conflict elites are mistimed or poorly enacted, or effective internal or external resistance to their attempts at creating conflict arises. As a consequence of elite communication and organizational failure, the planned violent campaign fails to materialize.

The strengths of this model include its multiple dimensions, including the often ignored variables of discourses, narratives and discursive structures and actions. Crucially, it maintains a central focus on agency and the key role of human actors in generating and sustaining violent conflict, a factor often unaccounted for in structural accounts based on correlation-based studies. Finally, it respects and accounts for contingency and the unique cultural, political and historical circumstances in which violent conflicts emerge (Alkopher 2005, p. 716), while retaining a useful degree of generalizability. The basic model can be effectively applied across cases.

The primary material (economic, political, demographic and social) structures identified in the literature to be correlated with intrastate war outbreak include factors such as: the presence of significant amounts of weapons, as well as high levels of military spending (Henderson and Singer 2000; Krause 1996); unprofessional militaries and a history of military interference in politics and/or a sense of continuing political crisis (Elbadawi and Sambanis 2000; Fearon and Laitin 2003); the presence of certain forms of lootable resources (Fearon 2004; Ross 2004a, 2004b); ethnic dominance of one or two groups by another; high levels of economic inequality and poverty, especially the onset of an economic crisis (Collier and Hoeffler 2002; Collier *et al.* 2004; Fearon and Laitin 2003); high levels of corruption and patronage politics, or, more accurately, the disruption of system-stabilizing patronage systems (Azam 2001); unconsolidated or transitioning democracies (Hegre *et al.* 2001; Reynal-Querol 2002); political exclusion and grievance (Chapter 3, this volume); weak state structures (Herbst 1990; Jackson 2002); and the like.

Such factors are insufficient on their own to generate intrastate war, but they do provide the precipitating structural conditions – together with the discursive structures described below – which conflict elites can easily exploit to generate the conditions necessary for the initiation of organized political violence. Importantly, these structures are not based on absolute thresholds after which violent conflict becomes impossible. As violent civil conflict in Northern Ireland, Spain and more recently the Ukraine demonstrate, it is sufficient that *relative* poverty, exclusion and grievances exist for violence to be possible. Similarly, it is not the case that all these structures must be present; a few can be sufficient to create structural conditions conducive to the onset of violent conflict. In particular, the availability of weapons is crucial to the outbreak of violent conflict, although in a globalized world awash with arms, rapidly obtaining such weapons for the purposes of a violent campaign is normally no obstacle, as the conflicts in Libya and Syria demonstrated.

The discursive structures which have been identified as key precipitants of intrastate wars (Jackson and Dexter 2014) include, among others: banal or open militarism and entrenched political values which accept the necessity of military force (Jabri 1996); exclusive and hostile social identities based on ethnicity, religion or nationalism (Bowman 2003; Fearon and Laitin 2000); collective narratives of historical grievance or dispossession (Kaufman 2001; Lemarchand 1994); national myths, historical narratives and truth regimes about an enemy other (Mertus 1999; Wilmer 2002); cultural reminders of conflict-generating discourses and narratives contained in memorials and commemorative practices, popular entertainment, music, films and art (Croft 2006); and the like.

In my view, the most significant discursive structure of intrastate wars, and one which is present in the vast majority of states today, is the well-established notion of the instrumental rationality of violence as a tool of politics (Jabri 1996). This is also referred to as the narrative or myth of redemptive violence. The fact is that most societies have accepted this narrative and it has been materialized in the institutionalization and centrality of the military to society, as well as all the cultural practices which support militarization such as popular entertainment, war remembrance and national commemoration. The belief that normative political goals –

such as national defense, liberation from oppressive regimes, saving strangers from genocide, resisting totalitarianism, and the like – can be obtained through military violence is at this historical juncture an almost universal, and deeply embedded, discursive structure, in part due to the well-established mythology of the 'good war' (Lawler 2002) of World War II. Once again, these discursive structures are insufficient on their own to generate organized political violence, but are highly amenable to elite manipulation and exploitation as a way of generating the necessary social consensus for organized violence.

The agents of intrastate wars are often referred to in the literature as 'ethnic entrepreneurs,' 'conflict entrepreneurs,' 'warlords' and the like (Lemarchand 1994; Reno 1998). They may be national-level political, religious or cultural leaders who have a platform for spreading their message, or they may be local-level elites who are able to generate conflict in a particular locality which then spreads. Sometimes, conflict elites receive material and political support from external actors. The other agents of intrastate wars are the so-called followers, the foot soldiers who actually fight and the broader populace who support or acquiesce to the violence. In the past, scholars have tended to assume that these actors were highly manipulated by conflict or ethnic entrepreneurs and exercised little agency in their own right (Demmers 2012, p. 35). However, we now understand that while many do follow the leaders and volunteer to engage in violence, often they actively resist the call to violence and may even choose to work against their own leaders' interests in the name of solidarity with their enemy.

Finally, within the context of the above-described material and discursive structures, conflict agents have to engage in a series of discursive practices aimed at generating violent conflict in order for it to take place. For example, they may engage in actual violence and oppression aimed at polarizing groups and creating contemporary grievances which justify militarization and conquest. Or, they may actively suppress groups and popular social narratives which pose an obstacle to the enactment of violent conflict, and/or engage in the mobilization of civilian actors trained in violence, such as militias and armed gangs. The key point is that such practices are constitutive of the actors and political institutions they operate in, and there is a clear relationship between means and ends. As Celestino and Gleditsch note (2013, p. 391), violent movements tend to lead to the concentration of power, centralization and polarization, effects that are extremely difficult to undo once the violent phase of the conflict is ended.

Simultaneously, conflict elites are required to articulate a series of key narratives designed to undermine prohibitions on violence and legitimize violent actions (Jackson and Dexter 2014), including: narratives of threat and emergency requiring self-defense and urgent military action to protect the community or some threatened political good such as a 'way of life'; narratives of grievance, exclusion and victimhood which justify redress or revenge, including in some cases national separation (Chapter 3, this volume); narratives of the evil, inhuman enemy deserving of violent opposition and punishment; narratives of the necessity of abandoning previous ethical constraints on killing and violence; and other similar narratives which may be historically and culturally contingent

(Ross 2003). An important point is that such narratives need to be skillfully articulated and widely disseminated so that they resonate with the target audience in order to produce the intended effect. Miscalculations about the public mood or miscommunicated narratives can fail to have the intended effect.

As argued, all these elements, at least to some degree, are assumed to be necessary in a given temporal and spatial context to initiate and sustain organized violent conflict; if any are mostly missing, or if elites lack the skills to enact them, the conflict is unlikely to ignite or be sustained. Importantly, while there are useful and important literatures which focus either on the material structural determinants of intrastate wars, or the discursive structures and processes of intrastate wars, there are few models or approaches which incorporate both of these elements whilst also acknowledging the importance and contingency of actors' agency. Even more importantly, at the official level, there remains a distinct lack of focus on the discursive structures and practices of intrastate war initiation, and consequently, most peacebuilding efforts are largely directed towards the material and institutional structures of conflict, such as economic, political and security aspects.

A critique of post-intrastate war liberal peacebuilding

The dominant peacebuilding model employed by the international community is recognized as having four main planks:

1 security sector reform (SSR), including disarmament, demobilization and reintegration (DDR) programs and the strengthening of law and order practices and institutions;
2 economic reform focused on the liberalization of the economy;
3 political reform in terms of the enactment of political participation and competition, national elections and constitutionally guaranteed civil liberties; and
4 in some instances, social reconciliation efforts in the form of truth commissions, lustration, amnesties or other transitional justice mechanisms (Bercovitch and Jackson 2009).

In many respects, this model is probably better conceived of as a state-building project (Chapter 4, this volume; Richmond 2013).

However, after at least two decades of peacebuilding theory and practice, there is by now a very large and sophisticated literature critiquing the dominant liberal peacebuilding model (Chandler 1999; Duffield 2001; Mac Ginty 2011, 2012a, 2012b; Paris 1997; Pugh 2005, 2013; Richmond 2013). Some of the main criticisms raised by scholars in recent years include: its one-size-fits-all template which is applied in every single case, regardless of local context and history; its ideological roots in, and commitments to, neoliberalism, and consequently, its neo-imperialistic character; its ideological consequences in relation to the production of liberal subjects, governmentality and biopower; its external imposition, elite-level

Discursive peacebuilding 81

focus and lack of concern or genuine partnership with local communities; its roots in conflict management and conflict resolution models, rather than a conflict transformation approach; its stabilization, state-building and negative peace orientation in terms of security reform; its poor record of implementation, lack of adequate resourcing, coordination failures and short-term commitment by donors; its imposition of Western values, particularly in relation to transitional justice and reconciliation; and its poor record of success.

In this chapter, I would add that the predominant failure of the current hegemonic model of liberal peacebuilding is that it rests on a faulty understanding of the causal processes of intrastate wars and therefore fails to deal with one of the most serious enabling conditions of violent conflict, namely, the discursive structures and processes which make organized violence possible. As a consequence, most resources and efforts are channeled into changing some of the important structural factors associated with conflict, such as economic underdevelopment, political participation, security sector reform and the like. Even here, though, the neoliberal economic model imposed on post-conflict states most often results in increased levels of economic inequality, while the rapid imposition of democratic institutions most often results in transitional instability associated with further violence.

In fact, the self-defeating nature of peacebuilding is that it attempts to construct a peaceful 'post-conflict' society while asserting and holding onto the doctrine and practice of 'legitimate' forms of political violence which enabled and precipitated the violence in the first place. That is, the international community tries to convince the warring parties to give up using violence to achieve political goals in the new post-conflict state, while at the same time, giving them a state structure in which violence may be used for a great many prescribed political goods (such as national defense, peacekeeping, humanitarian intervention, law and order, and so on). In addition, the international community insists on the right to use violence itself to enforce a peace, disarm the factions, maintain security, impose democracy, and the like, thereby demonstrating that political violence remains a crucial and legitimate tool of politics. In addition, as Laoutides in Chapter 4 of this volume clearly demonstrates, the peacebuilding community most often negotiates political pacts on the basis of nationalist identities and exclusionary identities (as at Arusha and Dayton, among others), creates institutions based on ethnic and religious identities, and establishes deliberative democratic institutions which exclude certain actors perceived to be illiberal, who are often the very actors fighting for a new political order (such as the Taliban in Afghanistan).

In other words, peacebuilding processes function to reinforce all the very same narratives and discourses which created hostile self–other identities and legitimized the use of political violence. Through the reification of the militarism and monopoly on violence at the heart of the modern state, peacebuilding actually *constitutes* an inherently violent form of politics anew rather than breaking the previous embedded cycle of violent politics. In this context, the frequent wars which follow the end of violent separatist campaigns, for example, such as the wars between North and South Yemen, the war between Eritrea and Ethiopia, the war between Georgia and Russia, the current civil war in South Sudan, among others, are not unexpected.

In short, there is an inherent paradox in the dominant model of peacebuilding, namely, that it attempts to create peace on the foundation and basis of the inherently violent Weberian state and international state order, whilst employing internationally-sanctioned, *legitimate* violence in an effort to create an essentially nonviolent domestic polity. From this perspective, it is no surprise that peacebuilding practice has such a poor empirical record of creating stable, positively peaceful, nonviolent societies. The problem is heightened in cases of separatist conflicts, especially when successful national separation is achieved by means of a violent campaign. In such cases, the nation-state is even more obviously constituted by war and violence, and the hostile identities constructed to make the violence possible in the first place, remain firmly in place.

Discursive peacebuilding

I propose 'discursive peacebuilding' as a potential answer, both theoretically and practically, to this inherently destabilizing and ineffective peacebuilding paradox. Discursive peacebuilding rests on two key sets of assumptions. First, it abandons the framework of conflict management or conflict resolution in favor of complexity theory and conflict transformation (Aggestam 1999; Botes 2003; Lederach 1997). This is more radical than it might sound, as it entails a commitment to accepting the permanent existence of social and political conflict and working towards its transformation into nonviolent and non-destructive forms. As such, it deviates from the assumption that conflict must be either controlled or minimized, or 'resolved' to the point where it disappears. A second set of assumptions revolve around the social construction of violent conflict and peace, and radical contingency (Demmers 2012). These assumptions recognize that conflict and peace is constituted in large part through social practice and discourse, rather than being a feature of, or exogenously caused by, structures or external agents.

On this foundation, discursive peacebuilding practice adds a range of contextually appropriate social interventions and support systems aimed broadly at discursive transformation. Practically, and depending upon the local context and history, such an approach might involve: reconstituting educational practices and histories which might be implicated in the generation of violence; the deconstruction of narratives, doctrines and institutions which legitimize the use of violence for political ends, and widespread anti-violence training; efforts to break down enemy images and narratives, and re-humanize and reconcile formerly hostile groups, including through the establishment of politically inclusive institutions; training in peace journalism for the media; the renegotiation of collective narratives and identities implicated in violence, including at the level of media and popular culture; the reconstruction of social practices of memorialization and commemoration when they are part of a cultural discourse which promotes othering and hostility; and the construction of institutions which support and sustain all these kinds of conflict transformation practices. In short, discursive peacebuilding goes beyond the political institutional, macro-economic and elite levels, as important as they are, and works with ordinary people and community groups to build upon and/or reconstruct cultural discourses and social practices, while also seeking to reconstruct elite-level political discourse.

At the political level, discursive peacebuilding is aimed at two key processes. In the first instance, it is aimed at the construction of agonistic forms of democratic participation and dialogic politics (Schaap 2006; Shinko 2008). The advantage of agonistic political forms and processes lies in its potential for including subaltern and marginalized groups who would normally be excluded under the terms of deliberative democratic forms and who might have undertaken violence in the very first place due to political exclusion. It is also potentially transformative in the way it turns violent military conflict into vigorous discursive conflict by turning enemies into opponents and antagonism into agonism. The Northern Ireland Assembly is held by some to be an example of a slow but tangible transformation of deeply antagonistic political conflict into something resembling agonistic democracy (Hayward and O'Donnell 2011).

Second, and more importantly, discursive peacebuilding aims at the complete disarmament and demilitarization of politics, or, the establishment of Gandhian nonviolent 'realism' in politics (Mantena 2012). In other words, it entails creating a genuine commitment to renouncing the final resort to force in the face of deadlock. The problem with the Weberian state form of politics, rooted as it is in the monopoly of legitimate violence, is that in a political crisis, the governing party can always resort to the use of violence as the final form of arbitration, as occurred in South Sudan soon after independence. This is the negation of politics and the basis for further outbreaks of violence. Without the ability or the legitimacy of any use of violence, politics instead becomes the arena for unfettered political discourse free from the threat of adjudication by violence. Institutionally, this entails the replacement of formal militaries with other nonviolent civilian forms of national defense and security.

These two main dimensions of discursive peacebuilding, the social and the political, are interdependent and necessary for constructing the boundaries of a functioning nonviolent politics. Without a social basis for the rejection of all forms of political violence, the political classes and institutions will fail to develop a truly nonviolent politics. Similarly, without leadership and commitment to nonviolence from the political institutions and classes, and the complete removal of the means of violent politics, the society will remain vulnerable to elite-led political violence. Clearly, such a situation would constitute a post-Weberian or post-state polity, making discursive peacebuilding a kind of 'Clausewitz in reverse' or Weber-in-reverse process.

The contours of discursive peacebuilding I have outlined here are not without foundation in the wider literature. There are a number of existing theoretical and empirical resources which could assist us to think through the theoretical basis of the concept. For example, Oliver Richmond, among others, has recently started to explore the concept and framework of 'peace formations,' which is a kind of 'grass-roots peacebuilding' where 'nonviolent, peaceful change is sought' in order to 'negate local violence' (Richmond 2013, p. 380). More specifically, he suggests that:

> peace formation processes, [are] where indigenous or local agents of peacebuilding, conflict resolution or development, in customary, religious, cultural, social or local political or local government settings, find ways of establishing peace processes and dynamic forms of peace, which are also constitutive of their state.
>
> (Richmond 2013, p. 383)

In other words, peace formation is a bottom-up approach to peacebuilding which builds on the kinds of nonviolent 'everyday peace' which exist in every society, and which is frequently ignored in large-scale, externally imposed peacebuilding missions.

Similarly, there are equally useful literatures exploring the potential of agonistic political forms for reconciliation (Schaap 2006; Shinko 2008), ways of dealing with radical disagreement (Dauphinee 2007; Ramsbotham 2010), the importance of narrative reconstruction in peace processes (Hayward and O'Donnell 2011) and dialogically-based forms of conflict resolution and transformation (Ramsbotham et al. 2011).

In addition to the theoretical bases for the formulation of discursive peacebuilding as a workable theory, there are also a number of empirically-based resources and studies which might inform its translation into peacebuilding practices. For example, Richmond (2013, p. 380) discusses a number of empirical examples of peace formations where local actors have mobilized and established forms of peace which I would associate with discursive peacebuilding, given that they are rooted in nonviolence, social justice, agonistic political forms and the like. Similarly, there are a number of nation-states without national militaries. Although most are small states and/or island states, such as Andorra, Samoa, Panama, Iceland, Haiti and others, this does not detract from the argument that it is possible to have a nation-state that does not accept the necessity of a formal military.

Costa Rica, for example, abolished its standing army in 1949 following a civil war, and has remained free of violent internal conflict since (Celestino and Gleditsch 2013, pp. 386–387). Its military budget was subsequently re-allocated to security, welfare and culture, and it has become one of the most peaceful, stable, democratic and prosperous nations in the region. Such examples lend weight to the argument that means and ends are not unrelated, but rather means prefigure ends (Arendt 1969; Schock 2013, p. 279). Therefore, real positive peace can only be achieved through nonviolent means, such as civilian defense rather than military defense. In addition to helping to constitute a more positively peaceful polity, the potential advantages of adopting civilian defense models rather than national military defense, include, among others: expanding democratic participation, civic education and inclusion in politics through dispersing and decentralizing power; breaking down hostile group identities and forging a new national identity; freeing up resources for welfare and human security; re-building trust between adversaries through a non-threatening external and domestic defense posture; building local capacity and strengthening local peace; and more.

Importantly, there is also a theoretical and empirical literature on civilian national defense models (Boserup and Mack 1974; Salmon 1988) which demonstrates possibilities for thinking beyond military forces as the primary tool for national defense, national identity, external engagement and the like. Directly related to this, there is a growing literature on the success and benefits of nonviolent civil resistance and reform campaigns (see Celestino and Gleditsch 2013; Schock 2013; Stephan and Chenoweth 2008). This literature demonstrates the potential for constructing mechanisms for political change and reform which do not rely on the use of violence. Importantly, it demonstrates empirically that not only can nonviolence be more effective than violence, a finding which challenges the myth of the instrumental rationality of violence, but it also demonstrates that nonviolence is correlated with more peaceful societies in the long-term. Once again, this reinforces the importance of the means–ends connection in peacebuilding.

Finally, there is an important but neglected literature on the success of unarmed peacekeeping and nonviolent peaceforces, including in situations of extreme government repression (Mahony and Eguren 1997; Schirch 2006; Schweitzer *et al.* 2001; Weber 1996). This literature suggests that there is real potential for thinking about forms of external intervention in civil wars and violent conflicts which does not rely on preponderant military force and the use of counter-violence to establish 'peace.' Developing and expanding the use of such an approach would go a long way towards de-legitimizing the use of force in international politics, and consequently in the peacebuilding phase as well. To this end, among other suggestions, the UN could establish a Department of Unarmed Peacekeeping in which personnel were trained and resourced for nonviolent interventions and peacebuilding, or provide support to existing groups. At the very least, peacebuilding after separatist and intrastate wars more generally, ought to include unarmed peacekeeping, demilitarization and disarmament, and the replacement of national militaries with civilian defense plans.

Conclusion

In this chapter, I have put forward the argument that current forms of peacebuilding after intrastate wars are, in many respects, 'failed by design' (Richmond 2013, p. 378). This is not only because they are rooted in neoliberal ideology and often poorly enacted, but because they tend to ignore the discursive structures and processes which trigger violent conflict and they contain an inherent contradiction over the role of military violence in politics. That is, because peacebuilding employs violence to create 'peace,' and because its vision of peaceful politics is rooted in the (inherently violent) Weberian state, it leaves untouched the central cultural belief that political goods can be obtained through violence. This narrative of the instrumental rationality of violence or myth of redemptive violence is one of the main discursive underpinnings or structures of organized political violence, and is likely one of the primary reasons why peacebuilding has been largely a failure in the post-Cold War period.

As a consequence, I have tried to argue that the current peacebuilding template ought to be replaced by discursive peacebuilding which aims to transform the discursive structures of violent conflict, including the central notion of the legitimacy of political violence. In practical terms, I have tried to argue that this entails the construction of nonviolent, pacifist political institutions and processes rooted in, and theoretically informed by, agonism and dialogical conflict transformation. In effect, discursive peacebuilding returns us to Johan Galtung's notion of 'cultures of peace' in which all forms of direct, structural and cultural violence have been de-legitimized and transformed. The number and variety of empirical examples which exhibit forms and aspects of discursive peacebuilding suggest that such an approach is far more than simple idealism, but could become reality with greater attention from scholars, greater efforts by peace workers, and a little bit of political will from key decision-makers.

Of course, a number of key challenges will need to be faced, including: the deep cultural acceptance of the necessity of military violence by both political elites and the general public, and by both states and international organizations; the determination of the great powers to maintain hegemony through military superiority; inertia, institutional interests and the embedded practices of liberal peacebuilding; and the material interests of the military-industrial complex, among others. However, the manifest success of nonviolent civil resistance in recent years, and a palpable sense of war weariness among global publics, suggests that the present historical juncture may be ripe for pushing this radical agenda forward.

References

Aggestam, K 1999, *Reframing and Resolving Conflict: Israeli-Palestinian Negotiations 1988–1998*, Lund University Press, Lund.

Alkopher, T 2005, 'The Social (and Religious) Meanings that Constitute War: The Crusades as Realpolitik vs. Socialpolitik,' *International Studies Quarterly*, vol. 49, no. 4, pp. 715–737.

Arendt, H 1969, *On Violence*, Harcourt Brace, Orlando.

Azam, J 2001, 'The Redistributive State and Conflicts in Africa,' *Journal of Peace Research*, vol. 38, no. 4, pp. 429–444.

Bercovitch, J and Jackson, R 2009, *Conflict Resolution in the Twenty-first Century: Principles, Methods and Approaches*, Michigan University Press, Ann Arbor, MI.

Boserup, A and Mack, A 1974, *War without Weapons: Non-Violence in National Defence*, Frances Pinter, London.

Botes, J 2003, 'Conflict Transformation: A Debate Over Semantics or a Crucial Shift in Theory and Practice of Peace and Conflict Studies,' *The International Journal of Peace Studies*, vol. 8, no. 2, pp. 1–44.

Bowman, G 2003, 'Constitutive Violence and Rhetoric of Identity: A Comparative Study of Nationalist Movements in the Israeli-Occupied Territories and Former Yugoslavia,' *Social Anthropology*, vol. XI, no. 3, pp. 37–58.
Celestino, M and Gleditsch, S 2013, 'Fresh Carnations or all Thorn, no Rose? Nonviolent Campaigns and Transitions in Autocracies,' *Journal of Peace Research*, vol. 50, no. 3, pp. 385–400.
Chandler, D 1999, 'The Limits of Peacebuilding: International Regulation and Civil Society Development in Bosnia,' *International Peacekeeping*, vol. 6, no. 1, pp. 109–125.
Collier, P and Hoeffler, A 2002, 'On the Incidence of Civil War in Africa,' *Journal of Conflict Resolution*, vol. 46, no. 1, pp. 13–28.
Collier, P, Hoeffler, A and Soderbom, M 2004, 'On the Duration of Civil War,' *Journal of Peace Research*, vol. 41, no. 3, pp. 253–273.
Croft, S 2006, *Culture, Crisis and America's War on Terror*, Cambridge University Press, Cambridge, UK.
Dauphinee, E 2007, *The Ethics of Researching War: Looking for Bosnia*, Manchester University Press, Manchester, UK.
Demmers, J 2012, *Theories of Violent Conflict*, Routledge, London.
Duffield, M 2001, *Global Governance and the New Wars: The Merging of Development and Security*, Zed Books, London.
Elbadawi, I and Sambanis, N 2000, 'Why Are There So Many Civil Wars in Africa? Understanding and Preventing Violent Conflict,' *Journal of African Economies*, vol. 9, no. 3, pp. 244–269.
Fearon, J 2004, 'Why Do Some Civil Wars Last So Much Longer Than Others?' *Journal of Peace Research*, vol. 41, no. 3, pp. 275–301.
Fearon, J and Laitin, D 2000, 'Violence and the Social Construction of Ethnic Identity,' *International Organisation*, vol. 54, no. 4, pp. 845–877.
Fearon, J and Laitin, D 2003, 'Ethnicity, Insurgency, and Civil War,' *American Political Science Review*, vol. 97, no. 1, pp. 75–90.
Hayward, K and O'Donnell, C 2011, *Political Discourse and Conflict Resolution: Debating Peace in Northern Ireland*, Routledge, Abingdon, UK.
Hegre, H, Ellingsen, T, Gates, S and Gleditsch, N 2001, 'Towards a Democratic Civil Peace? Democracy, Political Change, and Civil War, 1816–1992,' *American Political Science Review*, vol. 95, no. 1, pp. 33–48.
Henderson, E and Singer, J 2000, 'Civil War in the Post-Colonial World, 1946–92,' *Journal of Peace Research*, vol. 37, no. 3, pp. 275–299.
Herbst, J 1990, 'War and the State in Africa,' *International Security*, vol. 14, no. 4, pp. 117–139.
Jabri, V 1996, *Discourses on Violence: Conflict Analysis Reconsidered*, Manchester University Press, Manchester, UK.
Jackson, R 2002, 'Violent Internal Conflict and the African State: Towards a Framework of Analysis,' *Journal of Contemporary African Studies*, vol. 20, no. 1, pp. 29–52.
Jackson, R 2004, 'The Social Construction of Internal War,' in R Jackson (ed.), *(Re)Constructing Cultures of Violence and Peace*, Rodopi, Amsterdam and New York, pp. 61–77.
Jackson, R 2005, 'Internal War, International Mediation and Non-Official Diplomacy: Lessons from Mozambique,' *Journal of Conflict Studies*, vol. XXV, no. 1, pp. 153–176.
Jackson, R 2006, 'Africa's Wars: Overview, Causes and the Challenges of Conflict Transformation,' in O Furley and R May (eds), *Ending Africa's Wars: Progressing to Peace*, Ashgate, Aldershot, pp. 15–29.

Jackson, R 2009a, 'Conflict Resolution in Africa: A Comparative Empirical Analysis,' in M Meyer and E Ndura-Ouedraogo (eds), *Seeds of New Hope: Pan-African Peace Studies for the Twenty-First Century*, Africa World Press Inc., Trenton, NJ, pp. 229–248.

Jackson, R 2009b, 'Constructivism and Conflict Resolution,' in J Bercovitch, V Kremenyuk and IW Zartman (eds), *The SAGE Handbook on Conflict Resolution*, Sage, Thousand Oaks, CA, pp. 172–189.

Jackson, R and Dexter, H 2014, 'The Social Construction of Organised Political Violence: An Analytical Framework,' *Civil Wars*, vol. 16, no. 1, pp. 1–23.

Kaufman, S 2001, *Modern Hatreds: The Symbolic Politics of Ethnic War*, Cornell University Press, New York.

Krause, K 1996, 'Armaments and Conflict: The Causes and Consequences of "Military Development",' in L Van De Goor, K Rupesinghe and P Sciarone (eds), *Between Development and Destruction: An Enquiry into the Causes of Conflict in Post-Colonial States*, Macmillan, London, pp. 173–196.

Lawler, P 2002, 'The "Good War" after September 11,' *Government and Opposition*, vol. 37, no. 2, pp. 151–172.

Lederach, JP 1997, *Building Peace: Sustainable Reconciliation in Divided Societies*, USIP Press, Washington, DC.

Lemarchand, R 1994, *Burundi: Ethnocide as Discourse and Practice*, Woodrow Wilson Centre Press, Washington, DC.

McDonald, M 2009, 'Emancipation and Critical Terrorism Studies,' in R Jackson, M Breen Smyth and J Gunning (eds), *Critical Terrorism Studies: A New Research Agenda*, Routledge, London, pp. 109–123.

Mac Ginty, R 2011, *International Peacebuilding and Local Resistance*, Palgrave, Basingstoke.

Mac Ginty, R 2012a, 'Against Stabilization,' *Stability: International Journal of Security and Development*, vol. 1, no. 1, pp. 20–30.

Mac Ginty, R 2012b, 'Between Resistance and Compliance: Non-Participation and the Liberal Peace,' *Journal of Intervention and Statebuilding*, vol. 6, no. 4, pp. 167–187.

Mahony, L and Eguren, L 1997, *Unarmed Bodyguards: International Accompaniment for the Protection of Human Rights*, Kumarian Press, Connecticut.

Mantena, K 2012, 'Another Realism: The Politics of Gandhian Nonviolence,' *American Political Science Review*, vol. 106, no. 2, pp. 455–470.

Mertus, J 1999, *Kosovo: How Myths and Truths Started a War*, University of California Press, Berkeley, CA.

Paris, R 1997, 'Peacebuilding and the Limits of Liberal Internationalism,' *International Security*, vol. 22, no. 2, pp. 54–89.

Pugh, M 2005, 'The Political Economy of Peacebuilding: A Critical Theory Perspective,' *International Journal of Peace Studies*, vol. 10, no. 2, pp. 23–42.

Pugh, M 2013, 'The Problem-Solving and Critical Paradigms,' in R Mac Ginty (ed.), *Handbook of Peacebuilding*, Routledge, London, pp. 11–24.

Ramsbotham, O 2010, *Transforming Violent Conflict: Radical Disagreement, Dialogue and Survival*, Routledge, London.

Ramsbotham, O, Woodhouse, T and Miall, H 2011, *Contemporary Conflict Resolution*, 3rd edn, Polity Press, Cambridge, UK.

Reno, W 1998, *Warlord Politics and African States*, Lynne Rienner, Boulder, CO.

Reynal-Querol, M 2002, 'Ethnicity, Political Systems, and Civil Wars,' *Journal of Conflict Resolution*, vol. 46, no. 1, pp. 29–54.

Richmond, O 2013, 'Failed Statebuilding Versus Peace Formation,' *Cooperation and Conflict*, vol. 48, no. 3, pp. 378–400.

Ross, H 2003, 'Competing Narratives and Escalation in Ethnic Conflicts: The Case of Holy Sites in Jerusalem,' *Sphera Publica*, vol. 3, no. 1, pp. 189–208.

Ross, M 2004a, 'What Do We Know About Natural Resources and Civil War?' *Journal of Peace Research*, vol. 41, no. 3, pp. 337–356.

Ross, M 2004b, 'How Does Natural Resource Wealth Influence Civil War? Evidence from 13 Cases,' *International Organization*, vol. 58, no. 1, pp. 35–67.

Salmon, J 1988, 'Can Non-Violence be Combined with Military Means for National Defence,' *Journal of Peace Research*, vol. 25, no. 1, pp. 69–80.

Schaap, A 2006, 'Agonism in Divided Societies,' *Philosophy and Social Criticism*, vol. 32, no. 2, pp. 255–277.

Schirch, L 2006, *Civilian Peacekeeping: Preventing Violence and Making Space for Democracy*, Life and Peace Institute, retrieved July 25 2014, www.life-peace.org/wp-content/uploads/Civilian-Peacekeeping-Preventing-Violence-and-Making-Space-for-Democracy-Lisa-Schirch.pdf.

Schock, K 2013, 'The Practice and Study of Civil Resistance,' *Journal of Peace Research*, vol. 50, no. 3, pp. 277–290.

Schweitzer, C, Howard, D and Stieren, C (eds) 2001, *Nonviolent Peaceforce Feasibility Study*, Nonviolent Peaceforce, retrieved July 25 2014, www.nonviolentpeaceforce.org/english/resources/rstudy.asp.

Shinko, R 2008, 'Agonistic Peace: A Postmodern Reading,' *Millennium: Journal of International Studies*, vol. 36, no. 3, pp. 473–491.

Stephan, M and Chenoweth, E 2008, 'Why Civil Resistance Works: The Strategic Logic of Nonviolent Conflict,' *International Security*, vol. 33, no. 1, pp. 7–44.

Walter, B 2004, 'Does Conflict Beget Conflict? Explaining Recurring Civil War,' *Journal of Peace Research*, vol. 41, no. 3, pp. 371–388.

Weber, T 1996, *Gandhi's Peace Army: The Shanti Sena and Unarmed Peacekeeping*, Syracuse University Press, New York.

Wilmer, F 2002, *The Social Construction of Man, the State, and War: Identity, Conflict, and Violence in the Former Yugoslavia*, Routledge, New York.

Part II
Case studies

6 Recognition as a political act
Political considerations in recognizing Indonesia's annexation of East Timor

Clinton Fernandes

West Papua: prelude to East Timor

In 1969, after a sustained campaign of diplomatic and military pressure, Indonesia annexed the former Dutch colony of West Papua. Australian policy-makers had initially been opposed to Indonesian rule over the territory, which they regarded as occupying 'a position of great strategic and tactical importance, guarding as it does the western approaches to Torres Strait and the northern approaches to Darwin. Its western and northern coasts particularly contain a number of first-class harbors and airfield sites.' Accordingly, policy-makers believed that West Papua 'should not become subject to the control of any Asiatic authority,' but should 'remain a colonial possession of the Netherlands' (Dorling 1994, p. 82). However, as the Cold War developed during the 1950s, the Australian government came around to the view that it ought to rethink its support for Dutch control of West Papua. In December 1961, therefore, Australia's minister for external affairs finally abandoned support for the Dutch in a statement that referred to Australia's 'great interest in the ability of the indigenous people of West New Guinea to have the ultimate choice of their own future, whether it be for integration with Indonesia or for independence' (NAA 1961).

On August 15 1962, an agreement was signed between the Dutch and the Indonesians under the auspices of the United Nations. Known as the New York Agreement, it provided for the transfer of West Papua to an interim United Nations Temporary Executive Authority (UNTEA) from October 1 1962 to May 1 1963, followed by a longer period of Indonesian administration. The territory's inhabitants would be allowed before the end of 1969 'to participate in the act of self-determination to be carried out in accordance with international practice' (Fernandes 2006, p. 56). Seven months of UN administration duly occurred, after which Indonesia assumed administrative control of West Papua. There were rebellions against Indonesian rule and several thousand West Papuans sought refuge across the land border with the Australian-administered Territory of Papua and New Guinea (Saltford 2003).

While detailed research is yet to be conducted, it would appear that no Australian civil society groups supported the West Papuans, or campaigned for credible international supervision of the act of self-determination. Nor was there any significant public opposition to the Australian government's decision to 'discourage any interest by the United Nations High Commissioner for Refugees in the issue of West Papuan refugees' (Fernandes 2006, p. 61). In May 1969 two young West Papuan leaders, Clemens Runaweri and Willem Zonggonau, fled to Port Moresby. They attempted to board a plane to New York to brief the UN on Indonesia's conduct in West Papua. At the request of the Indonesian government, Australian authorities detained them on Manus Island when their plane stopped to refuel, ensuring that West Papuan voices were silenced. No Australian civil society groups appear to have opposed the government's actions.

Indonesia then conducted the Act of Free Choice, in which 1,022 West Papuans, approximately 0.1 percent of the population, voted unanimously to join Indonesia. Australian journalist Hugh Lunn saw Indonesian forces throw West Papuan demonstrators into trucks and drive them away. He raised the alarm but the UN representative did not intervene. The 1,022 West Papuans were handpicked without the supervision of the UN, the international press or other independent observers. A subsequent evaluation of the Act of Free Choice reported that it appeared to have been 'a sham, where a press-ganged electorate acting under a great deal of pressure appeared to have unanimously declared itself in favour of Indonesia' (Drooglever 2010, p. 758).

West Papuan separatist rhetoric today draws heavily on the flawed nature of what they refer to as the Act of No Choice. However, the international community's recognition of the annexation has been a major obstacle to separatist claims today. After Indonesia invaded the Portuguese colony of East Timor in December 1975, it hoped to secure international recognition of the annexation. Yet it was never able to do so successfully. Civil society groups in key countries played a crucial role in preventing international recognition.

Civil society support for East Timor before the invasion

In Australia, civil society support for East Timor came from groups and individuals who had been involved in previous social movements. Supporters included some former military personnel, members of aid organizations, academics, communists, members of the peace movement during the Vietnam War and members of some church groups. These supporters were in considerable disagreement on almost every issue except one, that the East Timorese be allowed to determine their own future. Former military personnel, for example, were often suspicious of, if not openly hostile to, those who had spent the decade before the Indonesian invasion opposing Australia's participation in the US attack on Vietnam. As the years went on, however, members of different groups developed personal friendships and better understanding of each other's motivations. As a consequence, their activities took on greater coherence.

Although not many Australians knew much about East Timor at the beginning of the 1970s, some former military personnel did. They were former members of the 2nd/2nd Independent Company and the 2nd/4th Independent

Company, who had seen action in East Timor during World War II. Many of these old soldiers visited East Timor as a group in 1973. The visit resulted in the renewal of many old friendships with their former Timorese comrades and the formation of new friendships as well. In order to help Australians communicate with the East Timorese, one of the veterans, Cliff Morris, compiled an English–Tetum dictionary. Morris also collected and published traditional East Timorese folk stories. A delegation of former soldiers led by a member of the 2nd/2nd Commando Association, Arthur Stevenson, would go to Canberra in 1975 to lobby for a peacekeeping force.

Some student activists began to support East Timor from 1968, when the National Union of Australian University Students published a report about Timor in the union newspaper *National U*, on July 22 1968. Until this report was published, East Timor was almost completely unknown to Australians outside the well-organized but insular network of former commandos. Other student activists in Melbourne were linked to a group known as Action for World Development, which was affiliated to the Australian Council for Overseas Aid. Australian academics and students in the field of international development were critical of the Indonesian development model, advocating instead a more self-reliant, participatory approach with local control, a greater emphasis on ecological issues and a specific focus on the emancipation of women. The Monash University academic Herb Feith was a particularly influential critic. He had pioneered the Volunteer Graduate Scheme with his visit to Indonesia in 1951, working as an interpreter in the Indonesian Ministry of Information. Feith's Indonesia credentials and his familiarity with the emerging discipline of development studies lent credibility to his criticism of the New Order's economic policies. Aid organizations became involved in the politics of the East Timor situation in February 1975, when Australian newspaper reports indicated that the Indonesian government was giving serious thought to a military operation against the territory.

Destabilization and invasion

There were three noteworthy political parties in East Timor at this time: UDT, FRETILIN and APODETI. FRETILIN and UDT enjoyed popular support, unlike APODETI, whose aim was integration with Indonesia. Both FRETILIN and UDT argued for an independent East Timor, with the former promoting rapid independence and the latter promoting gradual independence. In January 1975, FRETILIN and UDT united in what would be a short-lived political coalition. They agreed that a future transitional government would be led by members from both parties. However, their mutual suspicion proved to be too strong, and their political inexperience meant that they had no mechanisms to deal with their differences. In particular, the UDT was threatened by the growing popular support for FRETILIN, which was advocating land reform, an increase in educational expenditure, and support for small industries centered on primary products like coffee. UDT, dominated by conservative land-owning families, was opposed to some of this, and to a FRETILIN initiative called 'alphabetizacao' or basic literacy. The political inexperience of all the indigenous leaders, itself the result of years of living under Portuguese authoritarianism, manifested itself in the political contest that followed, when both sides attacked each other verbally and sometimes physically. Their political inexperience was manipulated by neighboring Indonesia, whose intelligence services fomented suspicion and conflict between them with the aim of eventual annexation of the territory.

In early August 1975, key figures in the UDT met Indonesian intelligence chief General Ali Murtopo in Jakarta. Soon after their return, they launched a coup against their FRETILIN opponents. FRETILIN fought back, and defeated its opponents by the end of August 1975. Its quick victory surprised Indonesian planners; they had fomented a civil war but the wrong side (from their perspective) won. Indonesia then resorted to military pressure on the border, conducting a terror and destabilization campaign in order to set up small enclaves just inside the territory. These enclaves would be used to mount small offensive actions against FRETILIN in order to make its position in East Timor untenable. All the while Indonesia denied it was involved and claimed instead that the fighting was between rival East Timorese factions. Under conditions of Indonesian destabilization, propaganda and military pressure, FRETILIN declared independence on November 28 1975. The next day, representatives of the UDT and three other small parties issued the so-called 'Balibo Declaration,' a proclamation requesting the Indonesian government to annex East Timor. Witnesses to its signing later testified that it was drafted in Jakarta and signed in a Bali hotel under coercive circumstances. While many foreign governments publicly attributed the conflict and its casualties to a 'civil war' rather than Indonesian military operations, they were aware, as a classified British diplomatic cable explained, that the

> so-called civil war from September to December was really only a clandestine Indonesian invasion and was confined to the border area with Indonesian Timor. It was the failure of this clandestine effort and the fear that FRETILIN, having declared East Timor independent of Portugal, might secure international recognition which prompted the Indonesian invasion.
>
> (NA 1979)

Indonesia invaded on December 7 1975 and attempted to repeat its earlier maneuver in West Papua. Accordingly, it chose 30 East Timorese, described them as a 'Popular Assembly,' and told them to endorse a petition to President Suharto asking for integration. Indonesia described this petition as the Act of Integration. It then installed 24 men as the so-called Provisional Government of East Timor, whose only role was to send another petition to President Suharto calling for integration with Indonesia. Although FRETILIN fought back, the Indonesian military was able to press its attacks thanks to the use of foreign aircraft: C-130 Hercules, F-51 Mustang, OV-10 Bronco, Iroquois and Choctaw

(USA), Sabre, Nomad and Sioux (Australia), Bolkow (West Germany), F-27 Fokker (Netherlands), Puma (France) and CASA-212 (Spain). Symbolically, the conventional war ended on December 31 1978 when FRETILIN President Nicolau Lobato was ambushed and killed. The Indonesian military declared that East Timor was pacified on March 26 1979. However, the territory was shut off from the outside world for considerably longer, with bans on foreign media and international aid agencies, and tight controls on official delegations. Yet it could never obtain international recognition of its annexation.

Civil society support for East Timor post-invasion

Australian activists first tried to take shiploads of aid to various ports of East Timor. In September 1976, four activists, Cliff Morris, Robert Wesley-Smith, James Zantis and Manolis 'Manny' Mavromatis, were arrested while trying to sail to East Timor with medical supplies. Collectively, these activists illustrate the diverse and highly contradictory nature of the early solidarity movement. Cliff Morris was an Australian dairy farmer in his mid-fifties from Deniliquin, New South Wales. At the age of 21, he had fought in East Timor during World War II as a commando with 2nd/4th Independent Company. By contrast, Robert Wesley-Smith was a peace activist and agricultural scientist who had worked on land rights with the Gurindji and Larrakia people and coached Aboriginal children in Australian Rules Football. James Zantis was a right-wing political activist from Bondi in Sydney's eastern suburbs. Manny Mavromatis had no overt political stance. He was a sailor and adventurer who believed that something should and could be done to help the Timorese, and that a trip to a war zone was exciting and worthwhile in itself. Their vessel, *Dawn*, had large supplies of medicines, some food, radio equipment and six firearms. They were charged with attempting to smuggle drugs (the medicines) and guns (the six firearms) to East Timor. On February 14 1977, after ten days in court, the four activists were convicted and placed on small bonds. The Northern Territory Supreme Court later overturned their convictions on appeal, but the attempt cost Wesley-Smith his life-savings.

Perhaps the most elaborate project undertaken by Australian activists in this period was the construction of an illegal radio link between the Northern Territory and East Timor. Warwick Neilley, the organizer of the North Australian Workers Union (later part of the Miscellaneous Workers Union) bought a few Single Side Band (SSB) radios from a store in Darwin. Some were sent to FRETILIN personnel, who mounted them on the back of a donkey after the Indonesian invasion began, and transmitted news and political messages to the outside world. An Australian man named Brian Manning, who was a key activist in the Communist Party of Australia, coordinated the effort to receive FRETILIN's radio transmissions. When the Australian government ordered that the transmissions cease, Manning and his colleagues set up a covert, and illegal, operation to keep the communications going. In a game of cat-and-mouse with the Australian police, sometimes the broadcaster would be caught and the radio confiscated, other times he would evade capture by stealth and deception. The illegal radio operation continued to operate until the end of 1978 as the only link between the external solidarity movement and the Timorese resistance.

A few Australian parliamentarians supported East Timor, too. Ken Fry, a backbencher from Canberra, spoke on behalf of East Timor at the UN Security Council in New York. Fry had been reluctant to go because he was a very new parliamentarian, and was quite intimidated by the prospect of speaking at the UN. However, he decided to go after receiving strong encouragement from his colleague, Senator Arthur Gietzelt, another supporter. Fry would be targeted by the Australian Security Intelligence Organization (ASIO), which monitored the telecommunications, bank accounts and other activities of East Timor activists. In addition, the Criminal Investigation Division of the Commonwealth Police (forerunner to the Australian Federal Police) investigated the ACT branch of the Australia East Timor Association, of which Fry was patron.

Australian government recognition of the annexation

Under Prime Minister Malcolm Fraser and Foreign Minister Andrew Peacock, the Australian government was keen to recognize Indonesia's sovereignty over East Timor. The problem was that there was considerable opposition from the Australian public. Informed that Indonesia planned to integrate East Timor on its independence day, August 17 1976, the Australian government requested it to bring the date forward by one month. It stressed to the Indonesians that 'the date of August 17 for any announcement involved them in particular embarrassment as it is the day on which Parliament is to reassemble' (NA 1976). Accordingly, Indonesia announced the integration on July 17 1976, during the Australian parliamentary recess.

Prime Minister Malcolm Fraser's visit to Jakarta in October 1976 presented him with a challenge, since his Indonesian hosts were keen to have him state publicly that Australia supported their takeover of East Timor. Indeed, the Indonesian Ambassador 'called on the Prime Minister before the visit to say on instructions that President Suharto would want to speak on the Timor question "as a first priority"' (NA 1976). When Fraser arrived in Jakarta, the Speaker of the Indonesian Parliament specifically invited him to comment on Timor. But Fraser was all too aware of the Australian electorate's hostility to the takeover. Thus, in his public statements on Timor:

> he merely repeated that Australia's position was well known and had been explained many times in Parliament by the Foreign Minister.... One of the members of [the Indonesian] Parliament told the American Ambassador that he regarded the speech as an excellent one for the Australian public, who were its intended audience.
>
> (NA 1976)

At his meeting with Suharto, Fraser asked for:

> understanding of Australia's difficulties in formally accepting integration and for time to overcome these.... Hence, supply boats organised by pro-FRETILIN groups were prevented from leaving Australian waters; attempts were made (with less success) to close off FRETILIN's radio-link with the Northern Territory; and most recently Ramos-Horta, the FRETILIN UN Representative, was refused a visa to visit Australia.
>
> (NA 1978)

As well-informed British diplomats in Australia observed, Foreign Minister Peacock wouldn't admit publicly that he intended to give de facto recognition of Indonesia's annexation due to:

> the long shadows cast by the past policies of both parties on Timor and [the way in which] the Timor issue has been and continues to be a party political football. The policy makers of both parties have indulged in tortuous somersaults and the accusations of moral turpitude, from either side of the House, have a strong lining of humbug.
>
> (NA 1976)

Australian newspapers reported that Indonesian Foreign Minister Adam Malik had claimed that Mr Fraser had reached a secret understanding on Timor with President Suharto during his visit. According to Alan Griffith, First Assistant Secretary in the Department of Prime Minister and Cabinet, Fraser 'had been so angry that he had almost blown Mr Griffith's head off.' Griffith confided that Fraser detested Malik, and asked 'could not someone tell the Indonesians to be quiet about Timor. What Australian/Indonesian relations needed was a couple of months of peace on East Timor.' Griffith offered 'some acid personal comments' on the Australian Ambassador to Jakarta, Mr Woolcott, saying that 'Mr Woolcott had contributed nothing on policy for the visit; he was a PR man and Mr Fraser had no regard for him' (NA 1978). So concerned was the Fraser government about the Australian public's hostility that Alf Parsons, First Assistant Secretary in the Southeast Asia and Papua New Guinea division of the Department of Foreign Affairs, said privately that the Department had been avoiding getting formal legal advice on the question of de facto recognition 'for fear of getting an embarrassing answer which would make it difficult to sustain the declared policy of the Australian government' (NA 1976). The level of public interest in East Timor in 1976 meant that when Australia abstained from the vote in the Fourth Committee, the news of the abstention, according to British diplomats, was carried on a prominent radio program 'as a news flash like a cricket score: 61 for, 18 against, 49 abstentions. As soon as Mr Peacock had finished his set address, the first questions put to him were about Timor and the reason for the Australian abstention' (NA 1976).

By 1978, however, policy-makers assessed that the political conditions would permit de facto recognition. A Cabinet recommendation dated 17 January 1978 advised that:

> on an early occasion the Government [should] announce that it fully accepts the reality that East Timor is part of Indonesia and that all future Government action [will] be based on the acceptance of the proposition that Indonesia exercises sovereign power so far as that territory is concerned.

It was able to do this because 'the volume of letters being received about Timor has dropped substantially over the past six months. It is currently running at the rate of about seven a month. This has been accompanied by a falling newspaper and television interest.' Consequently, on January 20 1978 Andrew Peacock announced that:

> the Government has decided to accept East Timor as part of Indonesia.... Since November 1975 the Indonesian Government has continued to extend its administrative control over the territory of East Timor. This control is effective and covers all major administrative centres of the territory.... This is a reality with which we must come to terms. Accordingly, the Government has decided that although it remains critical of the means by which integration was brought about it would be unrealistic to continue to refuse to recognise de facto that East Timor is part of Indonesia.
>
> (CPD 1978, pp. 25–26)

Peacock was acutely aware of public opposition to this decision even at this time. According to Alan Griffith and David Wilson, the First Assistant Secretary for South East Asia in the Department of Foreign Affairs, Australian officials had for months been seeking to find the right opportunity to get ministers to make a public announcement in respect of the Indonesian annexation of East Timor. Indeed, the Foreign Minister 'was said to have been extremely nervous right to the end.' He had 'apparently almost been ready to take the step later [in 1977] but the announcement of the election had intervened and the matter had been shelved during the campaign.' Wilson said that:

> because of past leaks of information on Timor the matter had been held extremely close; no more than six senior officials in the DFA had known about the move almost up to the time of the issue of the statement.... the Head of the DFA's Indonesian Section himself only found out in the middle of last week ... the Indonesian Government had been informed of the proposed announcement late last week; only then was the Australian Ambassador in Jakarta brought into the picture. Again, as few people as possible were in the know, possibly only the Acting Foreign Minister Mochtar and the Political Head of the Indonesian Foreign Ministry, Darusman.
>
> (NA 1978)

Australia's *de jure* recognition of Indonesia's annexation occurred on February 14 1979, when negotiations began with Indonesia over the seabed boundary between East Timor and Australia. Yet Australia remained the only Western state to recognize *de jure* the annexation of East Timor. European Community Heads of Mission in Jakarta acknowledged that Indonesia was in effective control of East Timor and that its control was irreversible. Yet, they saw 'no reasonable argument in favour of accepting an annexation that the UN are criticising, and in favour of calling an Indonesian fake procedure of "establishing the people's will" an act of democratic self-determination' (NA 1978). Accordingly, the EC Heads of Mission agreed that their governments should encourage Portugal to work with Indonesia directly to resolve the issue. Portugal took very little action until September 1980. In October 1979, for instance, its ambassador to the UN had been instructed 'not to actively solicit support' for the East Timor issue because of higher priority diplomatic objectives 'such as Portugal's acceptance into the EEC' (Smythe 2004, p. 82n). In time, Portuguese civil society efforts began to be reflected at the parliamentary level and a cross-party consensus in favor of East Timor emerged in the Portuguese parliament (Cabral 2003).

British civil society support for East Timor

Some civil society groups in the UK had become interested in East Timor even before the invasion. A number of human rights activists, academics and students had started an organization called the British Indonesia Committee in the early 1970s. This group supported those who had been persecuted by the Suharto regime. It worked on issues of political imprisonment, and also conducted a more general critique of Suharto's developmental and political approach. Since it tried from the very beginning to make alternative information about Indonesia available to the media, it had some connections to the media and members of parliament. It also had contacts among dissident Indonesians in Paris, who would send it information bulletins. John Taylor, who had written his PhD thesis on South-east Asia and Indonesia, was a founding member of the British Indonesia Committee. He became part of the British Campaign for an Independent East Timor (BCIET), which began in December 1975 just after the invasion. Its members tried to ensure that news about East Timor got into the press. They also lobbied members of parliament and built up some support in the Labour Party. They liaised with a group of parliamentarians who would respond to developments in Indonesia and East Timor.[1]

After the conventional military defeat of FRETILIN in 1979, the burden of the campaign was shouldered by TAPOL, the British Campaign for the Release of Indonesian Political Prisoners. Its advocacy on behalf of East Timor preceded the Indonesian invasion. It had written to the British government in August 1975 to urge an international initiative in favor of East Timor's right to self-determination. It argued that Indonesia's record of violence since 1965 indicated nothing but violence and terror for the Timorese. Its October 1975 Bulletin carried a report on the very first page, 'East Timor: Indonesian Takeover means

Bloodshed and Terror.' By 1979, the defeat of FRETILIN coincided with the release of Indonesia's political prisoners. TAPOL therefore decided to focus on East Timor. As its campaign began to expand, it adopted the subtitle of 'Indonesia Human Rights Campaign.'

British policy-makers consider recognition

By 1979, of course, Indonesian diplomats and their Western interlocutors were confident that East Timor was well on the way to joining West Papua and the Republic of the South Moluccas as uncontested parts of Indonesia. An Australian intelligence assessment had previously predicted that, while 'it will not surprise us if Indonesian servicemen are occasionally being shot in East Timor in 1986,' any resistance in East Timor:

> will lack an active sanctuary and they will not have substantive international support. The Indonesians have had long experience in incorporating dissident groups, for example those of Sumatra, the Moluccas and Irian Jaya, into the Republic, and this, together with a capacity to ignore world opinion, will stand them in good stead.... We consider that the vast majority of Timorese will accept the fait accompli provided by integration and that a sufficiently effective resistance to oust or severely embarrass the Indonesians will not develop.
>
> (NAA 1976)

These views solidified among British and other Western policy-makers. DF Murray of Britain's Foreign and Commonwealth Office expressed an influential view within the British diplomatic corps, writing that:

> East Timor has now been absorbed into Indonesia and I see no prospect that the actual situation will ever be different. By this I mean that Indonesia will exercise control and government, irrespective of what the world thinks about sovereignty and of the degree of unrest in the island.
>
> (NA 1979)

Murray solicited the views of other relevant British diplomats, explaining that Britain could give de facto recognition of the Indonesian takeover but refrain from giving *de jure* recognition on the analogy of the Baltic states. He asked, 'Is there any need for a formal recognition of de facto sovereignty?... What would be the precise disadvantages to the British attitude on Gibraltar, Belize and Falkland Islands of a formal announcement on recognition ...?' (NA 1979). He called for submissions from various posts. A rare display of concern for the East Timorese came from JK Gordon of the Southern European Department, who wrote that although 'there is no real danger that the Spaniards are going to seek anything other than a political solution to the dispute' in Gibraltar:

it is of course, for your department to judge on the moral issues, i.e. whether we should be recognising the claims of a regime which is alleged to have followed a policy which has led to the deaths of large numbers of East Timorese. These accusations may be entirely fallacious, but I wonder whether they should not at least be considered.

(NA 1979)

Britain's Central American colony of Belize was a different matter. It was protected by British troops,

> whose withdrawal could trigger a Guatemalan invasion regardless of what we say about Indonesia's annexation of East Timor. But here, too, if we were able to make some arrangements with Guatemala on which they subsequently reneged, the force of our protests might be somewhat weakened by our acceptance of Indonesia military action in East Timor.
>
> (NA 1979)

The FCO's South American Department assessed that although an Argentine invasion of the Falklands was unlikely, the possibility couldn't be ruled out due to 'a strong element of unpredictability in Argentine foreign policy ... [and] the normal Argentine ingredients of excessive national pride and over-attention to machismo.' There was physically 'little or nothing that we could do to prevent an Argentine invasion or to dislodge an invading force once there' and Britain's 'only recourse' would be to bring international diplomatic pressure to bear on Argentina. In that event, a British case at the UN would be 'seriously flawed' if they gave legal recognition of Indonesia's forcible takeover of Timor (NA 1979).

Meanwhile, British diplomats looked for ways to abstain in the vote at the UN's Fourth Committee, where FRETILIN's representative, Jose Ramos-Horta, was joined by American philosopher Professor Noam Chomsky. The *New York Times*' UN correspondent, Bernard Nossiter, refused to attend a press conference about East Timor on the grounds that the issue was 'rather esoteric,' and did not report a word of the UN debate, which also included testimonies from East Timorese refugees (Chomsky 1996, p. 286). The UK's mission to the UN reported that FRETILIN's representative was

> aware of their dwindling support in the UN and knows that a strongly-worded resolution is unlikely to pass in the Fourth Committee. They are said to be prepared to settle for a mildly-worded text concentrating on the humanitarian issues in order at least to keep this item on the UN's agenda.
>
> (NA 1979)

It reported that although

> the second draft resolution is even less contentious than the first ... we clearly wish to abstain in company with the other members of the [EEC],

both to maintain the common position for its own sake and, of course, to avoid upsetting the Indonesians just before [Suharto's] State Visit [to London].

UK civil society groups and sympathetic parliamentarians continued to apply pressure, with Lord Avebury demanding answers of the Foreign Secretary in the House of Lords. He described the reason given for not supporting resolutions on East Timor as 'not convincing.' He pointed out that resolutions had been passed on

> a variety of other matters in the U.N. such as Afghanistan, the Middle East etc. and none of these has ever done anything to improve the conditions of the people concerned yet we do not stand aside and abstain just because we think words are ineffective.
>
> (NA 1980)

British policy-makers were coming under pressure from all sides: civil society groups, their own need to uphold the principle of self-determination (because of the relevance to Gibraltar, Belize and the Falkland Islands) and their desire to please the Indonesian government. There could be no repetition of a quick recognition, as occurred in the case of West Papua. Nor could there be a sustainable method of finessing the distinction between de facto and *de jure* recognition. There was little support to be had from the US State Department, which had come under fire from US civil society groups. Under persistent questioning from US congressmen, George Aldrich, Deputy Legal Adviser in the State Department, was forced to admit that there had not been a valid exercise of the right to self-determination in East Timor. Aldrich also admitted that the Indonesian forces that invaded East Timor 'were armed roughly 90 per cent with our equipment,' and that 'as a legal matter, the right of self-determination continues to exist' (House of Representatives 1977).

The alteration of British policy and practice concerning recognition

In seeking a way out of the impasse, British policy-makers were also aware of the domestic controversies that arose when Britain recognized the new regimes in Iran and then Ghana while executions without trial were taking place in both countries. It decided, after considerable reflection and legal research, to abandon the policy of recognizing governments altogether. The Lord Privy Seal wrote to the Prime Minister, reminding him of the strident domestic criticism the government had encountered over some of its decisions to recognize certain governments. Accordingly, he wrote that Britain should change her practice on recognition, 'leaving the question rather to be inferred from the nature of our dealings with new regimes.' Such a change would, he argued, 'have practical advantages as well as giving us greater political flexibility and bringing us closer to our European partners without, however, sacrificing domestic or international legal requirements' (NA 1980).

Accordingly, the Foreign Secretary, Lord Carrington, advised parliament that Britain would 'no longer accord recognition to Governments.' Where an unconstitutional change of regime occurred, Britain's practice of announcing a decision to formally recognize the new government has 'sometimes been misunderstood, and, despite explanations to the contrary, our "recognition" interpreted as implying approval.' Henceforth, he said,

> we shall continue to decide the nature of our dealings with regimes which come to power unconstitutionally in the light of our assessment of whether they are able of themselves to exercise effective control of the territory of the State concerned, and seem likely to continue to do so.
> (HL 1980)

Several years later, Australia would also move in this direction.

The last 1982 General Assembly Resolution

In November 1982, the question of East Timor came up once again at the UNGA. It was an important moment for the East Timor cause, with Indonesia making a determined effort to win. It had almost won the year before, with 54 states voting in favor of East Timor's right to self-determination, 42 against and 46 abstaining. FRETILIN had never been given observer status at the UN, unlike Palestine and the South African liberation organizations ANC and PAC. Former Australian PM Gough Whitlam appeared before the UN Special Committee on Decolonisation, saying that 'It is high time that the question of East Timor was voted off the United Nations agenda and ceased to preoccupy and distract the nations of South-east Asia and the Pacific' (UN 1982).

He informed the Committee that he had visited East Timor in March that year, under the auspices of the International Committee of the Red Cross. He said he was

> convinced that what the Indonesian Government is doing in East Timor ... is visibly beneficial.... There's no denying the evidence of one's eyes. There are new schools, including secondary schools, there are new or reconstructed hospitals and dispensaries. There are now many more kilometres of asphalt road, and there is proper provision for increasing the amount of food.
> (UN 1982)

Whitlam was confronted by a well-organized opposition in the Committee room. First, he was questioned about his claim that his visit had occurred under the auspices of the International Committee of the Red Cross. A letter from the ICRC's Director of Operational Affairs was produced, stating that Whitlam's visit had been organized 'without having made any prior contact with our institution'

(Ramos-Horta 1987, p. 158n). Next, he was subjected to withering criticism by several members of the Committee, one of whom said that Whitlam had 'knocked on the wrong door' by coming to a decolonization committee to argue in favor of colonialism (Ramos-Horta 1987, pp. 129–131). He came under fire from Gordon McIntosh, an Australian Labor Party Senator from Western Australia, who had also flown to New York to testify before the Committee. McIntosh produced a letter in support of East Timor's right to self-determination, signed by an overwhelming majority of ALP parliamentarians. He played a tape of Australian journalist Greg Shackleton, who was one of a group of journalists murdered in 1975 by the Indonesian military. Seeing the damage being done to the diplomatic effort, the Australian government stepped in. A member of Australia's UN delegation threatened to cut off aid to Vanuatu because of that country's forthright support for East Timor on the Decolonisation Committee. When some of the activists threatened to make this threat public, the delegation tried to pass off the threat as a joke.

Portugal made a determined effort to prevent an Indonesian victory at the United Nations. Its National Assembly had created a Special Committee for the Accompaniment of the Situation in East Timor. President Ramalho Eanes appointed a team of diplomats to muster support around the world. Prime Minister Pinto Balsemao made East Timor the centerpiece of his speech at the UNGA. East Timor barely survived the vote: 50 states voted in favor, 46 against, and 50 abstained. The issue was taken off the General Assembly's agenda and referred to the 'good offices' of the UN Secretary-General, who was required to consult 'all parties directly concerned.'

Thus, despite making a costly, well-coordinated effort, and receiving the tacit support of influential Western states, Indonesia was never able to obtain international recognition of its takeover of East Timor. It attempted a repetition of its earlier actions in West Papua, but had not counted on the role of civil society groups that obstructed their governments from recognizing the takeover. The non-recognition removed a major obstacle to East Timor's eventual secession from its status as Indonesia's 27th province. In its attempt to navigate the tricky diplomatic waters of self-determination, diplomatic relations and domestic pressure, Britain eventually abandoned its policy of recognizing governments altogether.

Note

1 For example, Parliamentary Questions were asked by Ms Audrey Wise (July 7 1976), Mr Stanley Newens (January 28 1976, July 6 1976, June 30 1977), Mr David Knox (July 20 1977), Mr Cyril Townsend (July 21 1977), Mr Dennis Canavan (July 22 1977) and Mr William Wilson (July 25 1977).

References

Cabral, E 2003, 'Portugal and East Timor: From a Politics of Ambivalence to a Late Awakening,' *Portuguese Studies Review*, vol. 11, no. 1, pp. 29–47.
Chomsky, N 1996, *Powers and Prospects: Reflections on Human Nature and the Social Order*, Pluto Press, London.

Commonwealth Parliamentary Debates (CPD) 1978, *Statement by Andrew Peacock*, House of Representatives.

Dorling, P (ed.) 1994, *Diplomasi: Australia and Indonesia's Independence*, Document 82, Department of Foreign Affairs and Trade, Canberra.

Drooglever, P 2010, *Act of Free Choice: Decolonisation and the Right to Self-Determination*, Oneworld Publications, Oxford.

Fernandes, C 2006, *Reluctant Indonesians: Australia, Indonesia and the Future of West Papua*, Scribe Publications, Melbourne, Victoria.

House of Lords (HL) 1980, Statement by Lord Carrington to the House of Lords, April 28.

House of Representatives (US) 1977, *Human Rights in East Timor*, 19 July, pp. 59–64.

National Archives of Australia (NAA) 1961, *Statement by Sir Garfield Barwick*, Department of External Affairs, Current Notes on International Affairs, December 30.

National Archives Australia (NAA) 1976, Joint Intelligence Organisation Intelligence Report 12/76, Military Study, Indonesia.

National Archives – UK (NA) files: *1976: FCO 24/2208. 1977: FCO 15/2252; FCO 15/2253; FCO 15/2254; FCO 15/2255. 1978: FCO 15/2384; FCO 15/2385; FCO 15/2386. 1979: FCO 58/1608. 1980: FCO 15/2712; FCO 15/2713; FCO 15/2714; FCO 15/2715; FCO 15/2716; FCO 15/2697.*

Ramos-Horta, J 1987, *Funu: The Unfinished Saga of East Timor*, Red Sea Press, Laurenceville.

Saltford, J 2003, *The United Nations and the Indonesian Takeover of West Papua, 1962–1969: The Anatomy of Betrayal*, RoutledgeCurzon, London.

Smythe, P 2004, *The Heaviest Blow*, LIT Verlag, Münster, Germany.

UN 1982, Department of Public Information, GA/D/2334, November 9.

7 Containing separatism?

Control and resistance in China's Xinjiang Uyghur autonomous region

Terry Narramore

Introduction

The People's Republic of China's rapid rise in wealth and power has not lessened the ruling Communist Party's sensitivity to sovereignty over Taiwan, Tibet and Xinjiang. These areas constitute what China's officials routinely refer to as 'core interests,' implying they are non-negotiable and will be defended with force if necessary (Swaine 2011, pp. 7–8). Each territory is defined by the Party-state as integral to China's 'homeland' and therefore a link in the chain of sovereignty that cannot be broken. But each represents a challenge to the fundamental authority and legitimacy of the Party-state, especially given its historic mission of national unification to redress the privations of nineteenth-century imperialism.

Taiwan is considered part of the 'Han Chinese core,' whereas Tibet and Xinjiang have long been regarded as outlying (*waidi*) or border (*bianjiang*) territories (Taylor Fravel 2005, pp. 55–59). Despite China's strict enforcement of its 'one China' policy, the reunification of Taiwan remains unfinished business, unlike Hong Kong and Macao, whereas the Party-state's rule of Tibet and Xinjiang has faced resistance and revolt. The challenge of Taiwan is to deter *de jure* independence, which the Party-state sees as illegal secession, while not directly ruling the territory (Song 2003). The challenge of Tibet and Xinjiang is to prevent ethnic 'minorities' concentrated in border territories developing separatist movements that threaten the Party-state's direct monopoly rule. Although this threat has been contained in both cases, the Party-state's combination of repressive control and policies of national unity and development have the contradictory effect of fueling widespread discontent, sustaining separatist sentiment and identity, and provoking violent protests and conflict. Comparative studies of separatist conflict therefore place Tibet and Xinjiang within a category where 'military victory by the state' is 'successful but inconclusive' and there is 'ongoing or intermittent armed violence' (Heraclides 1997, pp. 704, 707). Violent conflict in these troubled regions escalated in 2008 and 2009, highlighting tragic failures in the Party-state's 'nationalities' policy of combining more open economic development with repressive political control.

Whereas the exiled Central Tibetan Administration's movement for 'genuine autonomy' enjoys a high international profile and won a period of regular, if fruitless, dialogue with the Party-state (He 2010; He and Sautman 2005/6; Ramos-Lynch 2010; Shakya 2008; Sperling 2004), Uyghur separatism is less prominent, lacks unity and the leadership of a Dalai Lama-like figure, and has not won any concessions to its cause. Soon after the '9/11' attacks on the United States, however, China declared itself a willing participant in the US-led 'global war on terror' and the Party-state lent Uyghur separatism a far higher profile by casting it in the mold of global Islamist terrorism. Both inside and outside Xinjiang, China apparently confronted a long-standing threat to national security from Uyghur 'terrorist forces' fighting for an 'East Turkestan' homeland, and official accounts of conflict with Uyghurs were now routinely described in this way (Office of the State Council 2002).

China's official propaganda, the various claims of exiled Uyghur groups and their supporters, and restrictions on academic field research in this sensitive area have long obscured the precise nature and extent of Uyghur separatism. The 'terrorist' appellation only further muddied the waters. Claims about Uyghur terrorists found a receptive audience in some political, media and academic circles. By December 2002 both the US administration and the UN had named the East Turkestan Islamic Movement (ETIM) in their lists of 'international terrorist organisations' with alleged connections to Osama bin Laden's al Qaeda and the Taliban. Twenty-two Uyghurs were taken from Afghanistan and Pakistan and detained in the United States' Guantanamo Bay facility, although they were never identified with a terrorist group and were released to six different third countries (Savage 2013; Worthington 2010). Academic studies also emerged (Acharya *et al.* 2010; Gunaratna and Pereire 2006; Reed and Raschke 2010; Wayne 2008) that uncritically linked China with the 'global war on terror,' a concept fraught with 'facile and ill-informed generalisations about Islam and Muslims' (Millward 2009, p. 348). While these studies did not condone the Party-state's repressive policies and saw them as contributing to Uyghur–Han conflict, they took for granted the terrorist threat to China. One argued that 'the Islamist terrorist threat to China is manifestly clear and is not ambiguous' and that, alarmingly, in addition to the Uyghurs, Hui or Chinese-speaking Muslim communities may offer a 'favourable environment' for 'breeding terrorism (Acharya *et al.* 2010, pp. 6, 105). Another was less alarmist but no less certain about the reality of terrorism, seeing China as one of the few successes in the global struggle against Islamic terrorism (Wayne 2008, p. 9).

A more judicious analysis of Uyghur resistance since 1949 shows that, despite regular violent incidents, an armed separatist insurgency in control of a territory or region, with a clear leadership structure and organization, has not been able to establish itself (Roberts 2012). Moreover, not all violent incidents can readily be identified with 'an explosion of separatist sentiment, much less as "jihadism" or "Islamic terrorism"' (Millward 2009, p. 355). Sources both hostile and sympathetic to Uyghur separatism have tended to reach the same exaggerated conclusion (Millward 2009, p. 349). Xinjiang is not a Chechnya, a Sri Lanka, an East Timor, nor even an Aceh. At the same time, a welcome skepticism about the capacity and conditions for separatism or 'terrorism' in Xinjiang

(Bovingdon 2010; Clarke 2008; Millward 2009; Roberts 2012; Shichor 2005) should not obscure the significant political challenge to Party-state authority that continuing Uyghur resistance represents. Like the Tibetans, Uyghurs may well have become more concerned about 'cultural autonomy' than the 'unattainable' goal of an independent state (Millward 2009, p. 357). But this lack of cultural autonomy is symptomatic of the Party-state's failure to 'win recognition as the sole legitimate representative of Uyghur interests and to make Uyghurs think of themselves as Chinese and citizens of the PRC' (Bovingdon 2002, p. 44). The sense of Uyghurs being 'strangers in their own land' has not been overcome (Bovingdon 2010). Echoing Kingsbury's chapter (Chapter 3), the Party-state is still failing to effect policies that move beyond a negative vertical discrimination that does not deliver equal treatment of all citizens. Despite concessions to the 56 'nationalities' making up the PRC, the 'multi-ethnic unification' of China has meant subordination or attempted assimilation of 'minorities' to the majority Han.

The Uyghur situation is not as explosive as the reality of an armed separatist movement or a 'national liberation' struggle, and therefore lacks the political 'legitimacy' of many separatist or secessionist claims. Conflict has been below the level that would stimulate calls for the peacebuilding discussed in Chapter 4 of this volume. Nor are the separatist fighters Laoutides notes much in evidence. But there is little doubt that Uyghur separatism is framed by identity politics, with a basic conflict between Han and Uyghur nationality claims. Non-territorial claims for 'autonomy' can be seen to have a normative legitimacy as a remedy for human rights abuses and the denial of the self-determination of 'minorities' (Bolton *et al.* 2010, pp. 4–5). If Uyghurs were to consolidate claims for autonomy within the international community, as exiled Tibetans have partially succeeded in doing, then they might begin to construct a case for 'remedial' separatism (Buchanan 2004, pp. 353–354; Buchheit 1978, p. 122) or a 'remedial right to self-determination' that does not require territorial separation (Weller 2009). Containing separatism in this sense requires the Party-state to recognize Uyghur minority rights enhancing their own sense of security, while Uyghurs would renounce claims to independence (Hechter 2000, p. 18). But, because 'host state recognition remains the most important factor' (Bolton *et al.* 2010, p. 12) determining remedial separatism the Uyghurs remain unlikely to attain it in the near future.

The Party-state and the dimensions of Uyghur separatism

In an 'exemplary high-capacity undemocratic regime' such as China's, a rapid decline or rise in the state's repressive capacity can increase collective claim-making and resistance (Tilly 2003, pp. 73, 174). The overwhelming capacity of China's Party-state defines Uyghur separatism. Claim-making is pushed into the 'forbidden range' towards violent encounters. There is a 'medium' level of violence, with 'great variability' in frequency, which demonstrates the 'high political stakes of contention' (Tilly 2003, pp. 50–53).

History and the institutional relationships between the central authorities and the periphery minorities can also play an important role in shaping the scope and intensity of separatist movements. If central authorities retain control over economic and political resources while not allowing potential separatists to muster sufficient resources to maintain national sovereignty claims, then separatism is unlikely to develop (Roeder 2007, pp. 262–279). Similarly, 'minorities' that have lost autonomous status are more likely to launch a secessionst campaign (Cuffe and Siroky 2013). The Uyghurs conform to a pattern of minimal resources for, and experience of, secession or separatism.

Xinjiang has not always been governed by a 'high-capacity' regime, and many of the Party-state's problems in governing the region are legacies from the past. Historically, China's hold on Xinjiang was always tenuous, despite the efforts to show lack of regional separate identity and continuous presence 'since 60 BCE' (Office of State Council 2002). The region was brought under China's control from 1759, but consolidation came only after a series of brutal conflicts and the pacification of both Turkic and Chinese Muslim rebellions under the last, Manchu, Qing dynasty (Chu 1966, pp. 163–197; Paine 1996, pp. 113, 118; Perdue 2005). Xinjiang was formally declared a province in 1884 (Lattimore 1950, pp. 47–51). If China's current territorial sovereignty can be said to be a legacy of 'empire' (Lattimore 1940), it is not surprising that they date from this period of the last dynasty's expansionary phase.

Some 65 years later when the People's Republic of China was established, Xinjiang 'remained culturally distinct and geographically remote' from the Han core (Bovingdon 2010, p. 3). The Communist forces inherited a fractious regional politics. From the 1920s to 1940s nationalism penetrated the politics of the Turkic-speaking peoples of the region, further consolidating the modern 'Uyghur' identity. Uyghur nationalists of the day actively cultivated an identity that was primarily 'political in motivation' (Lattimore 1950, p. 123), despite the official designation being a hybrid of invented adminstrative classification and Stalinist-style nationalities policy, believing that it enhanced their 'cultural autonomy' and solidarity vis-à-vis other Turkic 'nationalities' and Han Chinese (Lattimore 1950, pp. 103–128; Roberts 2009; Rudelson 1997, pp. 4–7).

During the same period the fragmented Nationalist (*Guomindang*) state experienced several rebellions and two periods of separatist government in the region. The first, centered on the southern city of Kashgar, declared itself the East Turkestan Islamic Republic in November 1933, but it was quashed by Chinese authorities by June 1934 (Forbes 1986, pp. 230–232; Millward 2007, pp. 201–206). A second, more successful East Turkestan Republic (ETR) was established in November 1944, centered on the north-west region of Ili and its capital, Ghulja. An amalgam of various Turkic nationalists who 'embodied both Islamising and secular modernising impulses' (Millward 2007, p. 226), the ETR managed to extract a concession of coalition government with the Nationalists, but had to renounce the goal of independece and drop the term 'Republic' as part of the deal. The remnants of the ETR leadership appeared to be on the verge of negotiating a similar compromise with the new Communist state when it was reported that they had perished in a plane crash on their way to Beijing (Benson 1990, pp. 155–166; Forbes 1986, pp. 193–195; Millward 2007, pp. 216–234; Whiting and Sheng 1958, pp. 98–112).

The Communist regime did not have to occupy Xinjiang through military conquest but small insurgent groups seeking independence persisted into the mid-1950s, underground parties continued into the post-Mao era, and sporadic protests and violence have occurred since the 1980s (Bovingdon 2010, p. 5; Dillon 2004, pp. 52–55; Millward 2007, p. 238). Although small-scale, these were obvious manifestations of a broader resistance to the Party-state's nation-building project in Xinjiang (Bovingdon 2010, p. 7). The new Party-state began constructing its own system for integrating the predominantly Muslim, Turkic-speaking peoples of the region, of whom the Uyghurs formed the majority. As part of their broader 'nationalities' policy for non-Chinese regions, in 1955 Xinjiang became the Xinjiang Uyghur Autonomous Region. Rather than the Soviet model of nominal federal 'republics,' they preferred a system of 'autonomy,' in theory allowing self-rule at local and regional levels.

The Party-state was nonetheless careful to counter any impression that autonomy implied independence. In practice the system was designed to facilitate partial self-rule while discouraging separatism. A divide-and-rule approach to the various 'nationalities' of Xinjiang resulted in 13 different groups being identified, with at least six of these given autonomous status at various levels of local government. Of the 27 autonomous units in Xinjiang, an identified nationality formed the majority in only 12. Being in the majority, the province as a whole was designated 'Uyghur,' but the parcelling out of autonomy to different groups at the local level diluted the potential political weight of this majority. This form of 'autonomy' translates to little more than the appointment of members of the recognized nationalities to local representative bodies and government offices. While the leaders of autonomous areas are drawn from the nationality with a demographic plurality, in a curious echo of Manchu Qing monitoring of Han officials, their 'deputies' are high-ranking Han Party members. All autonomous levels of government are under the authority of the Communist Party, whose leaders in Xinjiang are almost always Han. All major economic development and infrastructure projects in Xinjiang are determined from Beijing. Political authority in Xinjiang was thus more centralized than ever once it became an 'autonomous region' (Gladney 1991; Millward 2007, pp. 242–246).

In addition to the convoluted system for dividing the political authority of 'nationalities' at the local level, the Communist leadership adopted Han resettlement to Xinjiang. In the early 1950s the system was organized as the Production and Construction Military Corps and became the primary vehicle for recruiting hundreds of thousands of Han migrants sent down to the countryside and to Xinjiang through to the mid-1970s (Becquelin 2000, pp. 77–84; McMillan 1979, pp. 61–66; 1981, pp. 65–96; Millward 2007, pp. 251–254; Seymour 2000, pp. 174–175). They continue as the major instrument of Party-state policies for the development and integration of Xinjiang with the greater Chinese economy (Cliff 2009, pp. 84–85).

The mass Han in-migration is a major cause of Uyghur–Han tension and conflict. Although official population figures are shaped by Party-state sensitivity, it is estimated that the Han proportion is around 40 percent (8.75 million) in recent years, compared to the Uyghur 'minority' of about 46 percent (10.09 million) (Mackerras 2014, p. 247). The Han proportion may be significantly higher due to an itinerant workforce, with official estimates for 2000 of 790,000 considered conservative, and the movement of younger Uyghurs to wealthier coastal areas in search of work. The Han predominate in modern urban centers, mainly in the eastern and northern corridors, spreading outward from the captial, Urumqi, while the Uyghurs account for over 80 percent of the population in the more traditional southern cities of Kashgar, Khotan and Artush (Becquelin 2000, pp. 65–66, 75–77; Bovingdon 2002, pp. 47–52; Mackerras 2004, p. 8; Toops 2004, pp. 254–260). While claims that increasing Han in-migration undermines the identity of Uyghurs and other 'minorities' are not new, the scale and intensity of conflict that it generates varies according to the number of new arrivals and the extent of economic discrimination in their favor. The proportion of the Han population actually declined slightly in the 1980s as economic reforms drew Han and Uyghurs into the developing urban centers of eastern China. But policies designed to boost economic development in Xinjiang have discriminated in favor of immigrant and local Han employees. Large-scale state investments in cotton production during the 1990s and the massive infrastructure, energy and industrial projects of the 'great opening up of the West' policy tended to use local Han workers and attracted a further influx of immigrant Han (Becquelin 2004, pp. 358–378; Goodman 2004, pp. 317–334). Although these large injections of state funds boosted Xinjiang's rate of growth, the greater the Turkic population of a given area, the lower was the GDP per capita in that area (Becquelin 2004, p. 372; Wiemer 2004, pp. 177–178).

This socio-economic discrimination in large part follows from the rapid development model of the Party-state, which favors those with the work and language skills suited to urbanization. But at heart it is a consequence of the lack of precisely the sort of political autonomy that nationalities policy appears to promise. Many people in China have suffered the negative effects of arbitrary Party-state rule, intense ideological struggles, and such tragic policy failures as the famine of the Great Leap Forward and the violence of the Cultural Revolution. For many Uyghurs the system of autonomy itself became the main conduit for repression and regular abuse at the hands of 'outsiders' (Millward 2007, p. 237). This system is not one of monolithic repression or deprivation, but one in which the central authority of the Party-state attempts to control the dimensions of Uyghur identity. Many Uyghurs have taken this politically assigned identity and 'sought to define and exploit it on their own terms' (Gladney 2004, p. 225). As in other areas that potentially challenge its authority, such as Christian communities, the Party-state cultivates and co-opts an acceptable or 'patriotic' face of Uyghur identity. There are thus officially sanctioned standards of political appointment, economic opportunity, Islamic practice, and cultural, linguistic and educational attainment that are tolerated and promoted. It is the tightly controlled limits of this identity and the denial of genuine self-determination that causes contentious politics in Xinjiang. Apart from the more liberal reform period of the early 1980s, when there was some support from Beijing for local autonomy, for over 20 years the Party-state has followed a dual strategy of 'the loosening of economic policy with political tightening' (Bovingdon 2010, p. 53). This strategy was primarily a response to increased Uyghur separatist protest and violence in the wake of the creation of newly independent Central Asian states with the collapse of the Soviet Union in 1991. But it was ramped-up and intensified when Beijing declared itself to be part of the 'global war on terror' soon after the 9/11 attacks on the United States.

'Terrorism' and communal conflict post-9/11

China's rapid expression of support for the 'global war on terror' appeared to mark the Party-state's new frankness about what it described as 'terrorism' within Xinjiang. Just ten days before 9/11, the Secretary of the Communist Party Committee for the region declared that 'Xinjiang is not a place of terror' (AI 2002, p. 7). Such reticence had dissipated by January 2002, with the release of what remains the most comprehensive official report on China's brand of terrorism. 'Over a long period of time—especially since the 1990s,' the report stated:

> 'East Turkestan' forces inside and outside Chinese territory have planned and organized a series of violent incidents in the Xinjiang Uyghur Autonomous Region of China and some other countries, including explosions, assassinations, arsons, poisonings, and assaults, with the objective of founding a so-called state of 'East Turkestan.'
>
> (Office of State Council 2002)

The report claimed that from 1990 to 2001 these same unspecified forces were responsible for numerous terrorist 'incidents,' resulting in the deaths of 162 people and injuries to over 440 people, even though only 57 deaths were specifically enumerated. Perhaps most importantly from the perspective of the 'global war on terror,' the report also claimed that there were intimate links between East Turkestan terrorists, Osama bin Laden and the Taliban. Both bin Laden and the Taliban allegedly supported and trained the activities of a group called the East Turkestan Islamic Movement (ETIM), as well as other terrorist groups. Members of these groups, it was said, engaged in terrorist acts not only in Xinjiang, but also in Afghanistan, Chechnya, and other parts of Central Asia. The official report did not, however, directly link the ETIM to any 'terrorist' attack inside China (Office of State Council 2002).

The Party-state as 'member' of the 'global coalition' against terrorism redefined Xinjiang as part of the problem. The most immediate reason for doing so was to suppress separatism in Xinjiang without the fear of international condemnation. Although this response was hardly surprising, it was built upon a misleading representation of Xinjiang. The diversity among the people of Xinjiang and the Uyghur population, and the fragmentation of separatist groups, has assisted the Party-state in enforcing control through a divide-and-rule approach. But this diversity and division was entirely absent from China's post-9/11 report, which chose to tar all separatism with the same terrorist brush (Bovingdon 2010, p. 105; Clarke 2008; Shichor 2005). Association with the most lethal forms of global terrorism condemned purportedly widespread separatist violence in Xinjiang. Yet the government reassured the populace that its 'crackdown' on such violence 'targets only a few core members and criminals.' 'Toward the majority of the people involved, who have been hoodwinked,' the government claimed to adopt an 'attitude of educating and helping them, and welcomes them back to the true path' (Office of State Council 2002). The combination of alarm and reassurance suggests a level of political opportunism and the need to establish the bona fides of terrorism to an international audience while playing down its scope to law abiding Uyghurs and potential supporters of Xinjiang's economic development.

Moreover, the Party-state's own estimates of casualties over more than a decade of small-scale violence were low in comparison with the toll of separatist violence in such areas as Chechnya, Sri Lanka and Mindanao. Careful, scholarly studies of the claims of terrorism have cast doubt on the nature and extent of the violent incidents listed in this official report (Bovingdon 2010, pp. 113–128, 174–190; Clarke 2008; Millward 2004; Roberts 2012). The balance of evidence suggests that while the Chinese government has indeed experienced problems with periodic violent opposition and protest, including some terrorist-style attacks, it faces a more significant political problem in trying to contain and control broader hostility to its rule in Xinjiang.

At the same time, there has been a tendency in official reports to trawl for violent incidents and retrospectively cast them as separatist or terrorist (Bovingdon 2010, pp. 188–190). Leading up to the Beijing Olympics of 2008 there were reports of kidnappings and attempted hijackings by Uyghur 'terrorists,' whilst official media reports drew a link between Uyghur terrorism and the violent protests in Tibet in 2008 (Cumming 2008; Smith 2010, p. 7). The most intensive period of the 'global war on terror' was nonetheless not as restive or as violent in Xinjiang as the period of the 1990s. As Bovingdon (2010, pp. 133–134) notes, this relative decline in violence prior to the 2009 'riots' is indicative of more intensive repression rather than a measure of 'increasing satisfaction' among Uyghurs and other minorities.

The most significant incidents before the 'riots' of 2009 were the Baren incident of April 1990 and the Ghulja incident of February 1997, both of them demonstrate the close relationship between the Party-state's policies and Uyghur responses. China's official account presented the Baren incident as an organized 'counter-revolutionary rebellion,' led by Zeydin Yusup and his East Turkestan Islamic Party. Academic accounts suggest the riots were provoked by the closure of a newly built mosque in Akto, a town in Baren county, close to Kashgar, or complaints about the application (from 1988) of birth limits to minorities. Some estimates suggest over 120 were killed in the resulting violence (Millward 2007, pp. 326–327). The Ghulja riots in 1997 were the culmination of almost a year of clashes with security forces charged with implementing one of several 'strike hard' anti-crime campaigns often combined with broad security sweeps to warn against separatist activity or detain people for questioning (Bovingdon 2010, pp. 53, 131–134). A sweep through Ghulja in the Ili region in search of separatist forces sparked a violent protest on February 5–6 resulting in 100 deaths according to exiled Uyghur accounts (Chang 1997, p. 410). Other accounts claim that, over a two-week period, 3,000 to 5,000 people were arrested (AI 1999, pp. 18–25).

Post-9/11 the Party-state attempted to present these incidents as evidence of the East Turkestan terrorist movement linked to the global terrorism of al Qaeda and the Taliban. But the government's 2002 report manages to link only four incidents with particular groups. The Ghulja riots of 1997 are blamed on the East Turkestan Party of Allah, a group not mentioned in any other context. The East Turkestan Liberation Organization (ETLO) was the only group directly linked to a death in Xinjiang. The ETIM was accused of direct links with al Qaeda and the Taliban. These included a meeting with Osama bin Laden, funding and training from al Qaeda and the Taliban. However, there are serious doubts about ETIM's nature, capacity and alleged role in the 'jihadist' terrorism of Uyghurs (Roberts 2012, pp. 6–14). In 2003 China's Ministry of Public Security issued a new list of terrorist organizations linked to al Qaeda, which mentioned, in addition to the ETIM and ETLO, the World Uyghur Youth Congress and the East Turkestan Information Centre, based in Munich. No other state listed either group as 'terrorist' (Bovingdon 2010, p. 149; Millward 2004, pp. 22–28).

Strike hard campaigns have become a fixture of Party-state policy dealing with any form of organized opposition or separatist sentiment. One of the most extensive campaigns against Uyghur separatism was launched in 2001. According to Amnesty International (2002, p. 19), this resulted in over 3,000 arrests and 20 executions from 9/11 to the end of 2001. Later reports suggested that tens of thousands of people had been detained for investigation, with hundreds being charged and some being executed (UHRP 2007, p. 4). In 2005, 18,227 individuals were detained for endangering state security (UHRP 2007, p. 4). In more recent years these crackdowns have expanded to embrace the development of religious, cultural and language practices. The authorities have not been prepared to tolerate unauthorized gatherings for religious purposes, and they have strictly enforced rules prohibiting religious instruction or mosque attendance for children under 18 (Bovingdon 2010, pp. 71–72; Human Rights Watch 2006). The government has also reduced the amount of class instruction given in 'minority' languages and merged some dedicated Uyghur schools with mainstream Chinese schools (Dwyer 2005). These measures appear to be part of a more intensive policy to 'Sinicise' minority cultures, again raising the specter of cultural genocide (Ma 2014, p. 238). During strike hard crackdowns on separatism, Uyghurs seem to inhabit an Orwellian world of state control. A wrong word here, an anti-Chinese joke there, can sometimes be sufficient grounds for detention (Bovingdon 2002, pp. 76–78). The 'global war on terror' unfortunately provided a degree of tacit endorsement to the excessive application of Party-state powers. It also extended to China the opportunity to expand its influence in the Central Asian region and improve relations with the United States.

In addition to security crackdowns in Xinjiang, China's government presented the problem of their 'East Turkestan terrorist organisation' as a part of global terrorism (Millward 2004, pp. 26–28). China routinely linked separatist violence in Xinjiang with foreign support or 'hostile foreign' forces, from both exiled Uyghurs and states like the United States, which aimed to split or subvert China's sovereign territory. With these concerns in mind, China pursued a policy of wooing the Central Asian states on the borders of Xinjiang. This culminated in 1996 with the formation of the Group of Five (China, Russia, Kazakstan, Kyrgyzstan and Tajikistan; with the 2001 addition of Uzbekistan, the organization became known as the Shanghai Cooperation Organization). The original purpose of this group was to deal with border disputes, but it rapidly turned toward the regional suppression of trans-border Islamic insurgents. Through a combination of diplomatic pressure and increased trade and investment, China extended its influence throughout these Central Asian states (Sheives 2006, pp. 207–214). The initial reluctance of these states to comply with China's requests for control of exiled Uyghur separatists within their borders, changed dramatically after the 9/11 attacks by repatriating Uyghurs to China for trial and banning Uyghur political organizations operating inside their borders, particularly in Kazakstan and Kyrgyzstan (Millward 2007, pp. 336–338). The Central Asian states also had an interest in joining China's counter-terrorist campaign, given that many of them faced Islamic insurgencies. China helped establish a joint anti-terrorism center in Tashkent, gave military aid to Kyrgyzstan, and launched a series of joint military exercises with its SCO partners. The SCO itself now routinely reflects China's concern to work against all forms of 'terrorism, separatism and religious extremism' (Sheives 2006, p. 213).

The 'global war on terror' also sparked a revival in relations between the United States and China, which only a few months before 9/11 were 'on the verge of extinction' (Gittings 2001, p. 5). Perhaps the most remarkable concessions that China gained were those from the United States itself. The *Patterns of Global Terrorism 2001* (USDS 2002, pp. 16–17) report acknowledged China's cooperation with the 'international community' in fighting terrorism and praised the 'encouraging and concrete' results of counter-terrorism dialogue with China. The report also referred to Chinese concerns regarding 'Islamic extremists' operating in and around Xinjiang, and 'credible reports that some Uyghurs who were trained by al Qaeda have returned to China.' The United States subsequently established an FBI presence in its Beijing embassy as part of its global counter-terrorism operations. In 2002, the United States acceded to the appeals of the Chinese government and formally listed the ETIM as a terrorist organization reinforcing the impression that the ETIM was responsible for most of the terrorist attacks in Xinjiang (Millward 2004, pp. 13–14).

These concessions to China's view of its terrorist problem proved to be short-lived. US reports on global terrorism and those on religious freedom in China routinely point out that anti-terrorism measures should not serve to suppress the religious practices of Muslims in China. In 2003 the US government refused to list a second Uyghur group nominated by China, the East Turkestan Liberation Organization. In a later revision, the US State Department re-assigned the ETIM to a list of 'groups of concern,' taking it off the terrorist list (USDS 2007). In 2004 the National Endowment for Democracy awarded a grant in support of the Uyghur American Association. The Bush administration endorsed the role of Rabiya Kadeer in leading exiled Uyghurs, and President Obama has returned to the annual convention of raising concerns with China's human rights in relation to religious freedom (Mackerras 2009, pp. 139–144).

Perhaps the most devastating blow to China's change of policy towards the Uyghurs post-9/11 was the serious outbreak of violence associated with the July 2009 'riots' in Urumqi. Although clouded by a lack of independent evidence, events initially appeared to follow the pattern of previous demonstrations that turned violent. A small group of Uyghurs gathered in the northern parts of Urumqi, to protest against what they believed to be lenient treatment of Han Chinese accused of killing at least two Uyghur workers in a factory in the southern province of Guangdong. These workers were reportedly killed, and hundreds injured, after a false rumor spread that the Uyghur men had raped two Han women. News of this incident spread to Xinjiang through the Internet, sparking the July demonstration in Urumqi. When security forces attempted to push the demonstrators away from a public square, attacks upon shops and Han in the vicinity allegedly broke out. The 'rioting' that followed, and the actions of Han vigilante groups over subsequent days, led to the deaths of 197 people with thousands injured, the majority Han according to official reports. Communication networks with Xinjiang were shutdown and the events were considered serious enough for then President Hu Jintao to interrupt a state visit to Italy. In an unusual measure, the Urumqi Party Secretary was removed from his position. Some offical accounts linked the 'riots' to terrorism and the ETIM.

But the Uyghur demonstration was prompted by perceived injustice towards fellow Uyghur in the south of China and showed few overt signs of separatist sentiment or even demands for greater autonomy. The troubling development was the rapid escalation of communal violence between Uyghur and Han that set off large demonstrations of Han concerned with their security. This serious breakdown of relations between Uyghurs and Han, from which Urumqi has not yet fully recoverd, is in large part the legacy of the hardline policies against separatism since 9/11 and the increasing attempts to integrate Uyghurs into a Han-centric vision of national unity (AI 2010; Bovingdon 2010; Mackerras 2014; Millward 2009; Roberts 2012, pp. 15–17). Further violent clashes have occurred since then, mainly in and around Kashgar in the south, claiming around a hundred lives according to official reports. The Party-state's concern about these developments is reflected in a report issued after President Xi Jinping met with Xinjiang's provincial leaders in mid-2013 where they declared that 'ethnic separatist forces at home and abroad continue to intensify their activities, and deep-seated problems harming social stability in Xinjiang remain fundamentally unsolved' (Mackerras 2014, p. 248). High-profile incidents, such as the apparent explosion of a car that was driven into Tiananmen Square, towards the famous portrait of Mao, simply reinforce the now reflex official reporting of such violence as separatist Uyghur terrorism (Wong 2014). Relations between Uyghurs and Han 'will probably get worse in the near term,' with no significant improvement in sight for 'at least a generation, if at all' (Mackerras 2014, pp. 249–250).

Conclusion

China's Party-state continues to expand its national wealth and capacity for regional and global influence. Yet its nationalities policies appear to be further from achieving their goal of integration with the Han core than at any time since the Cultural Revolution. Uyghurs cannot in sober reality hope for the independence of a separate state, and the majority do now seek 'genuine autonomy' instead. Concessions in this direction would ameliorate Uyghur–Han conflict, but would also challenge the Party-state's monopoly on power and risk escalating demands towards separatism or secession. As Laoutides argues in Chapter 4, it is only when parties to conflict can be reassured of the security of their own position that meaningful reconciliation or peacebuilding can be achieved. The Party-state appears too committed to its one-party monopoly and hardline against genuine autonomy, and Uyghur resistance too weak and fragmented for this vital movement to occur. This at times tragic dilemma between an authoritarian state and one of its key 'minority nationalities' appears no nearer to satisfactory resolution.

References

Acharya, A, Gunaratna, R and Wang, P 2010, *Ethnic Identity and National Conflict in China*, Palgrave Macmillan, New York.

Amnesty International (AI) 1999, *People's Republic of China: Gross Violations of Human Rights in the Xinjiang Uyghur Autonomous Region*, Amnesty International, New York.

Amnesty International (AI) 2002, *China's Anti-Terrorism Legislation and Repression in the Xinjiang Uyghur Autonomous Region*, retrieved March 7 2003, http://web.amnesty.org/aidoc/aidoc_pdf.nsf/index/ASA170102002ENGLISH/$File/ASA1701002.pdf.

Amnesty International (AI) 2010, *Justice, Justice: The July 2009 Protests in Xinjiang, China*, Amnesty International, New York.

Becquelin, N 2000, 'Xinjiang in the Nineties,' *China Journal*, vol. 44, pp. 65–90.

Becquelin, N 2004, 'Staged Development in Xinjiang,' *The China Quarterly*, vol. 178, pp. 358–378.

Benson, L 1990, *The Ili Rebellion: The Moslem Challenge to Chinese Authority in Xinjiang, 1944–1949*, M.E. Sharpe, New York.

Bolton, G, McGivern, L and Steele, S 2010, 'Editorial Introduction: Secession, Sovereignty, and the Quest for Legitimacy,' *St. Antony's International Review*, vol. 6, no. 1, pp. 3–15.

Bovingdon, G 2002, 'The Not-So-Silent Majority: Uyghur Resistance to Han Rule in Xinjiang,' *Modern China*, vol. 28, no. 1, pp. 39–78.

Bovingdon, G 2010, *The Uyghurs: Strangers in their Own Land*, Coumbia University Press, New York.
Buchanan, A 2004 *Justice, Legitimacy, and Self-Determination: Moral Foundations for International Law*, Oxford University Press, Oxford.
Buchheit, LC 1978, *Secession: The Legitimacy of Self-Determination*, Yale University Press, New Haven, CT.
Chang, FK 1997, 'China's Central Asian Power and Problems,' *Orbis*, vol. 41, no. 3, pp. 401–415.
Chu, W 1966, *Moslem Rebellion in Northwest China, 1862–1878: A Study of Government Minority Policy*, Mouton, The Hague.
Clarke, M 2008, 'China's "War on Terror" in Xinjiang: Human Security and the Causes of Violent Uighur Separatism,' *Terrorism and Political Violence*, vol. 20, no. 2, pp. 271–301.
Cliff, TMJ 2009, 'Neo Oasis: The Xinjiang *Bingtuan* in the Twenty-first Century,' *Asian Studies Review*, vol. 33, no. 1, pp. 83–106.
Cuffe, J and Siroky, DS 2013, 'Paradise Lost: Autonomy and Separatism in the South Caucasus and Beyond,' in JP Cabestan and A Pavković (eds), *Secession and Separatism in Europe and Asia: To Have One's Own State*, Routledge, Abingdon, UK, pp. 37–53.
Cumming, C 2008, 'Quiet Death in Xinjiang,' *Guardian*, April 5, retrieved December 7 2012, www.guardian.co.uk/commentisfree/2008/apr/05/china.tibet.
Dillon, M 2004, *Xinjiang: China's Muslim Far Northwest*, Routledge/Curzon, London.
Dwyer, A 2005, 'The Xinjiang Conflict: Uyghur Identity, Language Policy, and Political Discourse,' *Policy Studies*, no. 15, pp. 1–88.
Forbes, ADW 1986, *Warlords and Muslims in Chinese Central Asia: A Political History of Republican Sinkiang, 1911–1949*, Cambridge University Press, Cambridge, UK.
Gittings, J 2001, 'Beijing Makes Mileage out of Bush's Anti-Terror Agenda,' *Guardian Weekly*, October 25–31.
Gladney, DC 1991, *Muslim Chinese: Ethnic Nationalism in the People's Republic*, Harvard University Press, Cambridge, MA.
Gladney, DC 2004, *Dislocating China: Muslims, Minorities and Other Subaltern Subjects*, Hurst & Co, London.
Goodman, DSG 2004, 'The Campaign to "Open up the West": National, Provincial-level and Local Perspectives,' *The China Quarterly*, vol. 178, pp. 317–334.
Gunaratna, R and Pereire, KG 2006, 'An al-Qaeda Associate Group Operating in China?' *The China and Eurasian Forum Quarterly*, vol. 4, no. 2, pp. 55–61.
He, B 2010, 'A Deliberative Approach to the Tibet Autonomy Issue: Promoting Trust Through Dialogue,' *Asian Survey*, vol. 50, no. 4, pp. 709–734.
He, B and Sautman, B 2005/6, 'The Politics of the Dalai Lama's New Initiative for Autonomy,' *Pacific Affairs*, vol. 78, no. 4, pp. 601–629.
Hechter, M 2000, *Containing Nationalism*, Oxford University Press, Oxford.
Heraclides, A 1997, 'The Ending of Unending Conflicts: Separatist Wars,' *Millenium: Journal of International Studies*, vol. 26, no. 3, pp. 679–707.
Human Rights Watch 2006, 'China: A Year After New Regulations, Religious Rights Still Restricted,' *Reuters Alertnet*, February 28, retrieved September 18 2007, www.alertnet.org/thenews/newsdesk/HRW/8e2d9ae1f5b37ae6b295e73bf81d3e50.htm.
Lattimore, O 1940, *Inner Asian Frontiers of China*, Oxford University Press, Hong Kong.
Lattimore, O 1950, *Pivot of Asia: Sinkiang and the Inner Asian Frontiers of China and Russia*, Little, Brown and Co, Boston.

Ma, R 2014, 'Reflection on the Debate on China's Ethnic Policy: My Reform Proposals and their Critics,' *Asian Ethnicity*, vol. 15, no. 2, pp. 237–246.

Mackerras, C 2004, 'Ethnicity in China: The Case of Xinjiang,' *Harvard Asia Quarterly*, vol. 8, no. 1, pp. 4–14.

Mackerras, C 2009, 'Xinjiang in Central Asia since 1990,' in C Mackerras and M Clarke (eds), *China, Xinjiang and Central Asia: History, Transition and Crossborder Interaction in the Twenty-first Century*, Routledge, Abingdon, UK, pp. 133–150.

Mackerras, C 2014, 'Xinjiang in 2013: Problems and Prospects,' *Asian Ethnicity*, vol. 15, no. 2, pp. 247–250.

McMillan, DH 1979, *Chinese Communist Power and Policy in Xinjiang, 1949–1977*, Westview Press, Boulder, CO.

McMillan, DH 1981, 'Xinjiang and the Production and Construction Corps; A Han Organisation in a Non-Han Region,' *Australian Journal of Chinese Affairs*, no. 6, pp. 171–193.

Millward, JA 2004, 'Violent Separatism in Xinjiang: A Critical Assessment,' *Policy Studies*, vol. 6, pp. 1–41.

Millward, JA 2007, *Eurasian Crossroads: A History of Xinjiang*, Columbia University Press, New York.

Millward, JA 2009, 'Introduction: Does the 2009 Urumqi Violence Mark a Turning Point?' *Central Asian Survey*, vol. 28, no. 4, pp. 347–360.

Office of the State Council 2002, '"East Turkestan" Terrorist Forces Cannot Get Away with Impunity,' Information Office of the State Council of the PRC, *People's Daily*, 21 January, retrieved March 7 2002, http://english.people.com.cn/200201/21/eng 20020121_89078.shtml

Paine, SCM 1996, *Imperial Rivals: China, Russia, and their Disputed Frontier*, M.E. Sharpe, Armonk.

Perdue, PC 2005, *China Marches West: The Qing Conquest of Central Eurasia*, Belknap Press of Harvard University Press, Cambridge, MA.

Ramos-Lynch, M 2010, 'Sino-Tibetan Dialogue: Much Misunderstanding, Little Room for Compromise,' *China Security: A Journal of China's Strategic Development*, vol. 6, no. 3, pp. 67–74.

Reed, JT and Raschke, D 2010, *The ETIM: China's Islamic Militants and the Global Terrorist Threat*, Praeger, New York.

Roberts, SR 2009, 'Imagining Uyghuristan: Re-evaluating the Birth of the Modern Uyghur Nation,' *Central Asian Survey*, vol. 28, no. 4, pp. 361–381.

Roberts, SR 2012, *Imaginary Terrorism? The Global War on Terror and the Narrative of the Uyghur Terrorist Threat* (Ponars Eurasia Working Paper), Institute for European, Russian and Eurasian Studies, Elliot School on International Affairs, George Washington University, Washington, DC.

Roeder, PG 2007, *Where Nation-States Come From: Institutional Change in the Age of Nationalism*, Princeton University Press, Princeton, NJ.

Rudelson, JJ 1997, *Uyghur Nationalism Along China's Silk Road*, Columbia University Press, New York.

Savage, C 2013, 'U.S. Frees Last of Chinese Uighur Detainees from Guantanamo Bay,' *New York Times*, December 31, retrieved January 11 2014, www.nytimes.com/2014/01/01/us/us-frees-last-of-uighur-detainees-from-guantanamo.html?_r=0.

Seymour, JD 2000, 'Xinjiang's Production and Construction Corps, and the Sinification of Eastern Turkestan,' *Inner Asia*, vol. 2, no. 2, pp. 171–193.

Shakya, T 2008, 'Tibetan Questions,' *New Left Review*, vol. 51, pp. 5–27.

Sheives, K 2006, 'China Turns West: Beijing's Contemporary Strategy towards Central Asia,' *Pacific Affairs*, vol. 79, no. 2, pp. 205–224.

Shichor, Y 2005, 'Blow Up: Internal and External Challenges of Uyghur Separatism and Islamic Radiacalism to Chinese Rule in Xinjiang,' *Asian Affairs: An American Review*, vol. 32, no. 2, pp. 119–135.

Smith, Jr WW 2010, *Tibet's Last Stand? The Tibetan Uprising of 2008 and China's Response*, Rowman & Littlefield, Lanham, MD.

Song, X 2003, 'A Unified China or an Independent Taiwan? A Normative Assessment of the Cross-Strait Conflict,' in B Coppieters and R Sakwa (eds), *Contextualizing Secession: Normative Studies in Comparative Perspective*, Oxford University Press, Oxford, pp. 228–251.

Sperling, E 2004, *The Tibet–China Conflict: History and Polemics*, East-West Center, Washington, DC.

Swaine, MD 2011, 'China's Assertive Behaviour, Part One: On "Core Interests",' *China Leadership Monitor*, no. 34, pp. 1–25.

Taylor Fravel, M 2005 'Regime Insecurity and International Cooperation: Explaining China's Compromises in Territorial Disputes,' *International Security*, vol. 30, no. 2, pp. 46–83.

Tilly, C 2003, *The Politics of Collective Violence*, Cambridge University Press, Cambridge, UK.

Toops, S 2004, 'The Demography of Xinjiang,' in S Frederick Starr (ed.), *Xinjiang: China's Muslim Borderland*, M.E. Sharpe, Armonk, New York and London.

United States Department of State (USDS) 2002, *Patterns of Global Terrorism 2001*, Department of State, Washington, DC, retrieved September 9 2002, www.state.gov/s/ct/.

United States Department of State (USDS) 2007, U.S. Designates 43 Terrorist Groups, April 30 2007, retrieved September 18 2007, http://usinfo.state.gov/xarchives/display.html?p=washfile-english&y=2007&m=April&x=20070425112939idybeekcm0.9128382.

Uyghur Human Rights Project (UHRP) 2007, *Persecution of Uyghurs in the Era of the 'War on Terror'*, October 16.

Wayne, M 2008, *China's War on Terrorism: Counterinsurgency, Politics and Internal Security*, Routledge, Abingdon and New York.

Weller, M 2009, *Escaping the Self-Determination Trap*, Brill, Leiden.

Whiting, AS and Sheng, S 1958, *Sinkiang: Pawn or Pivot?*, Michigan State University Press, East Lansing, MI.

Wiemer, C 2004, 'The Economy of Xinjiang,' in S F Starr (ed.), *Xinjiang: China's Muslim Borderland*, M. E. Sharpe, Armonk, pp. 163–190.

Wong, E 2014, 'Chinese Governor Signals Crackdown on Separatists,' *New York Times*, March 6, retrieved April 15 2014, www.nytimes.com/2014/03/07/world/asia/chinese-governor-signals-crackdown-on-separatists.html?_r=0.

Worthington, A 2010, 'Seized in Pakistan: The Remaining Guantanamo Prisoners,' *The Public Record*, September 26, retrived October 15 2010, http://pubrecord.org/law/8311/seized-pakistan-remaining-guantanamo/.

8 The anathema of partition
The quandary of division, secession and reunification in Cyprus

Michális S Michael

Introduction

Commenting on the aftermath of Turkey's 1974 invasion Greek Cypriot poet Kostas Montis (1987, p. 571), exclaimed that 'Now how can we die/With this worry behind us?/Necessarily we have to postpone.' Across the infamous Green Line, Turkish Cypriot poet Neshe Yashin (1979, p. 36) will confide in us that her 'father says/Love your country/My country is divided into two/Which part should I love?' Both exhortations encapsulate the pathology and the longevity of a partitioned/divided Cyprus. Such utterances are indicative of the embeddedness of partition in the everyday cultural milieu of Cypriots.

Reading the joint declaration by the two Cypriot community leaders Nicos Anastasiades and Derviş Eroğlu on 11 February 2014 one gets the impression that reunification of this tormented island is imminent (UN 2014). However, subsequent statements by both leaders render a more complicated and convoluted predicament. Specifically, Anastasiades at a press conference the following day, in reference to the 2004 referendum on the Annan Plan, acknowledged that:

> the experience of the past and the rejection of a plan proposed by the United Nations by 76% does not allow anyone to return it, even (with) decorative alterations, before the Cypriot people, because a second rejection will lead to partition, to the probable recognition of today's illegal regime ... [Journalist interjection: 'So with one word "no solution" means partition ... ']....
> Without a doubt, the consequences are even more serious for the existence and survival of Cypriot Hellenism. Let's not overlook the fait accompli created by (the passing of) time.
>
> (Anastasiades 2014, author's translation)

Similarly Eroğlu in an interview to the Greek political magazine *Crash* reminded us that:

> The ideal solution for us is, of course, different from the ideal solution for our Greek neighbors. The important thing here is an agreement that is sustainable, continuing, not creating new issues, and not dragging the two

people in Cyprus to another conflict, rather than an ideal solution. We call it the realistic solution. The realistic solution is to accept the existence of two people in Cyprus and to understand that a new joint state with two sections based on equality under the continuing guarantees will have to be established. [...] My advice to everyone is that they should digest the reality of having two peoples, two administrations and two sections in Cyprus, and if an agreement is reached by moving away from those realities, they should have confidence that it would be beneficial for both people and the region.

(Eroğlu 2014)

Although both narratives lend themselves to entrenched positioning that oscillate hostile rivalries (Rasler *et al.* 2013, p. 5), they provide us with an insight into each side's mindset in terms of ending/un-ending of the Cyprus conflict. However, at a more fundamental level, such narratives accentuate the dilemma compounding each attempt at reunifying a divided society and partitioned state (Michael 2005, p. 2): how to construct a legal-constitutional order, dictated by a set of historical determinants and the fundamental precepts of liberal democracy, including transitional justice, which reconciles human rights and group security, whilst fortifying the foundations for sequential integration/unification (Michael 2009, p. 191).

Contextualizing the above dilemma, this chapter sets out to explore several key questions pertaining to ending/un-ending of Cyprus' division: why despite endless negotiations and countless proposals, has there been no end to the Cyprus conflict? Does partition constitute an appropriate solution even as a second or third best solution, and if so how can it be justified, quantified and qualified? More to the point, to what extent does striving for a pragmatic settlement constitute a normative imperative to compromise for a second best solution in the Cyprus conflict? Are the underlying reasons to be found in the conflict's broader historical and endogenous/exogenous dynamics? Do the very structures and mindsets underpinning the negotiations render them incapable of facilitating a political settlement?

The answers lie in the complex web of interacting factors, internal and external to Cyprus, that have shaped the overall negotiating process.

The partitioning of history

Any serious examination of partition in the Cyprus conflict cannot take place without first considering its historical origins. If the history of the Cyprus conflict was reduced to a single schema, it would be a triangular trajectory of colonialism, nationalism and modernity. Nowhere is the clash between colonialism and nationalism more eloquently displayed than in the binary interaction between the Greek Cypriot demand for union (*énosis*) with Greece, its Turkish counter-claim of partition, and Britain's strategic and political interests in the island (Crawshaw 1978, p. 22).

In a sense, the clash between *énosis* and British strategic interests in Cyprus reflected the much broader historical confrontation between third-world nationalism and waning colonialism, within the dialectical compulsions of modernity. Unlike other national-liberation movements though, union was fundamentally an extension of Greek irredentist nationalism, and the subsequent struggles to incorporate Greek-speaking regions of the old Ottoman Empire into the modern Greek state. Although Greek nationalism first appeared in Cyprus as a consequence of the 1821 Greek Revolution, it was swiftly suppressed and did not manage to establish itself until the arrival of the British. By contrast, Turkish Cypriot nationalism, imbued by Kemalism, did not fully emerge until the 1940s.

One cannot appreciate Greek Cypriot nationalism, or Cypriot history for that matter, without grasping the effect of *énosis*. Moreover, one cannot understand the contradictions of modern Cyprus without first delving into the ideological underpinnings of British colonialism. Although, over time, various arguments were mounted by Whitehall rejecting *énosis* on security, strategic, political and economic grounds, underpinning British refusal was an unrelenting cultural ambivalence of whether Cyprus was indeed a Greek island (Holland and Markides 2006, pp. 187–188).

With the arrival of the British in 1878, the Greek Cypriot leaders promoted their aspiration for *énosis*, which was synonymous with national liberation for the Greek Orthodox Christian millet. However, from the very beginning two differing views of *énosis* emerged. Whereas Bishop Kyprianos welcomed the British with a succinct *énosist* message, Archbishop Sofronios, although hinting at *énosis*, stressed the people's attachment to the new administration and their expectation for a libertarian and equitable government (Kyrris 1985, p. 302). For the next 100 years these two tendencies would merge and divide, at various historical junctures, in their understanding and pursuit of *énosis*. Until the mid-1970s, *énosis* was the hallmark of Greek Cypriot political and cultural discourse.

The idea that *énosis* could be utilized first appeared in British policy when Foreign Secretary Edward Grey offered Cyprus to Greece in order that Greece enters World War I on the allied side (United Kingdom 1915, CAB 37/136/26). This offer was overturned and by 1931 the first riots against British authority took place on the island. The riots, however, were soon suppressed and emergency regulations enforced which targeted the Cyprus Church and the newly formed communist movement (Arnold 1956, p. 118). The 1931 riots entered the *énosis* lexicon, forming a reference point, sharpening the conflict and setting a precedent for the ensuing 1950s Greek Cypriot armed struggle.

World War II saw the island's domestic political environment largely shaped by external forces. The war persuaded all the political players in Cyprus (British, nationalists and communists) into cooperation, since their patrons had become allies. In the case of the *énosists*, the war determined the extent of pressure to be exerted against British rule, moderated by the belief that as allies, the British would 'reward' Greece by granting it Cyprus. The British capitalized on this sentiment by recruiting Cypriots with the slogan, 'Fight for Freedom and Greece.'

At the end of the war, the Greek government prepared its territorial claims, the acquisition of Cyprus was second on its list after the Dodecanese (Sulzberger 1944). The post-war also accentuated the Middle East's value to the West in terms of resources and geopolitics. In this highly contested region, Cyprus was the only territory under full British sovereignty. In 1946, the Attlee government viewed Cyprus as one of the six vital points in its global empire strategy, even 'more important than Haifa' (Browne 1946).

By late 1950s an intense international campaign for *énosis* by the Cyprus Church that involved an armed insurrection by EOKA on the island had forced the British government to seek a political solution to the Cyprus crisis. As the crisis quickly embroiled Greece, Turkey, NATO and the UN, British policy shifted towards relinquishing sovereignty over the whole island provided its military and political interests were safeguarded (UK 1958). By abandoning exclusive sovereignty over Cyprus, Britain could 'dovetail' its military requirements into any agreement (Harding 1958, p. 296).

One of Britain's 'exit strategies,' applied in similar decolonization situations that involved ethnic rivalry, was partition which had been an option as early as 1956, when then British Foreign Minister Harold Macmillan pondered that it 'might prove the only solution' (Macmillan 1971, p. 224). In more blunt terms, Prime Minister Anthony Eden's ultimatum was that 'Greeks and Turks could be associated with the British in control of the island, or the island could be partitioned' (Eden 1960, p. 415). The seriousness of the 'partition option' was such that Macmillan, a few days after becoming prime minister, 'sent a minute to the Foreign Secretary, reverting to the possibility of a settlement on the lines of partition.' Furthermore, he 'asked that the Minister of Defence ... set up an urgent inquiry into [British] military needs, and whether the base could be carved out of the territory without too much difficulty and effectively defended' (Macmillan 1971, p. 225).

The settlement that eventually prevailed was for a consociational independent state, the Republic of Cyprus. The idea of independence, albeit as a second-best solution, gained traction among various international third parties, including the British Labour opposition and the United States. By the time the London Conference (1959) took place to formally sign the Cyprus Agreement, Greece, Turkey and Britain had agreed on the main terms of a settlement. Britain had secured its strategic needs, with two sovereign bases of Akrotiri and Dekhelia. Greek Cypriot leader Archbishop Makarios' last-minute objections to certain aspects of the agreement were thwarted by Greek Prime Minister Kostantinos Karamanlis, who warned that Greece would not be responsible for the conference's failure, or for the consequences (meaning partition) (*Time Magazine*, March 2 1959, p. 17).

The 1960 Cyprus settlement introduced a new state of affairs. Cyprus became a presidential republic, the president being a Greek Cypriot and the vice-president a Turkish Cypriot with veto rights. The executive, legislative, public service and security forces comprised of 70 percent Greek Cypriots and 30 percent Turkish Cypriots; the High Court of Justice would have two Greek

Cypriots, one Turkish Cypriot and a neutral judge as president, with two votes; separate municipalities, created in the five largest towns with Turkish Cypriot inhabitants, were to be reviewed in four years; the 'total or partial union of Cyprus with any other State, or a separatist independence [was to] be excluded.' Finally, the republic's constitutional arrangement incorporated the Guarantee and Alliance treaties. The most significant and controversial of the two, the Treaty of Guarantee, between Cyprus, Britain, Greece and Turkey, undertook to ensure the republic's 'independence, territorial integrity, security and respect for its Constitution,' and prohibited 'all activity to promote directly or indirectly either union or partition of the Island' (UK 1960, pp. 86–87, 91–170).

Cypriot independence remained very much a consequence of its post-colonial constellation. Post-colonialism saw the emergence of a contradictory order, in which the Republic of Cyprus typified the irresolvable tension between the compulsion towards sovereignty and the benefits of limited self-determination under hegemonic oversight. By many Greek Cypriot nationalists independence was viewed as an intermediate step towards self-determination and *énosis*. On the other hand, despite its clumsiness, the Republic of Cyprus was an attempt at power-sharing among Greek and Turkish Cypriots. And although a second-best solution, the Republic of Cyprus would come to serve as both a source of dispute and a model for the future referral (Burton 1979, p. 108).

There is no doubt that along with transforming the Cyprus problem from a colonial to a regional dispute, British policy also accentuated it as an ethnic conflict. The process of ethnic division and segregation began with British colonial policies and practices that shaped the social system in such a way that the evolution of distinct Greek and Turkish nationalisms in Cyprus was inevitable (Given 2002; Pollis 1973, p. 599). In many respects, Cyprus partitional proposition is anchored in the legacy of British colonialism. A legacy that involved an impractical constitution that entrenched ethno-communalism, failing to account for 'the psychological and sociological fact that the power-protection system' increased 'suspicions, antagonism and conflict between the communities because of the discriminations and uncertainties involved' (Burton 1969, p. 34). The sectarian and divisive provisions of the 1960 arrangement constituted the seeds that led to its very collapse three years later.

From the beginning of the young republic, contentious issues emerged between the two communities. Each tested the effective functioning of the constitution. Against a background of constitutional gridlock, the political crisis flared to violent conflict when fighting broke out between armed irregulars. Turkish Cypriot withdrawal from the state apparatus, and their retraction into concentrated enclaves, rendered a political, social and demographic separation. As fighting threatened to escalate and embroil mainland Greek and Turkish troops stationed there, a UN ceasefire paved the way for the establishment of a peacekeeping force and a negotiation process (UNSC Resolution 186).

The 1964 crisis also saw US intervention into the conflict as it was determined to eliminate Cyprus as a constant irritant between Greece and Turkey, thus jeopardizing NATO's Mediterranean south-eastern flank. This involved US Under-Secretary of State George Ball and former Secretary of State Dean Acheson advancing various alternatives of 'double *énosis*' to solve the Greek–Turkish Cyprus problem (Acheson 1965; Brinkley 1992, p. 215). A less notorious intervention, but one which left an indelible impact on the future peace process, was that of the UN mediator on Cyprus, Galo Plaza (UN 1965 S/6253, pp. 19–28).

Plaza's recommendations led to UNSC Resolution 244 calling on the parties to enter into intercommunal talks via the 'good offices proffered by the Secretary-General' (UN 1967). Supported by Greece and Turkey, the first intercommunal talks (1968–74) saw the Greek Cypriots advocating for amendments to the 1960 Constitution while the Turkish Cypriots pressed for local government to entail the communal grouping of villages (Clerides 1989, p. 265; Necatigil 1989, p. 67; Polyviou 1976, p. 116). When the talks reached an impasse in 1971 it became apparent that the main obstacle to an agreement was over the nature and powers of local government and its correlation with the state apparatus (Denktash 1972, p. 10; Polyviou 1976, p. 138).

Despite the tense political climate of the 1970s, especially amongst the Greek Cypriots with the hardline *énosists* resorting to terrorism, a 'package deal' brought the talks very close to a settlement (UN 1974, S/11294, para. 60). However, increasingly the prevalent Turkish view was that a federal solution, based on a cantonal system, was a realistic compromise to the Cyprus problem (Karpat 1967, p. 51).

The road to partition

When the Cyprus crisis erupted in the summer of 1974, as Hitchens' (1984, p. 85) 'collusion theory' suggests, unevenly matched and differently motivated forces coalesced to partition the island. There is no doubt that the most important turning point in the modern incarnation of the Cyprus conflict were the events of 1974 and their dual significance: the socio-demographic impact of the ethnic partitioning on the island and the fact that all subsequent peace negotiations are geared towards addressing the consequences of those events.

The longstanding impact of 1974 on the Greek Cypriot psyche becomes ever so evident when we look at the period leading to the April 2004 referendum on the Annan plan. Soliciting support for the 'Yes' cause, US Secretary of State Colin Powell (2004) remarked during a television interview that '2004 (is) not 1974.' Powell's comment released insecurities concealed by the Greek Cypriots for three decades, exacerbated by parallels with the fall of Constantinople (1453) and the Asia Minor Catastrophe (1922). The year 1974 perpetuated the image of the 'unspeakable' Turk as Orthodox Hellenism's eternal enemy, out to expel them from their ancestral homeland, in a despondent fatalism skewed by betrayal, defeat and loss. Within this context, 1974 represents the apex of national treachery for Greek determinism, which reverberates through Greek Cypriot political culture and haunts their decision-making throughout the peace process.

Conversely, 1974 was heralded as a liberating 'peace operation' celebrated by the Turkish Cypriots as an antidote to Greek Cypriot domination. Psychologically 1974 served a therapeutic, almost cathartic, function for the Turkish

Cypriot community. Its egosyntonic resonance and its aggressive quality provided a liberating, cleansing sensation for a minority suffering from low esteem and a victim mentality (Volkan 1979, pp. 111–119).

The events of the summer of 1974 were set in motion eight months earlier, with a change of guard in the Greek junta. The new regime aggravated an already strained relationship between Athens and Nicosia and culminated on July 15 in a *coup d'état* ousting President Makarios. Citing its right to intervene under the Treaty of Guarantee, Turkey invaded the north of Cyprus five days later. As ceasefire negotiations took place in Geneva Turkish forces doubled the area under their control, unleashing the first wave of refugees.

When the Geneva conference reconvened, it became apparent that Turkey's plan was for a bicommunal independent state comprised of two autonomous zones, in which the Turkish Cypriot sector, of six districts, amounted to 34 percent of the island. When the talks collapsed, the Turkish military forces broke through the ceasefire line and gained control of nearly 37 percent of Cyprus. Turkey's prime minister Bulent Ecevit declared a ceasefire on August 16, stating that the 'foundations have been laid for the new federal state of Cyprus' (Hitchens 1984, pp. 164–165).

The challenge of reunification

Though the Cyprus conflict had engaged international diplomacy since the 1950s, it was the events of 1974 that dramatically changed the nature of the problem, compounding the difficulties facing all subsequent attempts at mediation. Partition, dislocation and militarization imposed a new set of variants and transformed the conflict from any previous incarnation. Well-versed in the post-1974 'new realities,' the UN-mediated intercommunal talks emerged as the dominant format for all future negotiations.

For the Greek Cypriots, the occupation of 37 percent of the island's territory by Turkish troops, and the exodus of approximately 200,000 Greek Cypriot refugees, had divided the island along demographic lines into two homogeneous parts. The Greek Cypriot community found itself in a more precarious position than prior to 1974, and in contrast to past seminal events, the social consequences of 1974 were felt beyond the traditional elite, shadowing an entire generation of Cypriots.

The Greek Cypriot political leadership quickly realized that these 'new realities' required a new policy and strategy. They became aware of their limited capacity to bring about a settlement, which was dependent on outside forces. They also realized that any attempt to continue the 1968 intercommunal talks was futile. UN resolutions, however, meant they could not reject the call for intercommunal talks, for fear of alienating the international community in general and the influential Western powers in particular. The intercommunal talks also operated within an environment where their negotiating counterpart was heavily dependent on Turkey. For the Greek Cypriots, Turkey would need to be pressured to instruct the Turkish Cypriots to make concessions at the negotiations. The main agents capable of applying such pressure in descending order were the United States, a core of Western European powers, and the international community.

The call to recommence intercommunal negotiations required an urgent reassessment of the Greek position. But a dilemma confronted the Greek/Greek Cypriot leaderships as to what kinds of objectives should, and could, be sought? It quickly became evident that their pre-1974 position was no longer feasible, especially given the threat that the existing de facto situation could become, in time, permanent.

This dilemma was resolved at a meeting in Athens in late 1974. The policy framework that emerged from the Athens summit became the bedrock of the Greek national position on Cyprus. Heavily influenced by a need for redemption, the Athens doctrine advocated for a (then multi-regional) bicommunal federation, with essential powers vested in the central government; that the total area under Turkish Cypriot administration should not exceed 25 percent of the island; repatriation of the Greek Cypriot refugees; the right of property and freedom of movement; and the withdrawal of the Turkish troops from Cyprus (Clerides 1989). The prevailing assessment was that comprehensive concessions were necessary if negotiations with the Turkish side were to have any chance of success. It was grounded in a policy of realism: accepting federalism as the basis for a negotiated settlement. Ambiguity, however, over the nature of Cypriot federalism and its implementation became the hallmark of the Cyprus dilemma for decades.

The events of 1974 also had a tremendous impact on the Turkish Cypriot community and its political transformation. The new security afforded to the Turkish Cypriots by the presence of Turkish troops, and their concentration in one geographical area, meant that internal differences soon emerged. The relocation of Turkish Cypriots into enclaves during 1964–74 had brought about a certain political homogeneity and united them as an isolated minority (Soysal 1992, p. 40). The effects on the political elite sharpened and solidified the partition ideology as advocated in the 1950s, which was the vehicle for separating the two communities. The Greek Cypriot economic and political embargo, aimed at preventing recognition of the Turkish Cypriot 'state,' only compounded the ideology of separateness.

Besides their military relationship, the Turkish Cypriot community was also heavily dependent on Turkish aid, which provided 80 percent of the community's budget. For Turkish Cypriots, Turkey's intervention in 1974 was legal under the Treaty of Guarantee, and morally justified as it protected them from the Greek *énosists*. Turkish Cypriots argued that since 1964 there had been two administrations on the island, and that the internationally recognized Republic of Cyprus had in essence been the Greek Cypriot state. In relation to Greek Cypriot refugee and territorial claims, these matters were supposedly settled with the August 1975 exchange of population agreement (Canefe 2002). Given the above situation, Turkish Cypriots argued that only a federation comprised of two equal peoples/states was feasible (Tamkoç 1988, p. 111).

Yet despite five rounds of intercommunal negotiations over a 40-year period there has been no settlement to the Cyprus problem (ICG 2014, p. 1). The

Partition in Cyprus 131

intercommunal talks generally treated the Cyprus problem as an ethnic conflict, and sought its resolution on this basis. Since the late 1950s, the two communities had been politically, economically, socially and psychologically separated over time, whilst the 1974 partition endowed this separation with a geographical, demographic and military dimension. The net effect of the physical division of the island has been to hamper communication, interaction and contact not only between the two communities but even between those forces which were prepared to pursue, or at least explore, common interests and objectives. In addition, postponement of a solution led at different times one or both parties to resort to unilateral actions outside the confines of the process, thereby exacerbating the conflict and further impeding negotiation and third party mediation.

A key conclusion from any analysis of attempts towards reconciliation is that both communities had, for different reasons and in different ways, become supporters of the status quo which they viewed as at least preferable to the uncertainties of any future regime that did not incorporate their maximum expectations. The Turkish Cypriots feared that reunification within a strong federation would see them revert to the pre-1974 situation as an isolated minority dominated by a larger and more powerful Greek Cypriot community. Conversely, the Greek Cypriots viewed any federal solution that did not encompass a strong central authority and the withdrawal of the Turkish troops, as no better than their existing predicament. They would be sacrificing their legitimacy as the sole recognized Cypriot state and would be risking the total occupation of the island. Though the motivation and the rationale may have differed, the position of both parties was similar in one important respect: they both considered the incentives for change weaker than the security of the status quo. Fear of worst-case scenarios paralyzed the will and the capacity to pursue a riskier but ultimately more promising course.

Another obstacle was that the 'linkage' approach to negotiations has meant that there could be no settlement unless all aspects of the Cyprus problem (e.g., constitution, territory and security) were simultaneously agreed upon. As talks progressed, they inevitably became more complicated with the introduction of greater detail and new points of disputation. In addition, talks were often hampered by the introduction of different interpretations to concepts that had previously been agreed upon. Further hindering the process throughout this period were the contrasting motives, priorities, preferences and objectives of the two sides, most starkly expressed in a series of dualisms: maintaining/changing the status quo, unification/separatism, federation/confederation, unitarism/decentralization.

The mutual insecurity and distrust created reluctance on both sides to risk any change to existing arrangements. This phenomenon was enhanced by the close relationship and interdependence between the two communities and their principal external powers (Greece and Turkey) respectively. The direct relationship also impeded the negotiations and altered the political environment forcing both sides to adopt confrontationist postures. This was especially so in the case of the

Turkish Cypriot community which had a different historical relationship with Turkey, was less self-sufficient, and lacked an opposition which could effectively challenge the prevailing orthodoxy. As the conflict became protracted both communities chose to pursue their respective interests, with the aim of strengthening or promoting their legitimacy as independent international political actors.

When the two sides abandoned communication and the intercommunal talks were no longer considered a priority, the Cyprus conflict inevitably reverted to tension. Placed in this context, unilateral actions designed to address military and/or political insecurities acquired potentially dangerous implications. The net effect was escalating military capabilities on both sides, intensification of international campaigns to bolster their respective causes, provocative statements and the re-emergence of nationalist sentiment.

Paradoxically it was these confrontational phases, often followed by a more co-operative mood, which injected into the negotiating process renewed impetus for change and encouraged the two communities to break from their previously entrenched positions. For example, the 1985 High Level Meeting came about after the 1983 Turkish-Cypriot UDI, the UN Secretary-General initiatives of the early 1990s were heavily influenced by the Greek–Turkish Aegean crisis of 1987, the CBMs were boosted by border clashes in 1993–4, the 2002–4 Annan initiative followed the S-300 missile crisis and the 2008–10 'Cypriot-led, Cypriot-owned' talks (Michael 2013) were instigated by the catalytic effect of Cyprus and Turkey's EU accession pathways, while current attempts come on the heels of the major financial crisis to hit the Republic of Cyprus and the ensuing row over gas and oil exploration in south-eastern Cyprus.

The overall conclusion arising from surveying the intercommunal talks is that, alone, they cannot overcome the structural and psychological obstacles to a negotiated settlement. The relative failure of the intercommunal talks stems from the fact that the negotiating process developed a logic and timing of its own, which did not necessarily correspond to the psychology of the political situation it was seeking to remedy. When, for example, dramatic developments occurred in the internal or external environment of the two parties, the intercommunal talks seemed incapable of capturing the conciliatory mood that ensued. The common interests shared by the two communities and the mutual benefits that could result from a negotiated settlement have not been sufficiently elaborated or communicated during the intercommunal dialogue.

A final assessment of the intercommunal talks leaves us with the conclusion that since the acceptance of a bicommunal/bi-zonal federation, negotiations followed a repetitious cyclical pattern where disagreements on the substantial issues saw both sides retreat to their entrenched positions. As a result the parties discussed all issues to the point of exhaustion, yet the two communities remained divided. In conceptual terms, disagreement over reunification fundamentally revolved around its structural form and, at least implicitly, the nature of power sharing. But underlying these differences was the intangible climate of mistrust between the two sides and their sense of insecurity, which meant the continuation of the status quo and contemplation of other unilateral options.

3 + 1 settlement scenarios: unitary, federal or two-state solutions

Forty years after Cyprus' territorial and demographic partition, we are able to visualize, more clearly, the contradictory trajectory of its peace process, characterized by the irresolvable tension between historical determinism and the unilateralist aspirations of omnipresent ethno-nationalist sovereignty. The tension between separatism and unification is expressed more tangibly in the new challenges posed by the doctrine of pre-emption during Cyprus' post-referendum/ post-EU accession. The difficulty of constructing a new peace paradigm in Cyprus is not only exacerbated by inter/intra-communal polarization, but is also vulnerable to internal and external tensions, particularly as they relate to European ambiguity over Turkey and northern Cyprus.

In this wider context, a survey of the Cyprus conflict over the last 40–50 year period suggests that the future of Cyprus is likely to unfold in the realm of either one of the following scenarios:

1. Cyprus's formal or informal annexation, in part or in whole, by either Greece or Turkey – this option implies high levels of instability and, given the volume of arms accumulated by both sides, the prospect of open hostility;
2. the current status quo is retained in perpetual ambivalence;
3. the island is united through some form of strong or loose federal arrangement resulting from a negotiated outcome.

By canvassing the three scenarios in this order, we are able to better assess the likelihood of their realization within different contexts and through the combination of various influences, domestic and international.

Since 1974 a ceasefire has technically been observed in Cyprus and all parties have recoiled from a war scenario. This is because the risks involved clearly overrode any potential benefits. Both sides argue that acquisition of sophisticated weaponry constitutes part of their defense system and the doctrine of mutual deterrence prevails. However, the main restraint against the outbreak of armed conflict in Cyprus has been the fact that it could quickly escalate into a broader Greek–Turkish war which would immediately force NATO, the United States, the Europeans and even the Russians to intervene.

Despite occasional ultra-nationalistic language, there has been no real evidence, thus far, that either Greece or Turkey wished to annex all of Cyprus, especially since this would burden them with a troublesome minority population that would, in turn, have far-reaching political repercussion for the aggressor. Annexation of northern Cyprus by Turkey was the most likely of the annexation scenarios and such a radical development would lead to high levels of bilateral tension and regional instability. If this was to occur, then Turkey would, effectively, establish another hostile frontier with Greece, and the EU, with a perpetually hostile neighboring population at its underbelly. It is also something that a majority of Turkish Cypriots seem to reject (*Cyprus 2015* 2010, p. 37).

Between the second and third scenarios, a fourth category saw a solution based on a two-state, 'loose federation,' or some other confederate arrangement. Promoters of minimalist models range from partitionists, who argued for the formalization of the status quo, to gradualists who advocated an evolutionalist approach to the Cyprus problem. For partitionists, historical experience suggested that co-existence between the two communities within a 'strong' federation was practically impossible. In this view, it was expected that the Greek Cypriots would make concessions on sovereignty in exchange for territorial concessions from the Turkish side (Bahcheli 2000, pp. 214–216; Gobbi 1993, pp. 49–55).

The gradualists did not preclude the prospect for future reintegration once confidence was established. Rather what was envisaged was a step-by-step transitional approach that addressed the minimum objectives of both sides. Initially this entailed a 'second-best' settlement, such as confederation or 'loose federation,' accompanied by a series of CBMs. Conceptually 'loose' federation rested on two interdependent propositions: that both sides voluntarily proceeded to the next level of engagement; and the need for a conducive climate to sustain commonalities, which within an EU framework, may lead to genuine unification (Theophanous 1996, pp. 175–177).

Building on such a socio-psychological premise, others argued that a long-term sustainable resolution to the conflict had to address the root causes of inter-communal friction and re-construct a shared Cypriot identity (Tocci 2000, pp. 23–26). This required Cyprus to undergo a 'conciliation' stage ('healing of wounds,' trust-building), followed by a 'testing' phase (e.g., evolutionary federalism), before arriving at a durable political accord (Hadjipavlou-Trigeorgis and Trigeorgis 1993, p. 342; Volkan 1998, p. 278). The outcome of such an initiative would be determined by the extent to which its proponents integrated the three aforementioned phases within a realistic timeline. Others, such as Bahcheli and Noel (2014, p. 668), skeptical over the viability of dyadic federations, suggest undertaking a series of modest steps between Greek and Turkish Cypriot state instrumentalities and civil society groups before attempting negotiating a 'full-fledged federal agreement.'

Since 1974 the status quo was considered by every party as a transitional conflicting phase and all negotiating efforts concentrated on the federal option. In essence negotiations over federalism were always impregnated with principles, surreptitiously competing with the parties' preferred positions (the Greek Cypriot penchant for a unitary state and the Turkish Cypriot preference for a two-state solution).

In the 2004 post-referenda context, uncertainty over federalism propelled a mood of despair and a readiness for both communities to surrender to the certainty of the status quo. Offsetting such contradictory developments are two opposing concepts: reinstituting the Republic of Cyprus as a metaphor for a unitarism, and a two-state solution. In what at first sight might appear as discontinuity, this approach in fact entails considerable continuity when projected in the conflict's entire historical continuum. Here, it is worth noting a number of qualifying differences between the old and new meanings of the unitary (Republic of Cyprus) and two-state solutions.

Dismissal of federalist solutions has always been prevalent amongst both communities. A series of opinion polls since the 2004 referendum reveal an increasing trend, particularly among younger generations, rejecting federalism and supporting unitarism and/or two-states (Lordos 2004, 2006; Webster and Christophorou 2004; UNFICYP 2007). Closer scrutiny, however, reveals a degree of volatility in attitudinal change and a distinct lack of clarity over what is understood by a unitary state or the difference between federal and two-state solutions.

In this context several aspects deserve closer attention. Greek Cypriot conceptualization of the unitary state is encapsulated in the Republic of Cyprus' pre-1974 milieu rather than its 1960 incarnation. Subsequently, rejection of the Annan plan affirmed the Republic of Cyprus' legitimacy as 'their' identity-based construct/polity. Such exclusivity has been challenged by the Turkish Cypriot integrationists who by utilizing the intercommunal space created by the Green Line corridor seek to resuscitate the republican project.

The other anomaly that emerged was the resonance of the two-state solution amongst constituencies that traditionally abhorred the notion. Where previously the two-state solution was associated with partition and the separatists, it emerged as a proposition seriously contemplated by a sizeable number of Greek Cypriots. Greek Cypriot distaste for Annan's plan, coupled with a revamped attachment to the Republic of Cyprus, has paradoxically converged with partition to produce a situation where the two-state solution threatens to dislodge federalism as the second-best solution. Looking past its implications, equally ominous are warnings that 'creeping divergence' would mathematically lead, by osmosis, to partition (SEES 2007, pp. 6–9).

Whilst Turkish Cypriots are returning to the Republic of Cyprus, increasingly Greek Cypriots are trading federalism for the two-state solution as their preferred second-best solution. By embracing the territory for sovereignty doctrine, provided that northern Cyprus dovetails its European fortune with that of Turkey's, the two-state solution becomes a historical end-game for Greek and Turkish nationalism in Cyprus.

Conclusion

Cyprus has many identities and problems (Bryant 2009). Divided and partitioned since 1974 its 'un-ending' demeanor stubbornly persists throughout its modern incarnation as it transgresses from colonial to post-EU accession discourses. As seen above, its history has been a contradictory interplay between separatist/(se) cessionist and unification/integrationist forces. Whether Horowitz's (1985, pp. 588–589) rendition of 'radical surgery ... separating the antagonists' or Heraclides' (1991, p. 24) partition by 'mutual consent,' prevails in Cyprus, these remain state-centric propositions that ignore the conflict's need for vertical integration (Chapter 3, this volume).

Attaining a sustainable peace within Cyprus requires reconciliation of competing values, interest and needs: these can only be addressed in a consolidated democratic environment. The issues in dispute pertain essentially to the terms of co-existence, the meaning of equality and the need for restorative justice. From a transformative perspective, any political settlement of the Cyprus conflict needs to meet two fundamental prerequisites: it has to satisfy all stakeholders by limiting further victimization, and thus to safeguard against future discord; and second, a successful settlement must incorporate mechanisms, incentives and processes for intercommunal integration rather than entrench communalism (Chapter 4, this volume).

Much is to be gained from joint bicommunal partnerships, ventures, institutions and projects that are diverse and conducive to more transparent and participatory processes. The re-establishment of contacts between political parties could help to advance a process from which might emerge common policies across a wide range of issues not usually associated with the troublesome core of the Cyprus problem (resources, environment, migration, combating racism, unemployment, industrial relations and gender equality).

The challenge confronting Cyprus ultimately lies in its capacity to transform itself into a post-modern society with a political arrangement that transcends its historical insecurities (Chapter 5, this volume). Often a climate of uncertainty and ambivalence demands risk-taking. In this sense, the EU could offer itself as a surrogate for creative politics. As Cypriots need to overcome their past and create their own history, there is the danger that continual rejections will prolong stalemate, and stalemate will ensconce partition (Özgür 2005).

References

Acheson, D 1965, 'Cyprus: Anatomy of the Problem,' *Chicago Bar Record*, vol. 46, no. 8, pp. 349–356.

Anastasiades, N 2014, *Press Release*, retrieved April 21 2014, www.presidency.gov.cy/Presidency/Presidency.nsf/All/C73BDD05C5693F0EC2257C7E0025047A?OpenDocument.

Arnold, P 1956, *Cyprus Challenge—a Colonial Island and its Aspirations: Reminiscences of a Former Editor of the 'Cyprus Post'*, Hogarth Press, London.

Bahcheli, T 2000, 'Searching for a Cyprus Settlement: Considering Options for Creating a Federation, a Confederation, or Two Independent States,' *Publius*, vol. 30, no. 1, pp. 203–216.

Bahcheli, T and Noel, S 2014, 'The Quest for a Political Settlement in Cyprus: Is a Dyadic Federation Viable?' *Publius: The Journal of Federalism*, vol. 44, no. 4, pp. 659–680.

Brinkley, D 1992, *Dean Acheson: The Cold War Years 1953–1971*, Yale University Press, New Haven.

Browne, M 1946, 'Britain Plans Her Global Defense,' *New York Times*, August 11.

Bryant, R 2009, 'The Many Cyprus Problems,' *Middle East Report*, no. 251, pp. 2–7.

Burton, J 1969, *Conflict and Communication: The Use of Controlled Communication in International Relations*, The Free Press, New York.

Burton, J 1979, *Deviance Terrorism and War: The Process of Solving Unsolved Social and Political Problems*, Martin Robertson, Oxford.

Canefe, N 2002, 'Refugees or Enemies? The Legacy of Population Displacements in Contemporary Turkish Cypriot Society,' *South European Society and Politics*, vol. 7, no. 3, pp. 1–28.

Clerides, G 1989, *Cyprus: My Deposition*, vol. 2, Alithia, Nicosia.
Crawshaw, N 1978, *The Cyprus Revolt: An Account of the Struggle for Union with Greece*, George Allen & Unwin, London.
Cyprus 2015 2010, *Next Steps in the Peace Talks: An Island-Wide Study of Public Opinion in Cyprus*, retrieved July 15 2014, www.interpeace.org/publications/cyprus/15-next-steps-in-the-peace-talks-english/file.
Denktash, RR 1972, 'The Problem of Cyprus,' *Review of International Affairs*, vol. 22, no. 544, pp. 9–11.
Eden, A 1960, *Full Circle*, Cassell, London.
Eroğlu, D 2014, 'We, too, are the Owners of Cyprus,' March 7, retrieved April 21 2014, www.kktcb.org/content02.aspx?id=1&sayfa=25&content=3510&select=&lang=en.
Given, M 2002, 'Maps, Fields, and Boundary Cairns: Demarcation and Resistance in Colonial Cyprus,' *International Journal of Historical Archaeology*, vol. 6, no. 1, pp. 1–22.
Gobbi, HJ 1993, *Rethinking Cyprus*, Aurora, Tel Aviv.
Hadjipavlou-Trigeorgis, M and Trigeorgis, L 1993, 'Cyprus: An Evolutionary Approach to Conflict Resolution,' *Journal of Conflict Resolution*, vol. 37, no. 2, pp. 340–360.
Harding, Lord of Petherton 1958, 'The Cyprus Problem in Relation to the Middle East,' *International Affairs*, vol. 34, no. 3, pp. 291–296.
Heraclides, A 1991, *The Self-Determination of Minorities in International Politics*, Frank Cass, London.
Hitchens, C 1984, *Cyprus*, Quartet Books, London.
Holland, R and Markides, D 2006, *The British and the Hellenes: Struggles for Mastery in the Eastern Mediterranean 1850–1960*, Oxford University Press, Oxford.
Horowitz, D 1985, *Ethnic Groups in Conflict*, University of California Press, Berkeley, CA.
International Crisis Group (ICG) 2014, *Divided Cyprus: Coming to Terms on an Imperfect Reality* (Europe Report 299), Brussels.
Karpat, KH 1967, 'Solution in Cyprus: Federation,' in *The Cyprus Dilemma: Options for Peace*, Institute for Mediterranean Affairs, New York, pp. 35–54.
Kyrris, CP 1985, *History of Cyprus*, Nicocles, Nicosia.
Lordos, A 2004, *Can the Cyprus Problem be Solved? Understanding the Greek Cypriot Response to the UN Peace Plan for Cyprus*, CYMAR, Nicosia.
Lordos, A 2006, *Building Trust: An Inter-Communal Analysis of Public Opinion in Cyprus*, CYMAR & KADEM, Nicosia.
Macmillan, H 1971, *Riding the Storm: 1956–1959*, Macmillan, London.
Michael, MS 2005, 'Cyprus and the Elusiveness of Modernity,' in MS Michael and AM Tamis (eds), *Cyprus in the Modern World*, Vanias, Thessaloniki, pp. 1–8.
Michael, MS 2009, *Resolving the Cyprus Conflict: Negotiating History*, Palgrave Macmillan, London.
Michael, MS 2013. '"Cypriot-led, Cypriot-owned" – Cyprus Talks Revisited,' *Australian Journal of International Affairs*, vol. 67, no. 4, pp. 526–539.
Montis, K 1987, *Apanta A: Poisi* (Collection A: Poetry), vol. 2, AG Leventi Foundation, Nicosia.
Necatigil, ZA 1989, *The Cyprus Question and the Turkish Position in International Law*, Oxford University Press, Oxford.
Özgür, Ö 2005, 'Rejection Provokes No Solution and No Solution Partition,' *Philelefteros*, 16 January.
Pollis, A 1973, 'Intergroup Conflict and British Colonial Policy: The Case of Cyprus,' *Comparative Politics*, vol. 5, no. 4, pp. 575–599.

Polyviou, PG 1976, *Cyprus in Search of a Constitution: Constitutional Negotiations and Proposals 1960–1975*, Nicosia.

Powell, CL 2004, 'Interview on MEGA TV with Michael Ignatiou,' April 16 2004, retrieved 12 May 2014, www.state.gov/secretary/former/powell/remarks/31532.htm.

Rasler, K, Thompson, WR and Ganguly, S 2013, *How Rivalries End*, University of Pennsylvania Press, Philadelphia.

South East European Studies at Oxford (SEES) 2007, *Cyprus after Accession: Getting Past 'No'?*, Workshop Report and Responses, retrieved July 15 2014, www.sant.ox.ac.uk/seesox/workshopreports/workshop_may2007.pdf.

Soysal, M 1992, 'Political Parties in the Turkish Republic of Northern Cyprus and their Vision of "the Solution",' in N Salem (ed.), *Cyprus: A Regional Conflict and its Resolution*, St. Martin, New York, pp. 39–43.

Sulzberger, CL 1944, 'Greeks Preparing Territorial Claims,' *New York Times*, August 8.

Tamkoç, M 1988, *The Turkish Cypriot State: The Embodiment of the Right of Self-Determination*, Rustem, London.

Theophanous, A 1996, *The Political Economy of a Federal Cyprus*, Intercollege Press, Nicosia.

Tocci, N 2000, *The 'Cyprus Question': Reshaping Community Identities and Elite Interests within a Wider European Framework*, Centre for European Policy Studies, Brussels.

UN 1965, 'Report of the United Nations Mediator on Cyprus to the Secretary-General,' March 26, retrieved July 20 2014, http://daccess-dds-ny.un.org/doc/UNDOC/GEN/N65/053/91/PDF/N6505391.pdf?OpenElement.

UN 1967, 'Resolution 244: The Cyprus Question,' December 22, retrieved July 15 2014, http://daccess-dds-ny.un.org/doc/RESOLUTION/GEN/NR0/240/96/IMG/NR024096.pdf?OpenElement.

UN 1974, 'Report by the Secretary-General on the United Nations Operation in Cyprus for the Period from 2 December 1973 to 22 May 1974,' May 22, retrieved July 15 2014, http://daccess-dds-ny.un.org/doc/UNDOC/GEN/N74/131/40/PDF/N7413140.pdf?OpenElement.

UN 2014, 'Joint Declaration,' February 11, retrieved July 15 2014, www.uncyprustalks.org/media/Good%20Offices/Photos%20For%20Main%20Articles/FEBRUARY_2014_JOINT_DECLARATION_FINAL.pdf.

UNFICYP 2007, *The UN in Cyprus: An Inter-Communal Survey of Public Opinion by UNFICYP*, media release, April 24, retrieved July 20 2014, www.unficyp.org/nqcontent.cfm?a_id=2170.

United Kingdom 1915, 'Cabinet meeting (Financial situation; Proposed cession to Greece of Cyprus without Cabinet consent; Need for smaller War Council)', CAB 37/136/26, October 21.

United Kingdom 1958, 'Cyprus: Statement of Policy Cmnd.', 455, HMSO, London.

United Kingdom 1960, 'Cyprus Cmnd.', 1093, HMSO, London.

Volkan, VD 1979, *Cyprus—War and Adaptation: A Psychoanalytic History of Two Ethnic Groups in Conflict*, University Press of Virginia, Charlottesville.

Volkan, VD 1998, 'Turks and Greeks of Cyprus: Psychopolitical Considerations,' in V Calotychos (ed.), *Cyprus and its People: Nation, Identity, and Experience in an Unimaginable Community, 1955–1997*, Westview Press, Boulder, pp. 277–284.

Webster, C and Christophorou, C 2004, 'Greek Cypriots, Turkish Cypriots, and the Future: The Day after the Referendum,' CYMAR Market Research, Nicosia.

Yashin, N 1979, *Hyacinth and Narcissus*, Cem, Istanbul.

9 Succeeding and seceding in Iraq
The case for a Shiite state

Benjamin Isakhan[1]

Following the invasion of Iraq in 2003, the Bush administration sought to define its success via the installment of an obedient and very Western type of 'democracy' (Jervis 2003). On the one hand, this project had some modest successes: a complex array of civil society movements emerged; undoctored news was enthusiastically produced and consumed across the nation; Iraqi citizens took to the streets to protest key government decisions; and millions of Iraqis voted in relatively free and fair national elections (Davis 2004, 2007; Isakhan 2008, 2011, 2012, 2014). On the other hand, the US project to democratize Iraq has also given way to a dramatic upsurge in ethno-religious factionalism in which a series of groups have sought to use 'democracy' to create or exacerbate division. Among these divisive political elements a relatively fringe idea held mostly by power-hungry elites has become a central driving force of much political debate within Iraq: separatism. These groups have developed sophisticated political rhetoric, policy and campaigns that speaks directly to their respective ethno-religious constituents, leaving Iraqis with little choice but to vote along sectarian lines. This has led to an Iraqi government which has been given a mandate by their constituents to fight in the interests of separatism and not towards a cohesive and collective Iraq (Baram *et al.* 2010; Little and Swearer 2006). Although there are many examples of political factions within Iraq which have called for territorial separatism since 2003 (such as some Sunni, Assyrian and Turcoman political parties), the most prominent calls came from the major Kurdish political parties (the Kurdistan Democratic Party and the Patriotic Union of Kurdistan) which have inherited a long tradition of calling, and fighting, for secession (McDowell 2000).

However, this chapter focuses on the less known case for a Shiite state. Specifically, it concentrates on the Shia Arab Islamist political party, the Supreme Council for the Islamic Revolution in Iraq (SCIRI), which differs from other Shia political factions in their calls for a decentralized federal Iraq with an autonomous Shia Islamic state in the south. It should be pointed out here that prior to 2003, the Shia Arab majority (constituting some 60 percent of the population) were routinely marginalized and often suppressed by the central Sunni-dominated state. However, with the fall of the Baathist regime the Shia have emerged as major political power-brokers and, since the elections of 2005, Iraq has emerged as the first ever Shia-dominated government in the modern Arab world. It is also worth noting that the Shia Arabs are largely concentrated in central and especially southern Iraq which is not only home to the important religious centers of Najaf and Karbala but also the mercantile and economic hub of Basra with its crucial port. More importantly, the Shia-dominated south is also home to the vast majority of Iraq's oil reserves with the three provinces of Nasiriya, Maysan and Basra alone holding around 71 percent of Iraq's oil (Munsoon 2009, p. 185).

In light of such factors, this chapter examines the extent to which SCIRI's calls for federalism and decentralization are motivated by its desire to establish a separate Shia Islamic state in the south of Iraq. Interestingly however, much recent literature has in fact claimed that there is no credible separatist movement in the south of Iraq. Indeed, Visser (2005) and others have gone to great lengths to explain away the potential for modern Shia Arab separatism arguing alternatively: that such ideas lack historical legitimacy (i.e., that the Shia Arabs have never mounted a credible secessionist movement in the past); that they lack popular contemporary support and are 'completely novel' or in the realm of 'intellectual marginality' for most of Iraq's Shia population; that the divides that do exist in Iraq should be understood in terms of regionalism rather than ethno-religious sectarian identities (i.e., that the Shia Arabs see themselves as 'southerners' not 'Shia'); and that the ethno-sectarian 'map' of Iraq is in fact a Western imposed construct that does not match Iraqi realities (Visser 2004, 2007, 2008a, 2008b; Visser and Stansfield 2008). While any nuanced account of prospective Shia separatism in Iraq must take into account the strength and depth of the work of Visser and his colleagues, they nonetheless underestimate the very real desire of certain elements of the Shia political elite to create a separate Shia-dominated Islamic state in the south of Iraq. Focusing specifically on the period of US occupation (2003–11), this chapter seeks to examine the extent to which SCIRI seized the opportunity inadvertently presented by the US project to democratize Iraq in order to advance its own separatist cause. As this chapter will demonstrate, SCIRI's contemporary claims are more than misunderstood rhetoric. They are premised instead on well-crafted (if modestly successful) political ideologies that, at the very least, provide tentative steps towards the creation of a separate Shia Islamic state in the south of Iraq. While this chapter is cautious not to argue that SCIRI is going to achieve such a goal any time soon, examining its claims and intentions does raise many important questions about the future of Iraq beyond the US occupation, the probability of Iraq maintaining (or achieving) a cohesive national identity and a robust democracy, and about the likelihood of secession succeeding in Iraq.

Foundation and principles

In the 1950s, the Shia Arab population of southern Iraq went through something of a political renaissance which included the emergence of the Shia religio-political entity, Hizb Al-Dawa Islamiyya ('The Islamic Calling', or more commonly referred to as Dawa, the 'Calling') sometime after 1957 (Batatu 1986, pp. 191–192; Nakash 2003, pp. 136–137). Under the charismatic leadership of Grand Ayatollah Muhammad Baqr al-Sadr (1935–80) and Ayatollah Sayed Mohammed Baqr Al-Hakim (1939–2003) the group grew rapidly in popularity and influence. However, little did the Dawa and its leaders know that Iraq was about to enter a decade of political turmoil following the *coup d'état* which toppled the British installed Hashemite monarchy in 1958. This uncertainty ultimately ended with the ascendency of the Baath Party in 1968 and then the emergence of Saddam Hussein in 1979. However, the Baath promptly set about utilizing their newfound powers to imprison, torture and execute what was left of Iraq's nascent opposition movements, including Iraq's Shia majority. Both Al-Sadr and Al-Hakim reacted by speaking out, leading to several arrests, stints in detention and bouts of torture throughout the 1970s. Part of the Baathist case against the Shia political movements was their argument that the Shia were in fact plotting to break up Iraq and create a separate Shia autonomous zone in the south under Iranian influence.

The Iran–Iraq War of the 1980s made the Sunni-Baathist state's relations with the Shia majority even more complicated as Iraq fought a protracted battle with its Shia Islamist neighbor. For example, many Dawa members supported the Islamic Revolution and spoke out against the war, even going as far as co-ordinating several assassination attempts on Saddam Hussein and other senior Baath Party members. Not surprisingly, Saddam banned the organization and, in 1980, he ordered the arrest, torture and execution of Al-Sadr. The Dawa movement continued under the authority of Al-Sadr's brother-in-law, Grand Ayatollah Mohammad Sadiq Al-Sadr, a charismatic and militant leader who sought to revitalize the Shia and engage them in political agitation against the state. He asserted his support for the Islamic Revolution in Iran and also called for the establishment of an Islamic state in Iraq (Duss and Juul 2009, p. 9). Saddam reacted predictably and had Al-Sadr assassinated in 1999, along with his two eldest sons (Stansfield 2007, pp. 61–62). This meant that the young and uneducated Moqtada Al-Sadr had suddenly inherited a considerable legacy, which he was to draw upon after the fall of Saddam in 2003 (Duss and Juul 2009, p. 9).

The persecution of Dawa by the Baathist state during the 1980s also had the effect of forcing many senior members of the party to flee to Tehran. Here they formed the SCIRI in 1982 under the leadership of senior Iraqi cleric, Ayatollah Mohammad Baqr Al-Hakim and his brother Abdul Aziz Al-Hakim (1953–2009) (Baram 1998, p. 52). With the backing of Iran's Ayatollah Khomeini and from the safety of Iran, SCIRI was able to set up a virulent opposition movement that repeatedly advocated the overthrow of the secular Baathist regime via a Shia-led Islamic Revolution and the establishment of a Shia Islamic state in Iraq under direct clerical rule. While such calls for 'revolution' are very different from secession, they nonetheless reveal the strength and depth of Iranian influence on SCIRI. This included the Iranian influence on SCIRI's political ideology, particularly that of Muhammad Baqr Al-Hakim. Abandoning his original position at the time of the founding of Dawa that a Shia Islamic state ought not be governed by clerics, Al-Hakim come to advocate the installment in Iraq of Khomeini's notion of the guardianship of the Islamic jurists, a decentralized form of government which included *Hukm Al-Wilayat* (the rule of the provinces) under the guidance of a supreme jurisprudent. Although subtle, the distinction is important: Al-Hakim came to both emphasize decentralization for Iraq and clerical style rule (Visser 2005, pp. 169–170).

SCIRI, however, increasingly distanced itself from calls for a decentralized Iraq under Shia Islamic clerical rule in the lead up to the US invasion in 2003. Instead, it began talking about 'democracy' and 'federalism' and the inclusion of all Iraqis. Al-Hakim's writings on democracy impressed the United States and qualified SCIRI as a legitimate part of the approved 'democratic opposition' (Ehrenberg *et al.* 2010, p. 318). As just one example, a statement issued by the Ayatollah in May 2001 demanded 'the humanitarian and legal rights for all Iraqi people ... those rights that the regime has confiscated without distinguishing between the Sunnis and Shiites, and between Arabs and Turkmen, for the regime has usurped all the rights of the Iraqi people' (Al-Hakim 2001, p. 319). However, the 2003 invasion has gradually exposed the thin veneer of SCIRI's commitment to democracy and federalism, revealing instead its goals for a separate Shia-dominated south.

Shiite separatism after 2003

Following the invasion and occupation of Iraq in 2003 key members of the SCIRI Party returned from their exile in Iran. After 23 years the movement's leader, Ayatollah Muhammad Baqr Al-Hakim, was back in Iraq along with prominent SCIRI figures such as his younger brother Sayeed Abdel Aziz Al-Hakim and the latter's son, Sayeed Ammar Al-Hakim. They brought with them years of exposure to the machinations of Iranian theology and politics, a handful of well-established media and propaganda outlets and a relatively sophisticated political ideology. They also brought their own private militia, the Badr Brigade, made up of 10–15,000 Iran-trained and funded elite Shia Arab soldiers. Upon their return, the SCIRI movement was at first well received by thousands of Shia, especially given Al-Hakim's call for an 'immediate end to the occupation, the transfer of power to Iraqis, and the formation of a constitutional government with Islamic, not secular, values' (Ehrenberg *et al.* 2010, p. 318). Such sentiments also received praise in an official welcome issued by the head of the Shia clergy in Iraq, Grand Ayatollah Ali Al-Sistani who called upon the Shia faithful to 'cooperate and support Ayatollah Al-Hakim' and praised him for having denounced the US Coalition Provisional Authority (CPA) original plan to install a puppet Iraqi government that would write the constitution under American auspices and be pliable to their interests in the region ('Ayatollah Al-Sistani's Decree' 2003, p. 3). Sadly, on August 29 2003, Al-Hakim was assassinated in Najaf by a massive car explosion believed to have been the work of Al-Qaeda in Iraq. This was a major setback for SCIRI as it relied heavily on his leadership, charisma and religious authority. The leadership then passed to his younger brother and the former head of the Badr Brigade, Sayeed Abdul Aziz Al-Hakim.

But SCIRI's real problem was not that of leadership but that years in exile meant it was barely known in Iraq and did not have a strong support base. Nonetheless, due to its strong US-backing, SCIRI formed a critical part of the CPA-appointed Interim Governing Council (IGC) that helped govern Iraq from July 2003 to June 2004. SCIRI was determined to put US rhetoric on 'democracy' to the test. It understood that by holding the United States to its promises it stood to gain an unprecedented degree of power and influence. So, in order to both widen its support base in Iraq and align itself with the US vision of Iraqi democracy, SCIRI had to radically transform itself from a revolutionary and militant movement into a democratic party. One way in which to do so was to flag SCIRI's democratic credential in its many media outlets. For example, *The SCIRI Bulletin* featured lengthy columns on 'Islam and Democracy' in which SCIRI argued that there was no disagreement between Shia religious theology and modern representative democracy ('Islam and Democracy' 2003a, 2003b).

On the one hand such sentiments are to be admired and certainly align with recent studies that have sought to demonstrate the similarities between democratic governance and the theology and practice of Islam (Sadiki 2012). On the other hand, however, it is revealing that SCIRI began to publish *The SCIRI Bulletin* in the same month that it was appointed by the United States to the IGC (July 2003) and that such pronouncements occurred in the context of the US plan to bring democracy to Iraq. Despite all of SCIRI's rhetoric about democracy and inclusion, it has always maintained an interest in creating a separate Shia Islamic state in southern Iraq. During the time of the Interim Iraqi Government (IIG) which governed Iraq from June 2004 to May 2005, SCIRI held several senior posts including having SCIRI loyalist Adel Abdul Al-Mahdi as Finance Minister of Iraq. Given such power, SCIRI renewed its interest in the establishment of an independent Shia territory by quietly promoting the notion of a SCIRI-dominated triangle in the provinces of Basra, Maysan and Dhi Qar in the far south of Iraq. These three oil-rich provinces were to be amalgamated into one federal entity, autonomous from the rest of Iraq. This would leave the rest of the Shia and most of Iraq (except for the Kurdish north) with very little oil (Visser 2008a, p. 2).

Then, in the lead up to the January 2005 national elections in Iraq, the divergent political factions of the Iraqi Shia population, including SCIRI, the Sadr Trend and Dawa, came together under the banner of the United Iraqi Alliance (UIA). SCIRI used its political savvy and its armed militia, the Badr Organization, to dominate the UIA. Its campaigns not only discussed the creation of a separate Shia state in the south, but used images of Sistani in order to persuade the Shia faithful that such ideas had been endorsed by the Grand Ayatollah (Duss and Juul 2009, p. 11). This strategy was to pay dividends. When the results were announced on February 14 the UIA had won 48 percent of the votes (Dawisha and Diamond 2006, pp. 93–94). Of the 275 seats that made up the Iraqi Transitional Government (ITG, May 2005–May 2006), the UIA had secured 140. SCIRI and the Badr Organization were the biggest winners with a combined total of 36 seats. This meant that SCIRI now had control of seven of the nine southern provinces (except Maysan and Basra) and that several SCIRI members ascended to positions of considerable influence and power. Al-Mahdi became one of two Vice Presidents of Iraq (until 2011) and another SCIRI loyalist, Bayan Jabr, took over the Interior Ministry, allowing the Badr Organization to deeply infiltrate the Iraqi Security Forces (ISF) (Duss and Juul 2009, pp. 11–12).

Following the January elections, the new Iraqi government was charged with the rather laborious task of drafting a permanent Iraqi constitution. Lengthy debates ensued over several complicated policy issues including that of federalism. From the very beginning of the post-Saddam era, the Kurds had made it very clear that their involvement in a post-Saddam Iraq was contingent on Sunni and Shia acceptance of a loose federal structure in which Kurdistan (itself comprising of a minimum of the three regions of Erbil, Sulaymania and Dohuk) would maintain its autonomy. This was in fact a dramatic toning down of some of the early post-invasion rhetoric which called for complete Kurdish secession from Iraq (Romano 2006; Sluglett 2010). By 2005 the Kurds had estimated, quite correctly, that they had more to gain from being autonomous within Iraq rather than seceding and pressured the new government towards such an end (Sluglett 2011).

SCIRI saw its opportunity and went on the offensive. With its enormous influence over Shia politics and over the Iraqi parliament, SCIRI ambitiously expanded its original idea of running an autonomous three-province southern region to include all nine of Iraq's central and southern Shia-dominated governorates. The goal was to create 'The Region of the Centre and the South' (*Iqlim Al-Wa-Sat Wa-Al-Janub*), a nine province oil-rich 'Shiastan' (Visser 2008b, p. 47). Cleverly, it began to frame its plan in terms of historical grievances, arguing that Iraq had for too long been dominated by a strong Sunni-led central government which had unfairly taken resources from the south with little recompense (Munsoon 2009, pp. 182–185). By July 2005, Al-Hakim had begun talking publicly about the plan via various outlets, including *Al-Jazeera*, where he claimed that:

> Over centuries, not decades, the central governments lead to a phenomenon of dictatorship. Today, we consider giving the opportunity to the regions, all regions in Iraq, to play a role in the administration of the country and [that to] reduce the central authorities is a contribution to the overall collective participation of all Iraqi people.
>
> (*Al-Jazeera*, July 10 2005)

Then, on August 11 2005, Al-Hakim addressed a rally of thousands of SCIRI loyalists in Najaf who had gathered to commemorate the second anniversary of the death of his brother and former leader, Ayatollah Muhammad Baqr Al-Hakim. He argued that the Shia must not miss their chance to create their own autonomous region in the south and that regional autonomy would in fact help to maintain Iraq's precarious political balance. He stated:

> We believe it is necessary to erect a single region of the centre and the south of Iraq due to the existence of commonalities between the inhabitants of

these areas, as well as the singularly oppressive policy with which the former regime confronted them. This opportunity of realizing such a holy project must not be let go of, and the necessary steps of implementing it must be taken ... the creation of a single region!

(cited in Visser 2008b, pp. 28–29)

Although Visser points out that this part of Al-Hakim's speech constituted only 40 seconds of his entire 34-minute address and is critical of the way it was drummed up in the media, it nonetheless gives us insight into SCIRI's ongoing agenda of creating a single and separate Shia region in the south of Iraq. Indeed, what Visser neglects to mention, and is arguably even more alarming, are the comments made by other senior SCIRI members at the same rally. For example, Hadi Al-Amiri, the secretary-general of the Badr Organization, extolled with great passion that the 'Shia should march forward towards establishing the southern region or else they will regret it.' He also stressed that the Shia 'should attain a federal region in the south to secure our rights which our enemies tried to deprive us from' and finished by asking the crowd rhetorically, 'what have we got from the central government except killing?' (*Al-Jazeera*, 11 August 2005).

Not surprisingly, such notions were not well received in Baghdad, especially among the Sunni minority who now faced the prospect of both Kurdish and Shia autonomy from the central government, a situation that would leave them with virtually no access to Iraq's rich oil reserves. All of this meant that the constitution that was ratified in October 2005 decentralized political authority, limited national power and privileged provincial, sectarian and ethnic interests over those of a unified Iraqi state. Arguably, this scenario became even more pronounced at the time of the December 2005 election in which the Iraqi people elected a permanent 275-seat government. A close look at the election results reveals that Iraqis had, almost without exception, voted along ethno-religious sectarian lines. In the nine predominantly Shia provinces, the UIA had won an average of 87 percent of the votes and of the 128 seats (of 275, 41 percent of the votes) won by the UIA, SCIRI had won the most with 30 (Katzman 2010, p. 21). When Maliki's government and the Dawa Party took the reins in May 2006, SCIRI continued to develop its power from behind the scenes, wielding far more authority than its limited popular base or international renown would suggest. SCIRI's Mahdi maintained his position as one of Iraq's two Vice Presidents, SCIRI also controlled the Finance Ministry, while Badr continued to infiltrate the ISF ironically enough with both Iranian backing and US support (Duss and Juul 2009, p. 3).

From 2006 Iraq descended into a particularly dark and unprecedented period with grim and complex battles fought between the occupying forces, the Iraqi armed services, various insurgent groups and terrorist organizations, as well as between competing ethno-religious sectarian militias (Dawisha 2009, pp. 258–271). The violence of 2006–7 in many ways helped galvanize support for SCIRI's vision of a united Shia region in the south. The bombing of the gold-domed Abbasid-era Al-Askari mosque in Samarra in February 2006, which is highly revered by the Shia Arab population and was deliberately targeted by Sunni insurgents, even led some Dawa members to voice their support for SCIRI's plan (Visser 2008b, pp. 44–45). Given such a climate, Al-Hakim sought to make his position clear when he addressed thousands of worshippers at the Imam Hussein shrine in Kerbala the following month (March 2006). Accompanied by senior members of SCIRI such as Vice President Mahdi and Iraqi MP Humam Hamudi, Al-Hakim asserted that in fact regionalism was a cure for Iraq's crippling ethno-religious sectarianism and violence. For Al-Hakim, 'my religious and patriotic responsibility makes me believe that the establishment of a central and southern Iraq region and Baghdad region is one of the solutions that will end those crimes against the innocent people' (Al-Hakim cited in Radhi 2006). Similarly, in a conference organized by SCIRI in June 2006 and attended by the Badr Organization, Al-Hakim explained that his belief in a southern Shia region in Iraq was modeled on the example of the Kurdish north. He claimed that 'federalism is the right choice in Iraq Kurdistan and it is the right choice in Iraq's centre and south, Baghdad and in any Iraqi city' (*Al-Jazeera*, June 11 2006). Capitalizing on this momentum in September 2006 SCIRI attempted to push through parliament a bill that would provide a legal framework for the creation of a Shia autonomous zone in the south (Munsoon 2009, p. 195). It failed initially, but a similar law was passed in October in which federalism was adopted. Marking a significant victory for SCIRI, the law does not impose any size restrictions on federal entities and permits a variety of configurations, bringing the notion of a nine-province southern region one step closer to reality (Visser 2008b, pp. 45–46).

In May 2007, SCIRI changed its name to the Islamic Supreme Council of Iraq (ISCI), losing the 'Revolution' to symbolically distance itself from Iran and its 1979 revolution. The newly badged ISCI did not however distance itself from its goal of an autonomous Shia zone in the south. Instead, Al-Hakim and his son Ammar Al-Hakim stepped up their campaign, appearing on several media platforms throughout 2007 advocating Shia autonomy. In one example the official ISCI television channel *Al-Furat* ('The Euphrates') aired a speech Al-Hakim had given before a large crowd in Kerbala. In it, the ISCI leader stated that:

> We renew our call for the activation of the constitutional authority that is given to the governorates. We should not stop at the theoretical belief in this constitutional right. However, this belief should be reflected through practical measures by the central government or any of the local governments in the governorates.... We will maintain our constitutional and legal movements towards a region of the centre and the south as it is a big guarantee for Iraq's progress and stability.
>
> ('The text of' 2007)

Along similar lines, Ammar Al-Hakim asserted in no uncertain terms that ISCI believes 'that the formation of federal regions in Iraq will solve a lot of political, economic and security problems by giving these regions more authority and budget for [the] reconstruction of those cities that were deliberately ignored during Saddam Hussein's era' ('Maad Fayadh Interviews' 2007).

In late 2008 and in the lead up to the provincial elections held across Iraq in January 2009, Prime Minister Maliki split those loyal to him in Dawa from the UIA to form the State of Law Coalition (SLC). This was a calculated political move by Maliki because he knew that without Dawa, the UIA would be in ruins. Maliki had effectively torn them apart and the constituent political parties, including ISCI, were forced to contest the 2009 provincial elections separately. The SLC emerged the clear winner of the 2009 provincial elections, winning 126 of 440 seats, as well as being the largest list in eight of the nine Shia provinces, severely weakening ISCI's position in the south. Indeed, ISCI received only 6.6 percent of the national vote and secured only 52 of the 440 seats available across Iraq's various provincial councils. These results can also be interpreted as a reflection of the dwindling support for ISCI's plan for a separate Shia state in the south. Part of Maliki's success was that he had been able to provide at least the guise of a non-sectarian and pro-nationalist agenda, while ISCI continued to talk the language of division. In a campaign speech transcribed in *The ISCI Bulletin*, for example, Al-Hakim argued that the provincial elections were in fact an opportunity to build 'a non-centralized state and establish Federal Regions in accordance [with] ... the constitution as Iraq being a Federal Union.... We call upon all people to make this experience a success for the good of the Iraqi interests' ('H.E. Al-Hakim Congratulates' 2008, p. 1).

In August 2009 Abdul Aziz Al-Hakim died and his son, Ammar Al-Hakim, was officially 'elected' to the leadership of ISCI at its tenth annual conference in October ('ISCI Tenth Conference' 2009, p. 4; 'ISCI Unanimously Elects' 2009, p. 5). Interestingly, Ammar Al-Hakim was initially very defensive about the issue of Shia autonomy in the south after taking office. In a series of interviews given shortly after his appointment, Al-Hakim argued that ISCI had in fact abandoned the plan of a nine-province Shia autonomous zone in the south some time ago and only advocated it because it was part of the constitution ('ISCI Does Not' 2009, p. 2; Spain's *El Mundo* 2009, p. 7). What he neglected to mention was that not only had ISCI been the central advocate of Shia federalism but also that it was because of ISCI's demands that it had made it into the constitution in the first place. Indeed, Al-Hakim was very cagey in several interviews when he is asked to clarify his actual position on federalism in the south ('Reuters Interviews Sayed' 2009, p. 5). In one instance he goes as far as stating that:

> All the governorates or more could be a region where the idea of forming a provincial group of people involved in culture, deprivation, aspirations and religion. [S]o [it] was the perception of ISCI in the southern regions that are involved in a unified culture that [they could] ... be eligible to participate in one region, [but] it is simply a proposal to the Iraqi people and [we stand by] what they choose.
>
> ('Spain's *El Mundo*' 2009, p. 7)

However, in 2009 ISCI had to further distance itself from its separatist agenda as the various Shia political entities re-ignited negotiations and formed a new coalition ahead of the 2010 national elections. This bloc was to be known as the National Iraqi Alliance (NIA), headed by former Iraqi Prime Minister, Al-Jaafari, and made up of ISCI, Badr, the Sadrists and other smaller political entities. This was quite an uneasy alliance, particularly given that ISCI and the Sadrists had clashed violently only the year before. Perhaps because of such divisions or because of their waning popularity, the NIA did not fare well in the elections with 70 (of 325) seats, only 18 of which went to ISCI (*Republic of Iraq: Legislative Election* 2010). However, none of Iraq's major coalitions had won the 163 seats needed to form a government in the 325-member parliament.

This meant that the various blocks and their constituent political parties would have to cobble together a coalition government. This saw the nation plummet into nine months of political stalemate before the deadlock was finally resolved in early November when an agreement was signed which would pave the way for the formation of a government. The new Iraqi government was announced in December of 2010 and much remained the same: Maliki would retain the position of Prime Minister (and actually extend his portfolio out to include the powerful defense and interior ministries); Mahdi would stay on as Vice President (before resigning in 2011); and many other key positions would rotate between a handful of familiar faces (Ottaway and Kaysi 2010). While ISCI did retain several prominent positions, its power and influence had been severely reduced. Also, no doubt due to its poor performance in the polls and its waning influence, the political stalemate of 2010 saw ISCI largely sideline its secessionist agenda. Instead, it advocated the need for a new unity government of national partnerships realizing that they needed to negotiate if they had any hope of retaining power. Tellingly, just days after the election, Al-Hakim argued in favour of an

> Iraq for all Iraqis ... we're the owners of the theory of real partnership. [I]n the campaign we stepped beyond the prospects of votes and we do not accept the principle of a political majority. We want a government of national partnership, were everyone participates, from all nationalities and affiliations, and it's not in the interest of Iraq to have a Shiite government. Iraq's interest is to have an Iraqi national government.
> ('Sayeed Al-Hakim Interview' 2010, p. 7)

In December 2010, as Maliki was announcing his new government in Baghdad, the earliest rumblings of the Arab Revolutions were beginning to send shockwaves out across the region (Isakhan *et al.* 2012). As long-lasting and deeply entrenched regimes fell across the region, Iraqis were confronted with the failures of their own democracy to deliver on the many promises made to them since 2003. This led to weeks of scattered protests across Iraq, culminating in the 'Day of Rage' (February 25 2011) in which thousands of protestors took to the streets in at least 17 separate demonstrations across the country following

Friday prayers. Unfortunately, Maliki reacted to these protests in ways similar to autocrats across the region: a potent cocktail of brutal suppression and modest political and economic concessions. This further exposed the increasingly authoritarian and violent nature of Maliki's government and its ever-shrinking support base among the Iraqi people. This provided ISCI with yet another opportunity to emphasize its 'silver-bullet' solution for Iraq's many complicated problems: decentralization and autonomy for the south. This time dressed up in the clothes of a National Initiative 'to reform the situation in the country' and move beyond 'the history of political and partisan interests' ('ISCI's National Initiative' 2011, p. 1) in March 2011 Al-Hakim called for the 'promotion of a decentralization administrative principle and the development of the laws in order to achieve true decentralization in the provinces. This would distribute the burden among the ministries and facilitates the task of accomplishing the people's issues' (ISCI's National Initiative 2011, p. 5).

This theme was reiterated several times throughout 2011 by ISCI in its publications ('Accumulation of Political' 2011, p. 5; 'ISCI Political Positions' 2011, p. 9; 'The Political Arena' 2011, p. 5). Tellingly, in July 2011 *The ISCI Bulletin* published an article entitled 'The Challenges of the Political Arena.' Challenge number one, according to ISCI, was the issue of federalism. In a thinly veiled critique of the Maliki government, it insinuated that it was yet another example of 'strong iron fisted central rule.' ISCI warned that such a system had historically created a 'pattern of unfair and oppressive regimes that exposed the national unity of Iraq to great dangers.' Such 'totalitarian' governments have also led to 'the arbitrary exclusion and long marginalisation of the majority population of Iraq,' the Shia Arabs. For ISCI such a situation creates a 'need to remove these types of unfair regimes that ruled Iraq and their damaging effects' and that they be replaced by 'the right of any one provinces or more to form a region based on a request for a referendum ... according to the regulations of the Iraqi constitution.' This would not only serve to 'protect the national unity considering that the Iraqi people consist of ethnic and sectarian and religious components' but would also 'reduce the influence of extreme centralization.' For ISCI the position is clear: 'Extreme centralization produces only dictatorship and totalitarian parties. Because federalism prevents partition, centralism encourages it' ('The Challenges of the Political Arena' 2011, p. 6). ISCI's motivation for such strong words is also clear: it has long desired to rule over an independent or autonomous Shia Islamic state in the south of Iraq.

Conclusion

The prospects of ISCI successfully achieving its goal of creating a Shia Islamic state in the south of Iraq are low. ISCI does not have a great deal of power or support and most of Iraq's Shia political elite see that they have more to gain from being included in a Shia-dominated central government than they would an independent state. However, this is a critical and unpredictable time in Iraqi history. The protracted political impasse of 2010, recent escalations in violence, the withdrawal of all US troops at the end of 2011 and the Arab Revolutions have all led to an Iraqi populace that is increasingly disillusioned about the efficacy of the US imposed model of democracy and its ability to meet their many urgent needs. Separatism (in the form of independence or at least autonomy) may yet emerge as a credible alternative for the Shia, especially if they were to lose power in Baghdad while watching the relative prosperity and stability of the Kurdish north. Indeed, if the various Shia political elite rallied behind the notion of Shia separatism, perhaps under ISCI leadership, a credible secessionist movement may yet emerge. They certainly meet many of the necessary criteria: the Shia Arabs have the resources (oil), relative degrees of homogeneity (Shia Arab), the means (both militarily and bureaucratically), legitimate historical grievances (against the Baath) and a strong ally (Iran). All of this raises serious concerns about the future of Iraq and points to the tensions between imposing a democracy by force and the realpolitik of the region.

Note

1 The author would like to acknowledge the research assistance and translation skills of an anonymous Iraqi colleague and friend.

References

'Accumulation of Political Crises/Absence of Solutions' 2011, *The ISCI Bulletin*, vol. 4, no. 14, pp. 1, 5–6.
Al-Hakim, MB 2001, 'Statement by Ayatollah Mohammed Baqir Al-Hakim,' in J Ehrenberg, JP McSherry, JR Sanchez and CM Sayej (eds), *The Iraq Papers*, Oxford University Press, Oxford, pp. 318–319.
'Ayatollah Al-Sistani's Decree' 2003, *The SCIRI Bulletin*, vol. 1, no. 1, p. 3.
Baram, A 1998, *Building Toward Crisis: Saddam Husayn's Strategy for Survival*, The Washington Institute for Near East Policy, Washington, DC.
Baram, A, Rohde, A and Ronen, Z (eds) 2010, *Iraq Between Occupations: Perspectives from 1920 to the Present*, Palgrave Macmillan, New York.
Batatu, H 1986, 'Shi'i Organizations in Iraq: Al-Da'wah Al-Islamiyah and Al-Mujahidin,' in JRI Cole and NR Keddie (eds), *Shi'ism and Social Protest*, Yale University Press, New Haven, pp. 179–200.
'The Challenges of the Political Arena' 2011, *The ISCI Bulletin*, vol. 4, no. 13, pp. 6–7.
Davis, E 2004, 'Democracy's Prospects in Iraq,' *Foreign Policy Research Institute E-Notes*, June, pp. 1–3.
Davis, E 2007, 'The Formation of Political Identities in Ethnically Divided Societies: Implications for a Democratic Transition in Iraq,' *The American Academic Research Institute in Iraq Newsletter*, vol. 2, no. 1, pp. 3–4.
Dawisha, A 2009, *Iraq: A Political History from Independence to Occupation*, Princeton University Press, Princeton, NJ.
Dawisha, A and Diamond, LJ 2006, 'Electoral Systems Today: Iraq's Year of Voting Dangerously,' *Journal of Democracy*, vol. 17, no. 2, pp. 89–103.
Duss, M and Juul, P 2009, *The Fractured Shia of Iraq: Understanding the Tensions within Iraq's Majority*, Centre for American Progress, Washington, DC.

Ehrenberg, J, McSherry, JP, Sanchez, JR and Sayej, CM (eds) 2010, *The Iraq Papers*, Oxford University Press, Oxford.
'H.E. Al-Hakim Congratulates the Muslim World for Eid Al-Adha' 2008, *The ISCI Bulletin*, vol. 2, no. 1, p. 1.
Isakhan, B 2008, 'The Post-Saddam Iraqi Media: Reporting the Democratic Developments of 2005,' *Global Media Journal*, vol. 7, no. 13, pp. 1–25.
Isakhan, B 2011, 'The Streets of Iraq: Protests and Democracy after Saddam,' in B Isakhan and S Stockwell (eds), *The Secret History of Democracy*, Palgrave Macmillan, London, pp. 191–203.
Isakhan, B 2012, *Democracy in Iraq: History, Politics and Discourse*, Ashgate, London.
Isakhan, B 2014, 'Protests and Public Power in Post-Saddam Iraq: The Case of the Iraqi Federation of Oil Unions,' in L Anceschi, G Gervasio and A Teti (eds) *Informal Powers in the Greater Middle East: Hidden Geographies*, Routledge, London, pp. 117–128.
Isakhan, B, Mansouri, F and Akbarzadeh, S (eds) 2012, *The Arab Revolutions in Context: Civil Society and Democracy in a Changing Middle East*, Melbourne University Press, Melbourne.
'ISCI Does Not Seek to Weaken PM Al-Maliki' 2009, *The ISCI Bulletin*, vol. 2, no. 4, pp. 1–2.
'ISCI Political Positions' 2011, *The ISCI Bulletin*, vol. 4, no. 9, pp. 8–9.
'ISCI Tenth Conference: Final Statement' 2009, *The ISCI Bulletin*, vol. 2, no. 13, pp. 3–6.
'ISCI Unanimously Elects Sayed Ammar Al-Hakim' 2009, *The ISCI Bulletin*, vol. 2, no. 11, p. 5.
'ISCI's National Initiative' 2011, *The ISCI Bulletin*, vol. 4, no. 5, pp. 1–5.
'Islam and Democracy' 2003a, *The SCIRI Bulletin*, vol. 1, no. 3, pp. 2–3.
'Islam and Democracy' 2003b, *The SCIRI Bulletin*, vol. 1, no. 4, p. 2.
Jervis, R 2003, 'Understanding the Bush Doctrine,' *Political Science Quarterly*, vol. 118, no. 3, pp. 365–388.
Katzman, K 2010, *Iraq: Politics, Elections, and Benchmarks*, Congressional Research Services Report for Congress, Washington, DC.
Little, D and Swearer, DK (eds) 2006, *Religion and Nationalism in Iraq: A Comparative Perspective*, Harvard University Press, Cambridge, MA.
Londono, E 2010, 'Shiite Blok Suspends Talks, Undermining Maliki's Chances to Remain Iraq's Leader,' *Washington Post*, August 2.
Maad Fayadh Interviews Ammar Al-Hakim 2007, *Al-Furat*, October 22.
McDowell, D 2000, *A Modern History of the Kurds*, 2nd edn, I.B. Tauris, London.
Munsoon, PJ 2009, *Iraq in Transition: The Legacy of Dictatorship and the Prospects for Democracy*, Potomac, Washington, DC.
Nakash, Y 2003, *The Shi'is of Iraq*, Princeton University Press, Princeton, NJ.
Ottaway, M and Kaysi, D 2010, 'Iraq's Long Road to a Government,' *Carnegie Endowment for International Peace*, Washington, DC.
'The Political Arena and Chronic Intersections' 2011, *The ISCI Bulletin*, vol. 4, no. 15, pp. 4–5.
Radhi, AM 2006, Speech at the Imam Hussein shrine, Al-Hakim, *Buratha News*, March 21.
Republic of Iraq: Legislative Election of 7 March 2010, Independent High Electoral Commission of Iraq, The Majlis.
'Reuters Interviews Sayed Ammar Alhakim' 2009, *The ISCI Bulletin*, vol. 2, no. 12, pp. 4–6.

Romano, D 2006, *The Kurdish Nationalist Movement: Opportunity, Mobilisation and Identity*, Cambridge University Press, Cambridge, UK.

Sadiki, L 2012, 'Islam,' in B Isakhan and S Stockwell (eds), *The Edinburgh Companion to the History of Democracy*, Edinburgh University Press, Edinburgh, pp. 121–130.

Sayeed Al-Hakim Interview with Al-Jazeera 2010, *The ISCI Bulletin*, vol. 3, no. 2, pp. 4–7.

Sluglett, P 2010, 'Common Sense, or a Step Pregnant with Enormous Consequences: Some Thoughts on the Possible Secession of Iraqi Kurdistan,' in DH Doyle (ed.), *Secession as an International Phenomenon: From America's Civil War to Contemporary Separatist Movements*, University of Georgia Press, Athens, GA, pp. 319–337.

Sluglett, P 2011, 'Kurdistan: A Suspended Secession from Iraq,' in A Pavković and P Radan (eds), *The Ashgate Research Companion to Secession*, Ashgate, London, pp. 539–541.

'Spain's *El Mundo* Interviews H.E. Ammar Alhakim' 2009, *The ISCI Bulletin*, vol. 2, no. 9, pp. 6–8.

Stansfield, G 2007, *Iraq: People, History, Politics*, Polity, Cambridge, UK.

The text of Sayed Al-Hakim's speech before the crowds in holy Kerbala 2007, *Al-Furat*, March 9.

Visser, R 2004, 'Shia Perspectives on a Federal Iraq: Territory, Community and Ideology in Conceptions of a New Polity,' in D Heradstveit and H Hveem (eds), *Oil in the Gulf: Obstacles to Democracy and Development*, Ashgate, Aldershot, pp. 125–166.

Visser, R 2005, *Basra, the Failed Gulf State: Separatism and Nationalism in Southern Iraq*, Lit Verlag, Münster.

Visser, R 2007, 'Ethnicity, Federalism and the Idea of Sectarian Citizenship in Iraq: A Critique,' *International Review of the Red Cross*, vol. 89, no. 868, pp. 809–822.

Visser, R 2008a, 'Introduction,' in R Visser and G Stansfield (eds), *An Iraq of Its Regions: Cornerstones of a Federal Democracy?*, Columbia University Press, New York, pp. 1–26.

Visser, R 2008b, 'The Two Regions of Southern Iraq,' in R Visser and G Stansfield (eds), *An Iraq of Its Regions: Cornerstones of a Federal Democracy?*, Columbia University Press, New York, pp. 27–51.

Visser, R and Stansfield, G (eds) 2008, *An Iraq of Its Regions: Cornerstones of a Federal Democracy?*, Columbia University Press, New York.

10 Secessionist aspects to the Buddhist–Muslim conflict in Rakhine State, Myanmar

Anthony Ware

Introduction

In June 2012, long-simmering Buddhist–Muslim tensions in Rakhine State, Myanmar, erupted into violence. The trigger this time was the rape and murder of a Buddhist girl by Muslim men. A Buddhist mob responded, seeking to take justice into their own hands, demanding police hand over the accused. While the police refused, another Buddhist mob soon thereafter attacked and killed Muslim pilgrims traveling on a bus, inflaming the ire and fears of the Muslim population. Rumors and recriminations spread quickly on both sides, requiring a curfew and state of emergency to contain the unrest. Order was eventually restored, but a second wave of attacks erupted in October, in multiple areas across Rakhine State. This time, though, most attacks were directed against Muslims, and appeared to be well-coordinated and well-planned (ICG 2013).

Buddhist–Muslim violence is nothing new in Myanmar, especially in this part of the country. However, this outbreak was particularly destructive, with official government figures showing 192 dead and 265 injured across 11 townships, and 8,614 homes plus almost 2,000 public buildings razed (UoM 2013). While the statistics show the death and injury toll was relatively evenly split between the two communities, over 86 percent of the houses destroyed were owned by Muslims, making Muslims the vast majority of the 140,000 people displaced by the conflict (UNOCHA 2013). Reports of violence have substantially decreased since then, with the exception of a flare-up connected with the April 2014 census, nonetheless, tensions remain high across the state and many regions are even now under curfew.

These clashes have most of the hallmarks of sectarian or communal violence, and were largely characterized as such in the ensuing political analysis. International commentary, in particular, characterized this as communal violence between Rakhine Buddhists and 'Rohingya' Muslims, the latter depicted as a minority ethnic group oppressed by a local Buddhist majority (the Rakhine), who were presented as being closely aligned with the national Buddhist majority (the Burmans) and supported by the Burmese military. In the process of highlighting the human rights situation of the 800,000 or so Rohingya, therefore, an international discourse emerged which conflated the history of the military government's human rights abuses with the actions of Rakhine against Rohingya. As a result, most international analysis has approached the conflict primarily in terms of the human rights and/or citizenship issues faced by the Rohingya. While these are major contributing factors, what is missed in most commentary is that this violence was a response to moves by the military government to grant citizenship to many 'Rohingya' in the lead up to the 2010 elections, in a move to gain support and thus weaken the electoral result of nationalist Rakhine Buddhists.

For these reasons, this chapter suggests that nationalist, even secessionist, aspects must be included in the analysis of this conflict. This is a very complex scenario driven by highly contested historical narratives and competing territorial claims. This chapter, therefore, explores these nationalist and secessionist aspects from a long, historical perspective, examining contested versions of the history of the region and their competing historical separatist claims, as well as the role these narratives play in sustaining the contemporary conflict.

It is widely theorized that a comprehensive military victory is one of the more likely routes to peace after separatist conflict (Chapter 4, this volume). The Myanmar government achieved a relatively secure victory over multiple separatist armies in the region more than five decades ago, which has been fairly comprehensively reinforced over the past two decades. Nonetheless, the underlying issues remain and the conflict continues. This chapter argues that the long subjugation of both protagonists under authoritarian Burmese military rule suppressed both the expression of and renegotiation of group identities, preventing resolution of the underlying grievances and perpetuating the long-standing structural violence. The transitional environment of the past couple of years, then, has created a context within which the long suppressed nationalist, extremist, sectarian and secessionist aspirations have been able to not only resurface, but in many cases even deepen. This chapter argues that the suppression, rather than resolution, of group grievances and rival territorial claims allowed the central government's military victory in the secessionist war to morph into communal, sectarian violence that continues to be driven by nationalistic, separatist-based fears and aspirations. Armed militant groups may have been contained and leaders removed, but both populations are still driven by the narratives of separatism. In response, it is argued, an entirely different, negotiated approach to peaceful reconciliation is required.

The remainder of this chapter is divided into three sections. The first provides a historical survey of the protagonists and conflict from ancient to recent times, culminating in competing secessionist claims for overlapping territory after the bitter violence of World War II and the continued rival self-determination struggles ever since. The second section provides an analytical discussion of the key narratives driving the contemporary violence, and the emergence of a 'double minority complex' in which, seen from a national/international and social-psychological perspective, both the majority Rakhine and the minority Rohingya feel as if they are threatened minorities struggling for their very survival. This section thus analyzes the competing narratives used by both sides from the perspective of separatist versus communal underpinnings, challenging the historicity and utility of both Rohingya claims to ethnicity as the basis of group rights and Rakhine narratives that the Rohingya are illegal immigrants and their identity is inherently separatist and jihadist. Implications are drawn on the transition between separatist and communal conflict in the context of external military suppression rather than resolution. The final section concludes with thoughts about alternative approaches required for a peaceful resolution to this conflict.

Historical development of competing narratives

Myanmar has been plagued by separatist insurgency and ethnic conflict since independence in 1948, claiming an estimated million casualties (Steinberg 2010). Despite ongoing attempts at a national ceasefire and some positive negotiations, 52 armed ethnic groups remain in place across the country (MPM 2014), with insurgent groups in Rakhine State including the nationalist Rakhine Arakan Liberation Army and the Rohingya Solidarity Organisation still recently active. While there is a strong post-colonial separatist character to all insurgency in Myanmar, what makes the Rakhine State Buddhist–Muslim violence distinctive is the 'double minority complex' overlay, with communal conflict related strongly to identities built on the competing historical narratives and territorial claims underlying the separatist causes.

Early history: Buddhist–Muslim co-existence

Arakan (Rakhine) was relatively independent of the Burmese empire until shortly before the colonial era, with trade and conquest bringing significant Muslim (and Hindu) influence and a substantial Muslim population to live alongside the dominant Buddhist people. Buddhist and Muslim identities, however, became increasingly polarized during the colonial era, as manifest in extreme communal violence during World War II, and in competing separatist struggles after independence, making the modern Buddhist and Muslim identities markedly different from those in pre-colonial times. The long-running insurgencies competing for territorial control over regions make a purely communal analysis of recent violence in Rakhine State insufficient. The following section explores the development of this polarization within the two communities, and the competing historical narratives used to justify the competing separatist claims.

Maritime trade and interaction between Arakan and Bengal date to the second and third centuries, well before the migration of the Rakhine (Arakanese) people into the region in the tenth century (Gutman 1976, 2001). The first confirmed Muslim settlements have long been dated to the founding of the Arakanese kingdom at Mrauk-U in AD 1430, when it was claimed the founder of the main dynasty regained the throne with military assistance from Bengal (where he had been exiled), who then stayed (Leider 2002; Yegar 1972). Recent scholarship, however, suggest this story is more legend than historical fact (Leider 2014a). Some accounts propose earlier settlements, and certainly Arab and Persian traders visited the area from the ninth century, so some resident Muslims in Arakan before Mrauk-U is not an unreasonable assumption (Yegar 1972).

The Mrauk-U kingdom, which began as a small agrarian vassal to Bengal, grew into a significant regional power by the early seventeenth century, which asserted influence across the Bay of Bengal (van Galen 2008). The expansion then disintegration of the kingdom was closely connected to its degree of control over south-eastern Bengal, and commercial and cultural ties with Chittagong, in particular, played a central role in Mrauk-U's history as a counterbalance to the growing power of the Burmese court at Ava (Charney 1998a, 1998b, 1999; Leider 2002; van Galen 2008; Yegar 1972). As van Galen (2008) expressed it, an 'Arakan-Bengal continuum' existed around the Bay of Bengal, both economically and culturally. The Arakanese rulers at Mrauk-U, with their dominance over Chittagong from the middle of the sixteenth century until 1766, adopted concurrent syncretic Muslim and Buddhist identities to draw on both sources of legitimacy, in what Charney (1999, p. 399) suggests is 'the Arakanese royal court's long-term indifference to the religious identities.'

A considerable Muslim minority thus developed in northern Arakan before the British took control. Most were slaves or the descendants of slaves captured by Mrauk-U (Smart 1917), or by the Portuguese and on-sold to Arakan (Yegar 1972):

> During Mrauk U's golden age in the seventeenth century, Chittagong was an economic pillar of the kingdom and Muslims formed a large part of the king's subjects and Muslim traders competed with Portuguese and Dutch traders. When Bengal fell into the hands of the Mughals in 1567, soldiers who had fought against the Mughals apparently took service at the court of Rakhine.
>
> (Leider 2014b, p. 223)

Charney (1999, p. 165) estimates at least 60,000 Bengalis were brought to live in northern Arakan by the end of the seventeenth century, possibly 30 percent of the total population, but this now appears a massive overestimate (Leider 2014a). This Muslim community appears to have maintained a distinct heritage and identity within the majority Buddhist environment, and there is little evidence of significant inter-religious tension between Buddhists and Muslims (Charney 1999; Tin Maung Maung Than and Moe Thuzar 2012).

Changing relations under Burmese and British conquests

Mrauk-U fell to the Burmese in 1784. The regional destabilization and insecurity during the waning of the kingdom, followed by the brutality of the Burmese conquest itself, resulted in a significant depopulation of Arakan, with a high death toll, a very large number of captives taken back to Ava and a mass exodus of refugees into British Bengal (Charney 1999; Leider 2002). There are claims the Burmese particularly targeted violence against Muslims and Hindus, fueling the exodus, including destruction of non-Buddhist religious structures and missionizing efforts towards all who remained (Charney 1999; Siddiqui 2012a, 2012c). Together with the Burmese invasion of Manipur, it was the stories of perhaps 40,000 refugees, who stayed in Bengal for a generation, that prompted the British invasion in the First Anglo-Burmese War of 1824–6 (Charney 1999; Harvey 1925; Tin Maung Maung Than and Moe Thuzar 2012). By the time of the British occupation, much of northern Arakan was sparsely populated despite widespread availability of high-yield paddy fields, an 'underpopulated agricultural frontier' (Charney 1999, p. 6; Yegar 2002).

After annexation in 1826, the colonial administration heavily promoted migration to develop agriculture in the sparsely-populated region. Arakan quickly became one of the most prosperous areas of Burma (Smith 1994), and high wages attracted both seasonal labor and economic migrants. Aye Chan (2005) argues that one of the underlying reasons for anti-Muslim resentment in Arakan was that the British administration granted 99-year leases to newly immigrated Bengalis, and when many of the Arakanese peasants returned they were deprived of the land that they formerly owned through inheritance. Charney (1999) argues that this time period was the point at which religious communalism most notably developed, both Buddhist and Muslim, in the competition between returnees and migrants, from Bengal and other parts of Burma, as the region was rapidly repopulated. In the absence of the traditional patron–client structures and established rural gentry, he suggests, people constructed new communal identities around religious leaders and spaces. In this sense, the emergence of the modern Rakhine Buddhist identity and what became the 'Rohingya' identity occurred concurrently and interdependently, such that 'one cannot talk of the emergence of [one without the other]' (Charney 1999, p. 13).

Chittagonian migrants concentrated in Akyab District (northern Arakan) and quickly became the dominant group in many areas, growing from 10 percent of the district in the 1869 census to 30 percent in the 1912 census, and 33 percent by 1931 (Baxter 1941; Leider 2014b; Smart 1917; Yegar 2002). In this massive wave of immigration, most of the ethnically-diverse original local Muslim population was 'absorbed by the newly immigrant Chittagonian Bengalis ... fundamentally transform[ing] the profile of the Muslim population in northern Rakhine ... [while] the Buddhist Rakhine were largely eradicated from the north of Akyab Division' (Leider 2014b, pp. 229, 231). By the end of the colonial era there were some Muslim communities who had maintained a distinct identity since pre-colonial times, such as the Kamans of Ramree Island and Myedus identified in the 1931 census (Tonkin 2014c), but the majority appear to have been absorbed into a melting pot of Chittagonian-Bengali immigrants and pre-colonial Muslim communities in northern Arakan, who adopted the history of the longer-established local Muslims as their own (Leider 2014b; Tonkin 2014a, 2014b, 2014c). The *Report on Indian Immigration* (Baxter 1941, p. 51) expressed concern that the high rate of Muslim migration into the region was problematic and 'contained the seed of future communal troubles.' Murray (1949, p. 2) likewise expressed concern at the long-term implications of '[Muslim immigrants] gradually displacing and over-running the Arakanese.'

Communal violence and separatist claims at independence

World War II marked a major turning point in Buddhist–Muslim relations. As the Rangoon British administration collapsed and the Allies beat a hasty retreat, the Arakan National Army (ANA) was formed by politically active Buddhist monks aligned with Aung San's Burma Independence Army (BIA), and hastily took control of most of Arakan until the Japanese arrived. Meanwhile, the BIA/ANA chased an estimated 500,000 colonial officials and sympathizers overland out of Burma, through Arakan (Smith 1994), while the British recruited Chittagonian volunteers into a 'V Force' to undertake guerrilla operations against the Japanese (Murray 1949, 1980). Naturally, such a confluence of nationalist Rakhine mobilization on the one side of the war and a Muslim mobilization on the other rapidly escalated tensions. There is a sense, therefore, in which the Rakhine Buddhists and Muslims became proxies of World War II powers.

The Japanese advanced to Akyab in May, but did not move north until October:

> in the meantime, the area of mixed population was the scene of repeated large-scale massacres in which thousands of people perished or died subsequently of starvation and exposure. Eventually the two communities separated into distinct areas, the Arakanese in the south supporting the Japanese and the Chittagongians in the north supporting the British. The area was a battleground for the next two years, and was thoroughly devastated by either side.
>
> (Murray 1949)

British officials in Arakan at the time, Murray (1949, 1980) and Mole (2001), attest to the almost complete segregation, as each community fled the anarchy and violence: Muslims to the north and Buddhists to the south. As Leider (2014, p. 16) notes, the violence 'created wounds that never healed and cemented the division between the Buddhist and Muslim communities in northern Rakhine,' reinforcing ideas that crystallized not only a strongly nationalist Rakhine identity, but also a nationalistic sense of shared identity amongst the Muslims, an identity which came to be described as 'Rohingya.' We will return to a discussion of the origins of this name and identity in the next section, but suffice to say that it does not appear to have been widely used before independence (Leider 2014b). Murray and Mole both note that during the war there was a good deal of talk about transferring the Muslim areas of North Arakan to the Chittagong Division of India, to become part of the future state of Pakistan rather than Burma. Both discount that this was ever seriously offered by the British, but the idea appears to have resonated. Mole claims an early map by Mohammed Ali Jinnah, architect of Pakistan's independence, included north Arakan in what is now Bangladesh.

Neither side was willing to surrender weapons at the end of the war (Smith 1994). Instead, a Muslim group calling themselves 'Mujahids' launched a separatist rebellion in 1946, two years before independence, then in April 1947, after the Aung San–Attlee Agreement had been signed granting Independence (but still nine months before it came into effect) a Rakhine nationalist rebellion seeking an independent Arakan began in concert with the Communist Party of Burma, the first of multiple major rebellions against the government (Smith 2007a; Tin Maung Maung Than and Moe Thuzar 2012). Thus, before independence both Rohingya and Rakhine separatist armies had rebelled in Arakan, both fighting for independence from the central government for competing territorial claims, the Rohingya fighting for north Arakan and the Rakhine nationalists fighting for the whole of Arakan, in addition to the multiple Rakhine communist groups. Serious instability continued until 1954, and each army had significant sympathy from both Muslim and Rakhine communities. By 1949 government control of the region was reduced to just Akyab (Sittwe) city (Murray 1949; Smith 1999; Yegar 2002).

The main Mujahedeen rebellion was militarily defeated in 1954, and the Rakhine nationalists were also significantly weakened during the 1950s. Nonetheless, a plethora of smaller armed separatist groups continued to emerge on both sides until insurgent action in Rakhine State virtually collapsed in the mid-1990s, in the face of sustained government operations. The military has conducted at least 13 major armed operations against the Rohingyas alone since 1948 (Selth 2004). In the face of defeat some Rakhine forces relocated to join Kachin and Karen rebel groups, while the remaining Rakhine and Rohingya forces moved across the Bangladeshi border (Smith 2007b). Since 2005 the Bangladesh authorities have also actively sought to contain both Muslim and Rakhine cross-border insurgency, resulting in virtually no rebel activity in Rakhine State for some years.

By the 2008, the remaining Rakhine nationalist groups were the Arakan Liberation Army (ALA, aligned with the Arakan Liberation Party) and the Arakan Army (AA, aligned with the National United Party of Arakan) (Smith 1999; South 2008). The ALA fought from 1968 until signing a ceasefire with the government in 2012. They still maintain four military camps with headquarters on the Indian border. The AA remain a combatant group, with troops currently fighting in Kachin State (BNI 2014). Both Rakhine armies joined the Arakan National Council in 2004, which espouses 'self-determination for the multi-ethnic Rakhine population' and 'peaceful co-existence' (BNI 2014), and have thus now changed much of their written documentation to reflect this more inclusive idea of Rakhine autonomy. However, the ALA were implicated in the coordinated October 2012 'communal' violence (ICG 2013), suggesting they have not all left ethno-nationalist ideas behind.

On the Rohingya side, the remaining militant groups were the Rohingya Solidarity Organisation (RSO) and the Arakan Rohingya National Organisation (ARNO) (Smith 1999; South 2008). The Rohingya Independence Force (RIF) was created in 1963, a decade after the collapse of the Mujahedeen rebellion, to re-ignite the fight for an 'independent Rakhine State' (Leider 2014b; Selth 2004; Smith 2007b). After the Rohingya were denied a state in the 1974 constitution, the RIF transitioned into the Rohingya Patriotic Front and launched new offensives.

The military, in response, used the 1978 census to launch massive military operations targeting 'illegal Bengali Muslims,' checking all identity cards (as the 1948 Union Citizenship Act had only provided citizenship for migrants whose families arrived before 1823). Over 200,000 Muslims fled into Bangladesh (Smith 1994, 2007b), provoking international outrage and the formation of new splinter groups, the Rohingya Solidarity Organisation and Arakan Rohingya Islamic Front, on the Bangladesh side of the border.

After the failed 1988 democracy uprising, the RSO and ARNO became increasingly active, although armed action was still extremely limited (Smith 1994). Nonetheless, this prompted major military operations, which led to another massive dislocation of some 260,000 Muslims into Bangladesh in 1991–2 (Smith 2007a), many of whom remain. By 2007 around 28,000 Rohingya refugees were still officially registered in UNHCR camps, with estimates 100,000–200,000 live illegally in Bangladesh (South 2008), figures virtually unchanged in 2014 (UNHCR 2014). Today, the Rohingya militants may still have a few camps near the Bangladesh–Myanmar border, but they have not been militarily active for some years (Bashar 2012; Smith 2007a; Vrieze 2013), and ARNO is now a London-based advocacy organization seeking 'the right of self-determination of the Rohingya people within the Burmese federation' (ARNO 2013b).

This historical survey of the protagonists and conflict has been deliberately detailed, to highlight the protracted nature of the issues and the complex secessionist aspects inherent in the rival territorial claims. The communal aspects to this conflict are obvious enough. However, the communities have become essentially segregated, all the more as security forces have separated communities to contain the most recent violence, and both harbor fears for their very survival in the face of the other. To ignore the recourse to armed separatist struggle over territory, self-determination and sheer survival by both sides is to overlook key dynamics of the conflict.

Analytical discussion: 'double minority complex' narratives

Michael (2007, 2011) coined the term 'double minority complex' to describe situations like the Sri Lanka, Northern Ireland, Israel–Palestine and Cyprus conflicts, in which, seen from a regional and social-psychological perspective, the majority in a country or region feel as if they are a threatened minority competing for territorial survival and nationalistic autonomy, locked in a deadly struggle with a local minority closely linked and (probably) supported by a powerful neighbor. This, he argues, creates a '*double (in)security* dilemma preoccupying both communities,' which requires accurate mapping of power relations and defies simplistic symmetrical-asymmetrical analysis (Michael 2011, p. 212, emphasis in the original). He uses this concept to analyze the competition between the Turkish Cypriot and the Greek Cypriot communities within the sub-regional context, arguing that: 'heightened insecurity created a defensive mindset that, in the absence of political dialogue, permeated throughout the social fabric of both communities ... [and] led to militarization that, coupled with hardening political rhetoric, contributed to the rise of ethno-nationalism' (Michael 2011, p. 148).

This analysis is particularly apt for the Rakhine Buddhist–Rohingya Muslim conflict in Myanmar. On one side, the Rohingya are a vulnerable minority whose rights have been significantly violated by both the Rakhine and the military-led Burman central government. The 'Rohingya' identity is underpinned by intense insecurity and extreme defensiveness forging a nationalistic sense of shared identity out of what even staunchly nationalist Rohingya authors agree was originally an ethnically diverse community of Muslims in Arakan,[1] in the sense of Anderson's (1983) *Imagined Communities*. One the other side, the Rakhine are also equally preoccupied with feelings of vulnerability and insecurity, stemming from Burman military-led rule over their state and demographic pressures from migration and neighboring one of the world's highest population densities. This feeling of being a threatened minority fighting for survival is often ignored, but should not be surprising after mass migration from Bengal and external colonial control for over two centuries, first by the British then by the Burmese. As Kyaw San Wai (2014, p. 2) argues, the Rakhine are reacting from a 'siege mentality' created by feelings of religious and territorial encroachment by their Muslim neighbors, 'acute sense of political, cultural, historical, economic, demographic and religious besiegement from the Bamar (main ethnic group in Myanmar)' and, more recently, perception that the international community ignore their concerns in preference for 'over-sensationalised propaganda' about the plight of Rohingya (ARDHO 2013).

Competing narratives: 'Rohingya' origins, ethnicity and intentions

Flowing from this mutual insecurity preoccupation are two conflicting, highly nationalistic narratives which drive this conflict, which are primarily about the origins, identity and place in history of the Rohingya, and thus their ability to claim group rights to territory and self-determination. This chapter challenges the historicity and utility of both narratives.

The Rohingya version argues Muslims settled in Arakan at a very early date, and that the level of Muslim influence in the Mrauk-U kingdom shows it to have been a principally Muslim kingdom, with Muslim rulers and some Rakhine subjects, until it was conquered by the Burmese Buddhists in 1784 (Islam, N, 2011; Islam, SS, 2007; Siddiqui, 2012a, 2012b). More to the point, this narrative argues that mass migration did not occur during the British colonial period, just a return of Rohingya to their land and an influx of seasonal workers from Bengal who went home after harvest, and thus the Rohingya are a long-established ethnic group in the country with rights to territory and self-determination.

The Rakhine version of the same history argues that the Muslim population and influence in the region was minimal prior to mass immigration during the British era, and that the 'Rohingya' identity adopts the history of a minority of Muslims remaining from pre-colonial times as being the history of all later migrants (ARDHO 2013; Aye Chan 2005; Khin Maung Saw 2005, 2011; Shwe Zan 2005). This history argues the Rohingya are virtually all Bengali immigrants from the colonial era or later, with the more extreme nationalist histories going so far as to argue that the majority of the Rohingya are refugees from the Bangladesh civil war and other natural disasters arriving illegally in Myanmar since independence, and are part of a coordinated Islamization of Myanmar. Independent scholarship takes a middle view between these two extremes: it does not deny significant Muslim influence in Mrauk-U, yet does not see evidence of Muslim rulers or a Muslim majority; likewise it sees both a significant Muslim minority in pre-colonial Arakan, without denying mass migration during the colonial period (Charney 1999; Gutman 2001; Leider 2002; Selth 2004; van Galen 2008; Yegar 1972).

Within both of these two narratives, a lot of importance has been placed on the historicity of the identity label 'Rohingya' as an ethnicity, or otherwise, as the basis for granting or denying group rights. At the heart of this nineteenth-century idea about fixed ethnic identity is the fact that the 1948 and 1974 Burmese constitutions give implicit recognition of group rights for 'ethnic minorities,' particularly those large enough to have a state named after them, based on an underlying federal idea of ethnic states and centrally-administered Burman-majority divisions. Detailed examinations of this issue have been well summarized by Leider (2014) and Tonkin (2014a, 2014b, 2014c), who conclude that while there are some early references that use the term 'Rooinga,' early use of the word appears to be a Bengali-derived term referring to geographical origin rather than ethnicity, and thus synonymous with 'Arakan' or 'Rakhine.' Tonkin (2014c, p. 3) finds that, 'In the 122 years between their conquest of Arakan in 1826 and Burmese independence in 1948, not a single reference to "Rohingya" is to be found in any British official report, regional gazetteer, census, legislation, private correspondence or personal reminiscence.' Leider (2014, p. 206), likewise, contends that, 'from their modern origins in the 1950s, the Rohingyas are best defined as a political and militant movement as its foremost aim was the creation of an autonomous Muslim zone.' As such, they both conclude that the label 'Rohingya' is a 'post-Second World War political label [created] in support of their political objectives' (Tonkin 2014c, pp. 1, 3). None of this analysis will sit well with Rohingya nationalists, however, such analysis does not, and should not be used to deny their human rights, citizenship or group rights claims.

Laboring this point for just a moment longer, it should be noted that regular reports about contact between Rohingya and Muslim extremist groups feed extreme Rakhine narratives about Rohingya jihadist intent, a fear which underlies a lot of Rakhine nationalist-initiated conflict. Historically, the Mujahedeen rebellion had at least Pakistan's tolerance of cross-border tactics, and was widely believed to be receiving some level of international support from other jihadist Mujahedeen groups (Callahan 2004; Smith 2007b). Some suggest they were incited by clerics calling for a jihad against the 'infidels' (Tin Maung Maung Than and Moe Thuzar 2012), and that they carried a Pakistani flag or fought for an independent 'Arakanistan' (Khin Maung Saw 1993, 2011). A decade ago

Selth (2004) found evidence that the Rohingya had had some contact with al Qaeda, the Taliban and Wahabist groups in Bangladesh and in Libya, although he urged caution about interpreting anything about Rohingya community sentiment from the contact of a few individuals (Selth 2013). Nonetheless, reports of such contact continue to surface (for example, the report by Jain 2013; refuted by Vrieze 2013, see also report on BNI 2014, p. 19), and continue to drive the fears of a large number of Rakhine. As such, it is interesting that Burma News International report a meeting of both Muslim and Rakhine leaders on 2 December 2013, as part of the Rakhine Inquiry Commission, suggesting disusing the term 'Rohingya' as a conflict control measure (BNI 2014, p. 69).

Path forward? Negotiating rights, citizenship and political identity

As Laoutides in Chapter 4 of this volume has shown, whilst victories in civil conflicts might generally enhance the likelihood of a durable peace where this means loser has a low capacity to return to armed conflict, negotiated settlements involving devolution options short of independence have been more effective in separatist conflicts, particularly in democratic countries. Conversely, Laoutides (Chapter 4) finds that, 'strategies of physical extermination of opponents, such as ethnic cleansing or genocide, and mass abuse of human or minority rights are more likely to follow outright military victory than a negotiated settlement.'

As can be seen from the preceding history, the Burmese central government, now transitioning from authoritarianism towards a more democratic form of some description, has won a fairly decisive military victory over both Rakhine and Rohingya militants. In many regards it could also be considered that the Rakhine nationalists have now won many of their claims against the central Myanmar government, in two stages: 1974 and post-2010. In 1973 Ne Win's Revolutionary Council sought public opinion while drafting the 1974 Constitution; the Rakhine submission was granted, changing Arakan Division into Rakhine State and thereby implicitly recognizing some degree of Rakhine group rights, while the Rohingya submission for the creation of a northern Arakan state was dismissed (Aye Chan 2005). Then, in the 2010 election the Rakhine Nationalities Development Party won a majority of the elected seats in the new state parliament, with a devolution of some powers to the states as part of the national political transition begrudgingly giving them some power over the territory they have sought to control. They also won the second largest bloc of seats in the national 'House of Nationalities' upper house, giving them significant new influence which they have used to develop a 'Buddhist solidarity' lobby, with Buddhist monks and a segment of the Burman elite now in support of Rakhine Buddhists in claims against the Rohingya (ICG 2013).

However, in the absence of a negotiated settlement, this strengthened position still leaves the Rakhine feeling vulnerable, and the double victory by both Burmese military and Rakhine nationalists over the Rohingya has left them in a very weak and vulnerable position, as human rights advocacy reports document (AI 2004; HRW 2013). The Rakhine clearly continue to respond from a 'double minority complex' position, as if a threatened minority competing for sheer survival despite their improved position. The outpouring of violence in 2012 has been linked to the military-backed Union Solidarity and Development Party's attempts to grant citizenship to many of the Rohingya prior to the 2010 elections, as part of the strategy to try to limit Rakhine success in the polls (ICG 2013). This failed, clearly, but the vehemence of the Rakhine response to both this, and then to the plan to allow self-identification as 'Rohingya' on the April 2014 Census, highlights the continuation of a siege mentality, with some credible analysis that one of the Rakhine separatist groups was behind the coordinated October 2012 attacks (ICG 2013).

Most contemporary international approaches to supporting development and democratization during a political transition are built around the idea of state-building, which in turn assumes that all parties can be brought to recognize that they all belong to the same political community. The biggest key challenge in Rakhine State will continue to be the denial of citizenship to the Rohingya, preventing any opportunity for any such democratization and for any coordinated political negotiation. The 1982 Myanmar Citizenship Law is often blamed as a reason for the lack of citizenship. Certainly, as has already been noted, the 1948 Citizenship Law only allowed migrants whose ancestors arrived before 1823 to become citizens of the country. However, if it had been applied without active discrimination by local officials, under the 1982 law a majority of the Rohingya would have achieved full citizenship long ago (ICG 2013). While discriminating classes of associate, naturalized and full citizens, under the Law, descendants of people who migrated before independence in 1948 should become citizens within three generations, as successive generations move from being associate or naturalized citizens to full citizens. Only those who have migrated post-1948 would be excluded. The problem has been local regulations making birth and marriage registration difficult, time-consuming and costly, especially for the poor, and therefore restricting access to citizenship. Still, the ICG (2013) estimate that 70 percent of Rohingya do (or did) have sufficient proof of descent to be eligible for some form of national identity documents, if Rakhine narratives about Rohingya Islamist separatism did not drive fear and active discrimination. Somehow, citizenship must be allowed to proceed, but in a way that de-escalates Rakhine fears.

Conclusion

This chapter argues that military victory and suppression have failed to deliver peace to Rakhine State, instead perpetuating and accentuating the intense 'double minority complex' sense of being a threatened minority competing for sheer survival in both Rakhine and Rohingya communities. Decades of suppression only perpetuated nationalist narratives, and the reduced censorship and control during the current political transition has allowed nationalistic sentiment to multiply. In a context where both groups have intense fears and feel under siege, some form of active renegotiation of identities and relationships is essential for peace, yet even commencing the conversation is highly provocative and problematic. This is all the more difficult given the Rohingya lack of citizenship and relative lack of organized leadership. Armed militant groups may have been all-but defeated, but conflict and violence remain just below the surface as the same nationalistic narratives driving the fears and aspirations of the separatist causes continue unabated. In this light, exclusion of Rohingya from the larger peace negotiations process, as is currently the case, does not bode well for resolution of the issues nor for lasting peace and stability. Rather, the Rakhine State conflict should not be treated as a special case completely independent from the broader discussions about national identities and possible semi-autonomous and federal state arrangement to ensure the voice of minorities in their own affairs, but that both Rakhine and so-called 'Rohingya' need to be part of this process if peace is to be achieved.

Note

1 Rohingya nationalists claim their ethnic origins trace back to the Arabs, Moors, Pathans, Moghuls, Bengalis and Indo-Mongoloid people (ARNO 2013a; CBRO 2014; Islam, N., 2011; Siddiqui 2014), although they would attempt to trace their history in Arakan much earlier than other authorities accept and argue that this sense of becoming a single community occurred at a much earlier date. See Leider (2014) for further discussion.

References

Amnesty International (AI) 2004, *Myanmar – The Rohingya Minority: Fundamental Rights Denied*, No. ASA 16/005/2004, May 18.

Anderson, B 1983, *Imagined Communities: Reflections on the Origin and Spread of Nationalism*, rev edn, Verso, London.

Arakan Human Rights and Development Organisation (ARDHO) 2013, *Conflict & Violence in Arakan (Rakhine) State, Myanmar (Burma): What is Happening, Why and What to Do*, Mae Sot, Thailand.

Arakan Rohingya National Organisation (ARNO) 2013a, *Facts About the Rohingya Muslims of Arakan*, retrieved February 16 2013, www.rohingya.org/portal/index.php/learn-about-rohingya.html.

Arakan Rohingya National Organisation (ARNO) 2013b, *Who We Are*, retrieved February 16 2013, www.rohingya.org/portal/index.php/who-we-are.htm.

Aye Chan 2005, 'The Development of a Muslim Enclave in Arakan (Rakhine) State of Burma (Myanmar),' *SOAS Bulletin of Burma Research*, vol. 3, no. 2, pp. 396–420.

Bashar, I 2012, *Rohingyas in Bangladesh and Myanmar: Quest for a Sustainable Solution*, RSIS Commentaries, S Pajaratnum School of International Studies, Nanyan Technological University, No. 108/2012, June 22, Singapore.

Baxter, J 1941, *Report on Indian Immigration*, Superintendent, Government Printing and Stationery, Rangoon, Burma.

Burma News International (BNI) 2014, *Deciphering Myanmar's Peace Process: A Reference Guide*, Chiang Mai.

Callahan, MP 2004, *Making Enemies: War and State Building in Burma*, Singapore University Press, Singapore.

Canadian Burmese Rohingya Organization (CBRO) 2014, *Facts About the Rohingya Muslims of Arakan*, retrieved 26 July 2014, http://rohingya.webs.com/arakanhistory.htm.

Charney, M 1998a, 'Crisis and Reformation in a Maritime Kingdom of Southeast Asia: Forces of Instability and Political Disintegration in Western Burma (Arakan), 1603–1701,' *Journal of the Economic and Social History of the Orient*, vol. 41, no. 2, pp. 185–219.

Charney, M 1998b, 'Rise of a Mainland Trading State: Rakhine Under the Early Mrauk-U Kings, c. 1430–1603,' *Journal of Burma Studies*, vol. 3, no. 1, pp. 1–35.

Charney, M 1999, 'Where Jambudipa and Islamdom Converged: Religious Change and the Emergence of Buddhist Communalism in Early Modern Arakan (Fifteenth to Nineteenth Centuries),' PhD thesis, University of Michigan.

Gutman, P 1976, 'Ancient Arakan: With Special Reference to its Cultural History between the 5th and 11th Centuries,' PhD thesis, Australian National University.

Gutman, P 2001, *Burma's Lost Kingdoms: Splendours of Arakan*, Orchid Press, Bangkok.

Harvey, GE 1925, *History of Burma from the Earliest Times to 10 March 1824, the Beginning of the English Conquest*, Longmans, Green and Co, London.

Human Rights Watch (HRW) 2013, 'All You Can Do is Pray: Crimes against Humanity and Ethnic Cleansing of Rohingya Muslims in Burma's Arakan State,' April 22.

International Crisis Group (ICG) 2013, *The Dark Side of Transition: Violence against Muslims in Myanmar* (Asia Report No. 251), Brussels.

Islam, N 2011, 'Muslim Influence in the Kingdom of Arakan', Kaladan Press Network, November 15.

Islam, SS 2007, 'State Terrorism in Arakan,' in ATH Tan (ed.), *A Handbook of Terrorism and Insurgency in Southeast Asia*, Edward Elgar, Cheltenham, UK, pp. 325–351.

Jain, B 2013, 'India Alerts Bangladesh about Rohingya Terror Training Camps in Chittagong Hill Tracts,' *The Times of India*, July 25.

Khin Maung Saw 1993, 'The "Rohingyas," Who are They? The Origin of the Name Rohingya,' in U Gärtner and J Lorenz (eds), *Tradition and Modernity in Myanmar*, Berliner Asien-Afrika Studien, Humboldt Universität, Berlin.

Khin Maung Saw 2005, *On the Evolution of Rohingya Problems in Rakhine State of Burma*, unpublished manuscript, Berlin.

Khin Maung Saw 2011, *Islamization of Burma Through Chittagonian Bengalis as 'Rohingya Refugees'*, unpublished manuscript.

Kyaw San Wai 2014, 'Myanmar's Religious Violence: A Buddhist "Siege Mentality" at Work,' S Rajaratnam School of International Studies [RSIS Commentaries], No. 037/2014, Singapore.

Leider, J 2002, 'On Arakanese Territorial Expansion: Origins, context, means and practice,' in J Leider and J Gommans (eds), *The Maritime Frontier of Burma: Exploring Political, Cultural and Commercial Interaction in the Indian Ocean World, 1200–1800*, Royal Netherlands Academy of Arts & Sciences, Amsterdam, pp. 127–149.

Leider, J 2014a, 'Man Saw Mwan's Exile in Bengal: Looking beyond the Legend,' *Association for Asian Studies 2014 Annual Conference*, Philadelphia, 29 March.

Leider, J 2014b, 'Rohingya: The Name, the Movement, the Quest for Identity,' in *Nation Building in Myanmar*, Myanmar EGRESS and Myanmar Peace Center, Yangon, pp. 204–255.

Michael, MS 2007, 'The Cyprus Peace Talks: A Critical Appraisal,' *Journal of Peace Research*, vol. 44, no. 5, pp. 587–604.

Michael, MS 2011, *Resolving the Cyprus Conflict: Negotiating History*, rev edn, Palgrave Macmillan, Basingstoke.

Mole, R 2001, *The Temple Bells are Calling: A Personal Record of the Last Years of British Rule in Burma*, Pentland Books, Oxford.

Murray, P 1949, 'Secret' Correspondence (Perspectives on the Troubles in North Arakan). To Robert W.D. Fowler, C.R.O., January 26 1949, UK Foreign Office SW1, F 1323/1015/79.

Murray, P 1980, *The British Military Administration of North Arakan 1942–43*, Private communication.

Myanmar Peace Monitor (MPM) 2014, 'Armed Ethnic Groups,' Burma News International, retrieved July 24 2014, www.mmpeacemonitor.org/stakeholders/armed-ethnic-groups.

Selth, A 2004, 'Burma's Muslims and the War on Terror,' *Studies in Conflict & Terrorism*, vol. 27, no. 2, pp. 107–126.

Selth, A 2013, 'Burma's Muslims: A Primer,' *The Interpreter*, Lowy Institute for International Policy, March 27.

Shwe Zan 2005, 'Study of Muslim Infiltration into Rakhine State,' in Shwe Zan and Aye Chan (eds), *Influx Viruses: The Illegal Muslims in Arakan*, Arakanes in United States, New York, pp. 3–20.

Siddiqui, H 2012a, 'Letter from America: The Rohingya Question – Part 1,' *Asian Tribune*, November 25.

Siddiqui, H 2012b, 'Letter from America: The Rohingya Question – Part 2,' *Asian Tribune*, December 2.

Siddiqui, H 2012c, 'The Rohingya Question – Analysis,' *Eurasia Review*, December 20.

Siddiqui, H 2014, 'Rohingya: The Forgotten People,' *Kaladan Press*, June 27.

Smart, RB 1917, 'Akyab District,' *Burma Gazetteer*, Vol. A, Government Printing, Rangoon.

Smith, M 1994, *Ethnic Groups in Burma: Development, Democracy and Human Rights*, Anti-Slavery International, London.

Smith, M 1999, *Burma: Insurgency and the Politics of Ethnicity*, 2nd edn, Zed Books, London.

Smith, M 2007a, 'Ethnic Conflicts in Burma: From Separatism to Federalism,' in ATH Tan (ed.), *A Handbook of Terrorism and Insurgency in Southeast Asia*, Edward Elgar, Cheltenham, UK, pp. 293–321.

Smith, M 2007b, *State of Strife: The Dynamics of Ethnic Conflict in Burma Since Independence*, Institute of Southeast Asian Studies, Singapore.

South, A 2008, *Ethnic Politics in Burma: States of Conflict*, Routledge, London.

Steinberg, DI 2010, *Burma/Myanmar: What Everyone Needs to Know*, Oxford University Press, Oxford.

Tin Maung Maung Than and Moe Thuzar 2012, 'Myanmar's Rohinga Dilemma,' ISEAS Perspective, July 9, Institute of South East Asian Studies, retrieved February 16 2013, www.iseas.edu.sg/documents/publication/ISEAS%20Perspective_1_9jul121.pdf.

Tonkin, D 2014a, 'The "Rohingya" Identity – Further Thoughts,' *Network Myanmar*, April 19.

Tonkin, D 2014b, 'The "Rohingya" Identity – Arithmetic of the Absurd,' *Network Myanmar*, May 9.

Tonkin, D 2014c, 'The "Rohingya" Identity – British Experience in Arakan 1826–1948,' *Network Myanmar*, April 9.

Union of Myanmar (UoM) 2013, *Final Report of Inquiry Commission on Sectarian Violence in Rakhine State*, July 8, Yangon.

United Nations High Commission for Refugees (UNHCR) 2014, *Bangladesh Fact Sheet*, March 2014, Bangladesh.

United Nations Office for the Coordination of Humanitarian Affairs (UNOCHA) 2013, *Rakhine Response Plan (Myanmar) July 2012 – December 2013*, Yangon.

van Galen, SEA 2008, 'Arakan and Bengal: The Rise and Decline of the Mrauk U Kingdom (Burma) from the Fifteenth to the Seventeeth Century AD,' PhD thesis, Leiden Universiteit.

Vrieze, P 2013, 'Experts Reject Claims of "Rohingya Mujahideen" Insurgency,' *The Irrawaddy*, July 15.

Yegar, M 1972, *The Muslims of Burma: A Study of a Minority Group*, Otta Harrassowitz, Wiesbaden.

Yegar, M 2002, *Between Integration and Secession: The Muslim Communities of the Southern Philippines, Southern Thailand, and Western Burma/Myanmar*, Lexington Books, Lanham, MD.

Conclusion

Costas Laoutides and Damien Kingsbury

The introduction to this volume outlined the central argument and the key contributions of this book which is concerned with two main tasks. The first aim was to situate the question of separatism within the broader socio-political context of the international system, arguing that a set of historical events as well as local, regional and global dynamics have converged to provide the catalysts that often trigger separatist conflicts. The second aim of this book was to situate progress towards a new conceptual framework for the study of territorial separatism. The latter links, in many interesting ways, the survival of communities in international politics with the effective control of territory and the consequent creation of new polities. The paradox in the logic embedded in the current model of independent states is that the state is designed to preserve its territorial integrity and hence oppose separatism. This is contrasted with communities seeking to separate in order to effectively survive and, in turn, to establish a new sovereign state. The independence, territorial sovereignty and international recognition of such new states is thus seen to be the conditions that can overcome the shortcomings the political community experiences under the pre-existing state. As such, separatist conflicts challenge conventional wisdom concerning conflict resolution within the context of international relations by unpacking a number of questions with regard to conflict transformation. Key issues include the role of democracy, international law, intervention, post-conflict peacebuilding and the creation of new political entities.

These aims and themes are prominent in the book. All of the authors refer to territorial separatism as a complex socio-political phenomenon that stands at a crossroads of several lines of inquiry whilst they call for progress towards a new conceptual framework for the study of territorial separatism. In Chapters 1 and 2 Pavković and Radan highlight, albeit in different ways, the nature of territorial separatism as an essentially contested concept that can join a wide group of similar concepts in social sciences, law and humanities spanning from the notion of democracy to the definition of war and genocide (Collier *et al.* 2006; Gallie 1956). For Aleksandar Pavković diverse definitions of secession agree that secession involves the creation of a new state by the withdrawal of territory and its populations from an existing state. Restrictive definitions focus on withdrawals carried out by force or to withdrawals subject to rational choice.

Thus their number is too small to concern any moral assessment. Alternatively, permissive definitions allow almost any withdrawal of territory/population to count as secession, such definitions favor moral assessment of the ways in which secessions are carried out or the means used to do so. In search for a common ground between definitions of secession found across a number of disciplines permissive approaches show a leeway for a possible integration. Peter Radan confirms the terminological uncertainty vis-à-vis secession in the sphere of international law (Kohen 2006). It is unclear in international law as to whether there is a limited right of unilateral secession or whether secession is purely a question of fact. It has been argued that the right of peoples to self-determination grants a limited, 'remedial,' right of secession. In 2010, in its advisory opinion relating to Kosovo's secession from Serbia, the International Court of Justice had, but declined to grasp, an opportunity to clarify international law in relation to secession. Thus, the opportunity for a decontestation of secession as far as international law is concerned went astray.

In a similar vein Kingsbury, Laoutides and Jackson (Chapters 3, 4 and 5) emphasize the present reluctance for a substantial academic, political and legal decontestation of separatism, calling for a revisiting of the phenomenon under a new analytical and interpretative schema that can inform separatist conflict transformation and resolution. Damien Kingsbury, drawing on five case studies, underlines the principle of equality that the state must adhere to in regard to all of its citizens, alluding to the liberal premises of an identity-neutral and citizen-centered state. Equal regard in relation to benefits, opportunities and safeguards that the state has the capacity to provide is of cardinal importance to maintain peace and justice in the society. Failure by the state to perform this basic civic function equally leads to alienation and, within an ethno-geographic context, separatist rebellions which are seen as the avenue to remedy such 'injustice.' Costas Laoutides takes his cue from Kingsbury and examines how sustainable peace is pursued in separatist conflicts and what are the challenges for peacebuilding operations. He argues that secessionist conflicts are a particular type of internal conflict that raises issues of territorial control and survival of the communities in question. Separatist conflicts are more amenable to negotiated settlements than other types of internal conflict but the implementation of peace accords faces two key challenges: the need for establishing a common political foundation for the distinct community that will foster trustful relations, and the transition of former fighters to agents of peace through a paradigmatic departure from identity politics and the ethnic security dilemma. Richard Jackson follows in the same theme as he problematizes the prevailing peacebuilding template which international institutions currently apply dogmatically to societies emerging from separatist war, thereby opening up analytical and normative space for the consideration of radically alternative peacebuilding approaches. By outlining a constructivist model of separatist war initiation, Jackson argues that, among others, discursive factors, social structures, histories, narratives and discursive practices play a central role that is relatively under-valued in most quantitative and structurally-based approaches to separatist war explanation, as well as in most institutional understandings of the causes of separatist war. To remedy this oversight he proposes a peacebuilding approach which takes a post-Weberian or post-state polity as its normative goal, a radically alternative approach to 'discursive peacebuilding' after separatist war which encompasses conflict transformation, agonistic democracy and dialogic politics, and the demilitarization of politics and its replacement with nonviolent and pacifist politics.

Attuned to this call the contributors in the second part of the book, through their respective analyses, rehearse and question the paradigmatic ethno-centric analysis of separatist conflicts situating anew their case studies in the dynamic context of a changing international environment that has to break away from mono-dimensional approaches, accustomed to scholars, policy-makers and politicians, in order to explore alternative foundations of political organization that can promote peaceful co-existence. Clinton Fernandes (Chapter 6) considers the powerful effect of international recognition of annexation and incorporation, with particular reference to East Timor. He argues that when Indonesia invaded East Timor in 1975 and annexed it in 1976, it followed a precedent established in 1969 during the 'Act of Free Choice' in West Papua, when it denied the population the right to self-determination through a referendum. Instead, it chose a group of 'representatives' who would vote unanimously to join Indonesia. As Fernandes notes, Indonesia expected the international community to extend official recognition of the annexation of East Timor, as had occurred with West Papua. Wide international recognition would have generated a powerful dynamic that could have extinguished East Timor's bid for freedom. However, Indonesia failed to obtain widespread *de jure* recognition of its takeover of East Timor, with Australia being the only Western state to recognize the annexation. In this contest of recognition, Fernandes unfolds the set of dynamics that informed the relationship between civil society and policy-makers highlighting the broader socio-political context, domestic and international, that dominated the recognition debate which ultimately led to the creation of independent East Timor.

Terry Narramore (Chapter 7) turns his attention to the internal dynamics that influence separatist conflicts as he considers how the policies of a government can actually exacerbate centrifugal tendencies, in this case considering the case of Xinjiang in China's north-west. As he notes, violent resistance of Uyghurs to the Chinese Communist Party's rule in Xinjiang provides a stark reminder that while China's sovereignty over Xinjiang is not in jeopardy and its policies have contained separatist movements, it is these same policies that continue to provoke separatist sentiment and Uyghur–Han (Chinese) tensions and violence. The July 2009 'riots' in Xinjiang's capital, Urumqi, were tragic demonstrations of this policy failure. Xinjiang thus remains an intractable case of the successful but inconclusive containment of separatism (Heraclides 1997), while Uyghur resistance has entered a phase marked by more intense Uyghur–Han conflict. Thus, Narramore contributes to the discussion about the limitation of conventional wisdom in separatist conflict resolution, calling for new avenues of conflict transformation and resolution.

Cyprus presents a paradigmatic case of separatism within the broader socio-political context of the international system given that the state has been partitioned between approximately ethnic communities, each strongly supported by, or a client of, an external state. As Michális Michael notes (Chapter 8), partition has always had an ominous presence in Cyprus's political discourse.

It is a case where a set of historical events, as well as local, regional and global dynamics, have converged to provide the catalysts that often trigger separatist conflicts. For Michael, if the history of the Cyprus conflict could be deduced to a single schema, that it would be as the antithetical, often-violent, interplay between separatism/secession/division and unification/integration/reconciliation. Michael examines one of the world's most protracted international conflicts and he analyzes how attempts at bringing the antithetical elements into a synthesis/resolution have fared, especially the normative challenge of how to construct a legal-constitutional order that is dictated by a set of historical determinants. These are said to include the desire to rectify past injustices which reconciles human rights and group security with the expectation of upholding the fundamental precepts of liberal democracy, while at the same time fortifying the foundations for sequential integration/unification and negating the paradigm of secession, division and partition. In doing so Michael marks the need for progress towards a new conceptual framework for the transformation and resolution of the Cyprus case but also for the study of territorial separatism at large.

One of the key consequences in the aftermath of the war in Iraq is that the arbitrarily constructed state, a product of the Sykes–Picot Agreement of 1916, with a loose sense of unity, has begun to unravel. A combination of domestic, regional and international factors in post-war Iraq have triggered separatist tensions that challenge Iraqi territorial integrity. Benjamin Isakhan (Chapter 9) discusses one of these challenges, namely the calls by the Supreme Council for the Islamic Revolution in Iraq (SCIRI) for an autonomous Shia Islamic state in the south of Iraq. While such calls have deep historical roots and have long formed part of SCIRI's complex political and ideological history, they achieved a renewed momentum following the US attempt to bring a form of democracy to Iraq after its 2003 invasion. While the prospects for Shia secession in Iraq remain low, Isakhan finds that it nonetheless forms an ongoing and central part of SCIRI's political agenda and thus constitutes a key element in the make-up of the fractured Iraqi state. Centrifugal tensions in Iraq confirm clearly the inherent paradox in separatist conflicts which associates community survival in international relations with state creation. Thus the call is for a transformation of the conflict with the aim to bring about positive peace by implementing a new type of political organization.

The need for progress towards a new conceptual framework for the study of territorial separatism is clearly evident in the case of the Rakhine State in Myanmar. Anthony Ware (Chapter 10) explores the secessionist aspects to the Muslim–Buddhist conflict in Rakhine. From one perspective, the secessionist struggle in Rakhine was largely won by the Burmese military in the

1950s–1960s, as the major, separate armed rebellions by both Rakhine Buddhists and Rohingya Muslims were put down. Yet, despite being significantly weakened, armed groups have continued to form and still remain. More to the point, however, Ware argues that the broader socio-political context of the international system in combination with a set of historical events as well as local and regional dynamics have provided the catalysts that led to separatist conflict. Communal violence turned to separatism in the ferocity of World War II, and the suppression, rather than resolution, of group grievances and rival territorial claims under decades of military rule have perpetuated and accentuated a 'double minority complex' in which, seen from a national/international and social-psychological perspective, both the majority Rakhine and the minority 'Rohingya' feel as if they are threatened minorities struggling for their very survival. In a context where both groups feel under siege, some form of active renegotiation of identities and relationships is essential for peace, yet even commencing the conversation is highly provocative and problematic, particularly given the 'Rohingya' lack of citizenship and lack of organized leadership.

The contributors to this volume considered how and why separatism arises and, potentially, how its claims can be addressed. In doing so they covered a range of perspectives and a number of case studies that provided a reasonable sense of the breadth of the separatist spectrum. The chapters in this book argued collectively that approaches to tame separatism can only endure and bring about positive outcomes if they are developed organically from the bottom up and in isolation from ideological agendas. In doing so there is a need to (re-)emphasize the fundamental complexity of territorial separatism which in turn calls for the integration of different disciplinary perspectives into a coherent interdisciplinary framework of study (Repko 2012). The etiology for territorial separatism is subject to historical, ethnic, economic, political and structural factors (Toft 2012) and therefore it has to be analyzed from different perspectives in order for us to reach a holistic understanding of it. Analysis and understanding are the first steps towards an integrated approach that would seek to remedy separatist conflict and alleviate harm and suffering from both physical and non-physical violence. This is a basis from which international legitimacy and endurance can be generated, leading to an outlook for state formation that can transcend some of the absolutist characteristics of the Westphalian model.

This volume is also a springboard for the expansion of the research agenda on the intertwined issues of separatism, the state, political identity and the possibilities for the resolution of such conflicts. Thus, in the final part of the conclusion it is worth mentioning four themes towards which future research should be directed:

- The recognition of the range of motives that drive separatist organizations to armed conflict.
- The role of political will in peace accords of separatist conflicts.

- The respective capacities to fulfill a peace agreement in separatist scenarios.
- The role of external involvement in enhancing the peace process.

Together, these four themes combine key dimensions for separatist conflict resolution.

Recognition of the range of motives that drive separatist organizations to armed conflict

There are four key sets of theories as to why separatist movements develop which are based on material grievance (Collier 2009; Collier and Sambanis 2007; Hale 2000), identity distinction (Connor 1994; Horowitz 1986; Kaplan 2005), geographic conditions (Brown 2001; Fearon and Laitin 2003) and political contexts (Bookman 1992; Boyle and Englebert 2008). The proposition is that each of these is usually present in separatist conflicts, although varying in causal proportion from case to case. Therefore, successful negotiated settlements recognize and deal with the motives that trigger separatist violence in the first place. What is important to establish is the ways this recognition is achieved within the framework of a peace process.

Political will in satisfying sufficient of separatists' goals

The capacity for and extent to which separatist demands can be satisfied is a critical factor in determining the level of political accommodation in the peace process. Lijphart (1977) stresses the crucial role of political will in the peace process but how political will is built both at the elite and grassroots levels is unexplored. Solutions to separatist claims include state independence, degrees of autonomy, types of power-sharing/dividing mechanisms (Coakley 2010, pp. 194–202; Sisk 1996), policies of integration of dispersed communities, and recognition of multiculturalism and minority rights (Esman 2004; Guelke 2012, pp. 82–88). However, in cases of successful political accommodation there has not been established correlation between demand satisfaction and implementation of peace processes.

The respective capacities to fulfill a peace agreement

The capacity for implementing and maintaining peace agreements constitutes a key challenge in resolving separatist claims. Peace agreements resolving separatist conflict may be derailed by frail state institutions, weak rule of law, inability/unwillingness of the security sector to maintain peace, lack of progress in political freedoms and civil rights (Kingsbury 2011; Walter 2002). Institutional capacity can perform three valuable functions that facilitate the construction of an enduring peace (Hartzell and Hoddie 2007, 2010). The first is that institutions should be designed to address the power distribution among the disputants, a theme that Kingsbury raised in Chapter 3 of the present volume. Second, the design and implementation of institutions in the aftermath of a negotiated agreement highlights the commitment by the parties to build a long-lasting peace, both Laoutides and Jackson in this volume (Chapters 3 and 4) touched upon aspects of this dimension. Third the institution designed as part of a separatist war settlement set the framework and the means with which social conflict is to be managed in the post-war state, both Michael and Ware in their case studies alluded to this need.

The role of external involvement in facilitating separatist peace processes

The main focus in the literature has been on explaining the causes and consequences of external involvement as a contributing factor to the dynamics of secession (Heraclides 1990; Saideman and Ayres 2008). However, emphasis on unilateral involvement is not sufficient to understand the complexity of succeeding in multi-party and multi-layered peacebuilding programs; conception and implementation; formal and informal interventions negotiating intra-elite conflict; and the modes of facilitating transitions to open political participation.

References

Bookman, M 1992, *The Economics of Secession*, St. Martin's Press, New York.
Boyle, K and Englebert, P 2008, 'The Primacy of Politics in Separatist Dynamics,' *African Perspective*, vol. 2, pp. 31–63.
Brown, M 2001, *Nationalism and Ethnic Conflict*, rev edn, MIT Press, Cambridge, MA.
Coakley, J 2010, 'Ethnic Conflict Resolution: Routes towards Settlement,' in J Coakley (ed.), *Pathways from Ethnic Conflict: Institutional Redesign in Divided Societies*, Routledge, Abingdon, UK, pp. 201–222.
Collier, D, Hidalgo, FD and Maciuceanu, AO 2006, 'Essentially Contested Concepts: Debates and Applications,' *Journal of Political Ideologies*, vol. 11, no. 3, pp. 211–246.
Collier, P 2009, *Wars, Guns and Votes: Democracy in Dangerous Places*, Harper, New York.
Collier, P and Sambanis, N 2007, *Understanding Civil War*, 2 vols, The World Bank, Washington, DC.
Connor, W 1994, *Ethnonationalism: The Quest for Understanding*, Princeton University Press, Princeton, NJ.
Esman, M 2004, *An Introduction to Ethnic Conflict*, Polity Press, Cambridge, UK.
Fearon, J and Laitin, D 2003, 'Ethnicity, Insurgency, and Civil War,' *American Political Science Review*, vol. 97, no. 1, pp. 75–90.
Gallie, WB 1956, 'Essentially Contested Concepts,' *Proceedings of the Aristotelian Society*, vol. 56, pp. 167–198.
Guelke, A 2012, *Politics in Deeply Divided Societies*, Polity Press, Cambridge, UK.
Hale, HE 2000, 'The Parade of Sovereignties: Testing Theories of Secession in the Soviet Setting,' *British Journal of Political Science*, vol. 30, no. 1, pp. 31–56.
Hartzell, CA and Hoddie, M 2007, *Crafting the Peace: Power-Sharing Institutions and the Negotiated Settlement of Civil Wars*, The Pennsylvania State University Press, University Park, PA.

Hartzell, CA and Hoddie, M (eds) 2010, *Strengthening Peace in Post-Civil War States: Transforming Spoilers into Stakeholders*, University of Chicago Press, Chicago.

Heraclides, A 1990, 'Secessionist Minorities and External Involvement,' *International Organization*, vol. 44, no. 3, pp. 341–378.

Heraclides, A 1997 'The Ending of Unending Conflicts: Separatist Wars,' *Millennium: Journal of International Studies*, vol. 26, no. 3, pp. 679–707.

Horowitz, D 1985, *Ethnic Groups in Conflict*, University of California Press, Berkeley, CA.

Kaplan, R 2005, *Balkan Ghosts: A Journey Through History*, Picador, New York.

Kingsbury, D 2011, *Sri Lanka and the Responsibility to Protect: Politics, Ethnicity and Genocide*, Routledge, London.

Kohen, MG (ed.) 2006, *Secession: International Law Perspectives*, Cambridge University Press, Cambridge, UK.

Lijphart, A 1977, *Democracy in Plural Societies: A Comparative Exploration*, Yale University Press, New Haven.

Repko, A 2012, *Interdisciplinary Research: Process and Theory*, 2nd edn, Sage Publications, London.

Saideman, SM and Ayres, W 2008, *For Kin or Country: Xenophobia, Nationalism and War*, Columbia University Press, New York.

Sisk, T 1996, *Power Sharing and International Mediation in Ethnic Conflicts*, United States Institute of Peace, Washington, DC.

Toft, MD 2012, 'Self-Determination, Secession and Civil War,' *Terrorism and Political Violence*, vol. 24, no. 4, pp. 581–600.

Walter, BF 2002, *Committing to Peace: The Successful Settlement of Civil Wars*, Princeton University Press, Princeton, NJ.

Index

9/11 attacks 109, 114

Abbasid-era Al-Askari mosque, Samarra 145–6
Aceh, Indonesia 44, 47, 48, 55
Acheson, Dean 127–8
Act of Free Choice, West Papua 94
Act of Integration, East Timor 96
Action for World Development 95
agonistic democracy 83, 84
al Qaeda 114, 116, 142, 163
Albania 34–5
Aldrich, George 104
Al-Amiri, Hadi 145
Amnesty International 116
Anastasiades, Nicos 123
Anderson, Benedict 161
Anderson, Glen 17, 19, 20, 21, 22, 23, 26
Annan Plan, Cyprus 123, 128, 132, 135
annexation 19, 20; Cyprus 133; West Papua 93–4; see also East Timor
APODETI, East Timor 95
Aquino, Corazon 52
Arakan Army (AA) 159
Arakan Liberation Army (ALA) 155, 159
Arakan National Army (ANA) 158
Arakan National Council 159
Arakan (Rakhine) see Buddhist–Muslim conflict, Myanmar
Arakan Rohingya Islamic Front 160
Arakan Rohingya National Organisation (ARNO) 159, 160
Argentina 103
armed groups, transition to political parties 68–70
ARNO see Arakan Rohingya National Organisation (ARNO)
asymmetric conflicts 5, 59
Athens doctrine 130
Aung San 158

Australia 93–5, 97–101
Australia East Timor Association 98
Australian Council for Overseas Aid 95
Australian Security Intelligence Organization (ASIO) 98
Ayres, R.W. 61

Baath Party, Iraq 141
Badr Organization, Iraq 142, 143, 144, 145, 146, 148
Balibo Declaration 96
Ball, George 127–8
Bangladesh 4, 22, 23, 30, 34, 160
Baren riots, Xinjiang 115–16
Belize 103
Bemis, Samuel Flagg 30
Beran, Harry 26
Berdal, M. 53–4
Biafra 30
bin Laden, Osama 114, 116
Bodea, C. 55
Bolshevik ideology 2
border adjustment 19
Bosnia-Herzegovina 35, 64–5
Boutros-Ghali, Boutros 62
Bovingdon, G. 115
Braithwaite, J. 54
Britain see United Kingdom
British Campaign for an Independent East Timor (BCIET) 101
British Indonesia Committee 101
Buchanan, Allen 26
Buddhist–Muslim conflict, Myanmar 153–65; double minority complex narratives 160–4; historical development 155–60
Burma Independence Army (BIA) 158
Burton, J. 127
Cançado Trindade, Antônio A. 38, 39
Carrington, Lord 105

Cassese, Antonio 32
Celestino, M. 79
Central Asian states 117
Charney, M. 156–7
China 108–19
Chomsky, Noam 103
civic failure 53–7
civic opportunity 48–53
civil society: and East Timor 94–5, 97–8, 101–2, 104; and West Papua 93–4
civil wars 1, 53–4, 55, 60–1, 78
civilian defense models 84–5
class-based rebellions 54–5
Coleman, Andrew 39–40
Collier, P. 53, 55
Communist Party, Burma 159
Communist Party, Philippines 55
complexity theory 82
Confederate States, USA 30
conflict agents 77, 79–80
conflict transformation 82–5
conflict trap 53
Congo 30
consensual secession 18–19
constructivist model of intrastate war initiation 76–80
Costa Rica 84
Crawford, James 17–18, 23, 25, 26, 29, 32, 36–7
Crimea 20
Croatia 34, 35
Cyprus 30, 123–36, 160–1; partition 124–9; reunification 123–4, 129–32, 133, 134–5; settlement scenarios 133–5

Dahl, Robert A. 51
Damian 20
Darul Islam rebellion 55
Dawa, Iraq 140–1, 143, 145, 146, 147
Day of Rage, Iraq 148–9
Dayton negotiations 35, 64
Declaration on Friendly Relations 30–4, 38–9, 41
decolonization 3, 16, 21, 23–4, 25, 26; Burma 158–9; Cyprus 126–7
demilitarization of politics 83, 84–5
demobilization 69, 80
democratization 49, 50–3, 62, 63–6, 67, 68, 69–70, 80, 81; Iraq 139, 140, 142, 143; Myanmar 164
devolution 61
Di Palma, Giuseppe 51
disarmament, demobilization and reintegration (DDR) 80
discursive peacebuilding 82–5, 86

discursive structures of intrastate wars 77, 78–9, 81
dissolution of host state 16, 22–3, 25
Diu 20
double minority complex narratives 160–4
Drooglever, P. 94
Dugard, J. 32, 41

Eanes, António Ramalho 106
East Timor 4, 48, 56, 94–106; and Australia 94–5, 97–101; civil society support 94–5, 97–8, 101–2, 104; destabilization and invasion 95–7; independence referendum 44–5, 51; national identity 47; and United Kingdom 101–4; United Nations resolutions 103, 105–6
East Turkestan Information Centre 116
East Turkestan Islamic Movement (ETIM) 109, 114, 115, 116, 117, 118
East Turkestan Liberation Organization (ETLO) 116, 118
East Turkestan Republic (ETR) 111–12
Ecevit, Mustafa Bulent 129
economic crises: Cyprus 132; Indonesia 51
economic liberalization 62, 63, 64, 65, 80, 81
Eden, Anthony 126
Elbadawi, I. 55
elections 54, 80; Bosnia-Herzegovina 64–5; Iraq 139, 143, 145, 148; Kosovo 65–6; and peacebuilding 63–6, 68
énosis (union), Cyprus 125, 126, 127, 128
EOKA, Cyprus 126
equal rights principle 30–4, 38–9, 44
Eritrea 4
Eroğlu, Derviş 123–4
ethnic cleansing 62
ethnic conflict 55–6
ethnic groups, and nations 45
ETIM see East Turkestan Islamic Movement (ETIM)
ETLO see East Turkestan Liberation Organization (ETLO)
ETR see East Turkestan Republic (ETR)
European Community 100
European Union 35

Falkland Islands 103
federalism: Cyprus 130, 131, 133, 134–5; Iraq 144, 146
Feith, Herb 95
Fernandes, Clinton 93–106
force, use of 15, 16
fragmentation of host state 16, 22–3, 25

Index 179

Fraser, Malcolm 98–9
FRETILIN, East Timor 95–7, 101, 103, 105
Fry, Ken 98

Galtung, Johan 86
genocide 62
Germany 21
Ghulja riots, Xinjiang 116
Gietzelt, Arthur 98
Gleditsch, S. 79
global war on terror 109, 114–19
Goa 20
Golan Heights 20
Gordon, J.K. 102–3
Greece 50, 124–6, 127, 128, 130, 133
greed and grievance thesis 53–4
Greek Cypriot nationalism 125
Grey, Edward 125
Griffith, Alan 99, 100
Group of Five 117
Guantanamo Bay 109

Haas, E. 67
Habibie, B.J. 50, 52
Al-Hakim, Sayed Mohammed Baqr 141–2, 144
Al-Hakim, Sayeed Abdul Aziz 141, 142, 144–5, 146, 147
Al-Hakim, Sayeed Ammar 142, 146–7, 148, 149
Haverland, Christine 19, 23
Hechter, Michael 22, 23, 25, 27
Helman, Gerald B. 62
Heraclides, Alexis 1, 5, 8, 18, 61, 63, 68, 108, 135, 171, 175
Herodotus 46
Hitchens, C. 128, 129
Hizb Al-Dawa Islamiyya *see* Dawa, Iraq
Holbrooke, Richard 35
Holsti, K. 3, 67
Homestead program, Philippines 55
horizontal distinction 54
horizontal legitimacy 67–8, 69–70
Hukbalahap Rebellion, Philippines 54
human rights abuses 3, 5, 44, 55–6, 62, 153–4
Hussein, Saddam 141

independence referenda: Crimea 20; East Timor 44–5; Kosovo 34
India 20, 30
Indigenous Peoples' Rights Act, Philippines 55
Indonesia: Aceh 44, 47, 48, 55; economic crisis 51; regime change 50, 51, 52; regional disaffection 48; state creation 47; West Papua 44, 47, 48, 55–6, 93–4; *see also* East Timor
institutional capacity 48, 49, 51, 55, 56, 174–5
instrumentalist understanding of nations 46
Interim Governing Council (IGC), Iraq 143
Interim Iraqi Government (IIG) 143
International Commission of Jurists 34
International Committee of the Red Cross 105
International Court of Justice (ICJ) 29, 35–40
international law: Declaration on Friendly Relations 30–4, 38–9, 41; Kosovo Advisory Opinion 35–40; regulation of secession 26, 27, 29; United Nations Charter 2, 3, 16, 21, 30, 60
international recognition 4, 29–30, 48; annexation of East Timor 94, 98–101, 102–4, 105–6; annexation of West Papua 93–4
Iran 141–2, 146
Iran–Iraq War 141
Iraq 139–50
Iraqi Security Forces (ISF) 144, 145
Iraqi Transitional Government (ITG) 143
Irish Free State 22, 23
irredenta 19, 20, 26
Isakhan, Benjamin 139–50
ISCI *see* Islamic Supreme Council of Iraq (ISCI)
ISCI Bulletin, The 146, 149
Islamic Revolution, Iran 141
Islamic Supreme Council of Iraq (ISCI) 146–50; *see also* Supreme Council for the Islamic Revolution in Iraq (SCIRI)
Israel 20

al-Jaafari, Ibrahim al-Eshaiker 148
Jackson, Richard 75–86
Janatha Vimukthi Peramuna (JVP – Peoples' Liberation Front), Sri Lanka 54

Kadeer, Rabiya 118
Karamanlis, Kostantinos 126
Katanga 30
Kaufmann, D. 53
Kazakstan 117
Kemalism 125
Kingsbury, Damien 1–9, 44–57, 169–75
KLA *see* Kosovo Liberation Army (KLA)
Kooijmans, P.H. 32

Koroma, Abdul G. 38–9
Kosovo 4, 34–40, 65–6
Kosovo Advisory Opinion 35–40
Kosovo Liberation Army (KLA) 35
Kurds, Iraq 139, 144, 146
Kyaw San Wai 161
Kyprianos, Bishop of Kitium 125
Kyrgyzstan 117

language 45–6
Laoutides, Costas 1–9, 59–70, 163, 169–75
Latin America 30
legitimacy, state 67–8, 69–70
Leider, J. 157, 158, 162
Liberation Tigers of Tamil Eelam (LTTE) 44
Libya 78
Licklider, R. 60
Lijphart, A. 174
Lincoln, Abraham 30
Lobato, Nicolau 97
Lunn, Hugh 94
Luttwak, E. 61

McIntosh, Gordon 106
Mackerras, C. 118–19
Macmillan, Harold 126
Al-Mahdi, Adel Abdul 143, 144, 145, 146, 148
Makarios III, Archbishop of Cyprus 126, 129
Malik, Adam 99
al-Maliki, Nouri 145, 147, 148–9
Malone, D 53–4
Manning, Brian 97
Marcos, Ferdinand 51, 52
market economy *see* economic liberalization
Marxism 49
Mavromatis, Manny 97
Michael, Michális S 123–36, 160–1
military: and regime change 50–1, 52; replacing with civilian defense models 83, 84–5
military victory 5, 60–1, 62, 154
Mill, John Stuart 67
Millward, J.A. 109
Mindanao, Philippines 44, 47, 48, 55
minority identity 2, 3
modernism 54, 67
modernist development theory 49–50
Mole, R. 158
Montis, Kostas 123
Moro Islamic Liberation Front (MILF) 44
Morris, Cliff 95, 97

motives, for separatist movements 174
Mrauk-U kingdom 155–6, 161
Mujahedeen rebellion, Burma 158–9, 162
Murray, D.F. 102
Murray, P. 157, 158
Myanmar *see* Buddhist–Muslim conflict, Myanmar
Myanmar Citizenship Law 164
myth of redemptive violence 78–9

Narramore, Terry 108–19
narrative reconstruction 82, 84
National Endowment for Democracy 118
national identity 2; constructed 46–7
National Iraqi Alliance (NIA) 148
National Union of Australian University Students 95
nationalism 2, 3
nations 45–7
NATO 35, 65, 126, 127
negotiated settlements 60–3, 174–5; *see also* peacebuilding
Neilley, Warwick 97
New York Agreement 93
Nigeria 30
normative theories of secession 26
Northern Ireland 78
Northern Ireland Assembly 83
Norway 22
Nossiter, Bernard 103

Obama, Barack 118
O'Donnell, G. 52

Pakistan 22, 23, 30, 34
Parsons, Alf 99
partition *see* Cyprus
Pavković, Aleksandar 15–27
peace agreements 174–5
peace formations 84
peacebuilding 62–70, 75–6; critique of post-intrastate 80–2; discursive 82–5, 86
peacekeeping, unarmed 85
Peacock, Andrew 98, 99, 100
Philippines: class-based rebellions 54–5; Mindanao conflict 44, 48, 55; regime change 50, 51, 52; state creation 47
Pinto Balsemao, Francisco 106
Plaza, Galo 128
political accommodation, of separatist demands 174
political transitions 50–3; *see also* democratization
politics, demilitarization of 83, 84–5
Portugal 50, 101, 106

Index 181

poverty, and civil wars 53–4, 55, 78
Powell, Colin 128
primordialist understanding of nations 45–6
procedural democracy 50, 64, 65, 68, 69–70

Radan, Peter 17, 18, 19, 20, 21, 22, 23, 26, 29–41
Rakhine Buddhists, Myanmar 153–5, 158, 159, 161–4
Rambouillet Peace Conference 35
Ramos-Horta, Jose 103
rational choice theory of secessions 22, 25
Ratner, Steven R. 29, 62
rebel transition 68–70
recognition *see* international recognition
referenda: Crimea 20; Cyprus 123, 128, 135; East Timor 44–5; Kosovo 34
refugees: Burmese 156–7, 160; Greek Cypriot 129, 130; West Papuan 94
regime change 50–3
resettlement policies, China 112–13
Responsibility to Protect (R2P) 16
Richmond, Oliver 83–4
Rohingya Independence Force (RIF) 159
Rohingya Muslims, Myanmar 153–5, 157, 158–60, 161–5
Rohingya Patriotic Front 159
Rohingya Solidarity Organisation (RSO) 155, 159, 160
Rostow, W. 49
Roth, Brad 41
RSO *see* Rohingya Solidarity Organisation (RSO)
Runaweri, Clemens 94
Russia 20, 117
Rustow, D.A. 67

Al-Sadr, Mohammad Sadiq 141
Al-Sadr, Moqtada 141
al-Sadr, Muhammad Baqr 141
Sadr Trend, Iraq 143, 148
safeguard clause, Declaration on Friendly Relations 31, 32–4, 38–9, 41
Sambanis, N. 53
Sandole, D. 70
Schmitter, P. 52
SCIRI *see* Supreme Council for the Islamic Revolution in Iraq (SCIRI)
SCIRI Bulletin, The 143
secession 15–27, 29–41; continuity versus fragmentation of host state 16, 22–3, 25; Declaration on Friendly Relations 30–4, 38–9, 41; Kosovo Advisory Opinion 35–40; normative assessment of 24–6;

permissive definitions 15, 19–22, 23, 25, 27; rational choice theory 22, 25; restrictive definitions 15, 17–19, 23, 25
security sector reform (SSR) 80
self-determination 2–3, 29, 62; of colonized peoples 16; Declaration on Friendly Relations 30–4, 38–9, 41
Selth, A. 163
separatist conflicts 1, 3, 4–5; military victory 5, 60–1, 62, 154; negotiated settlements 60–3; peacebuilding 62–70; third party intervention 4
separatist organizations, transition to political parties 68–70
Serbia 34, 35
Shackleton, Greg 106
Shanghai Cooperation Organization 117
Shiite separatism, Iraq 139–50
Al-Sistani, Ali 142, 143
Sloss, David 39, 40
Slovenia 34
social contract 48, 51–2
social divisions 53–7
social reconciliation 80
Socialist Federal Republic of Yugoslavia (SFRY) 22
Sofronios III, Archbishop of Cyprus 125
softline military approach 50–1, 52
South Sudan 4, 83
sovereign purchase 19
sovereignty 2, 20–2, 48, 60
Spain 78
Sri Lanka 44, 47, 48, 54, 55
state-building 62
state creation 4, 19, 20–2, 47, 59
State of Law Coalition (SLC), Iraq 147
states 47–8; civic failure 53–7; civic opportunity 48–53; continuity versus fragmentation 16, 22–3, 25; legitimacy 67–8, 69–70; rational choice theory of secessions 22, 25; voluntary cessation of territory 18–19; *see also* territorial integrity principle
statism 2
Stepan, A. 50
Stevenson, Arthur 95
Suharto 51, 52, 96, 99, 101
Supreme Council for the Islamic Revolution in Iraq (SCIRI) 139, 140, 141–6; *see also* Islamic Supreme Council of Iraq (ISCI)
Supreme Court of Canada 29, 34
survival, and territorial control 3, 59–60
Sweden 22
Syria 20, 78

Taiwan 108
Tajikistan 117
Taliban 114, 116, 163
Tamil Tigers 44
TAPOL (British Campaign for the Release of Indonesian Political Prisoners) 101–2
Taylor, John 101
territorial integrity principle 1–2, 16, 60, 62; safeguard clause 31, 32–4, 38–9, 41
territory: transfer of 19, 20, 26; voluntary cessation of 18–19
terrorist organizations 4, 35, 109–10, 114–19
Tibet 108–9
Timor-Leste see East Timor
Toft, M. 3, 5, 60–1, 173
Tonkin, D. 162
transitional democracy see democratization
transitional justice 80
Treaty of Guarantee, Cyprus 127, 129, 130
tribes 45
Turkey 30, 123, 126, 127, 128, 129–30, 133
Turkish Cypriot nationalism 125
two-state solution, Cyprus 134–5

UDT, East Timor 95–6
UIA see United Iraqi Alliance (UIA)
Ukraine 20, 78
unarmed peacekeeping 85
unification 21; Cyprus 123–4, 129–32, 133, 134–5
Union Solidarity and Development Party 163
United Iraqi Alliance (UIA) 143, 145
United Kingdom 23; and Burma 157, 158–9; and Cyprus 124–7; and East Timor 101–4; policy on recognition 104–5
United Nations: and Cyprus 126, 127, 128, 132; Declaration on Friendly Relations 30–4, 38–9, 41; doctrine of decolonization 16, 21; and East Timor 103, 105–6; Fiftieth Anniversary Declaration 33; and Kosovo 35, 36, 37, 65–6; peacebuilding 62–3; and secession 16, 18; Special Committee on Decolonisation 105–6

United Nations Charter 2, 3, 16, 21, 30, 60
United Nations Interim Administration Mission in Kosovo (UNMIK) 65–6
United Nations Peacebuilding Commission 62
United Nations Security Council 98; Resolution 244 (Cyprus) 128; Resolution 1244 (Kosovo) 35, 36, 37, 65
United Nations Temporary Executive Authority (UNTEA) 93
United States 30, 62; and China 109, 117–18; and Cyprus 127–8; and East Timor 104; and Iraq 139, 142
Urumqi demonstrations, Xinjiang 118
Uyghur American Association 118
Uyghur separatism 109–19
Uzbekistan 117

van Galen, S.E.A. 156
vertical legitimacy 67–8, 69
violence, myth of redemptive 78–9
Visser, Reidar 140, 145
voluntary cessation of territory 18–19

Wahid, Abdurrahman 52
Ware, Anthony 153–65
weapon availability 78
Wellman, Christopher H. 26
Wesley-Smith, Robert 97
West Papua 44, 47, 48, 55–6, 93–4
White, R.C.A. 33
Whitlam, Gough 105–6
Wilson, David 100
Wilson, Woodrow 3
Wood, John R. 22–3, 25–6, 27
World Uyghur Youth Congress 116
World War II: Burma 158; Cyprus 125–6

Xinjiang, China 108, 109–19

Yashin, Neshe 123
Yudhoyono, Susilo Bambang 52
Yugoslavia 22
Yusuf, Abdulqawi A. 37–8, 39

Zantis, James 97
Zonggonau, Willem 94